PENGUIN BOOKS

DRAFT ANIMALS

Phil Gaimon was a professional cyclist from 2009–2016, including two years in the WorldTour with Garmin-Sharp (2014) and Cannondale (2016). He is the author of *Pro Cycling on $10 a Day* (2014) and *Ask a Pro* (2016) and an ordained minister, amateur comedian, podcaster, entrepreneur, and host of Phil's Fondo. Phil is retired from racing but still rides his bike for fun and Strava.

DRAFT ANIMALS

*Living the Pro Cycling Dream
(Once in a While)*

Phil Gaimon

PENGUIN BOOKS

PENGUIN BOOKS
An imprint of Penguin Random House LLC
375 Hudson Street
New York, New York 10014
penguin.com

Photograph credits:
Page xix: VeloImages
Page 62: Laura Meseguer
Page 233: Nate King
Page 236: Doug Earnest
All other photos taken by the author.

LIBRARY OF CONGRESS CATALOGING-IN-PUBLICATION DATA
Names: Gaimon, Phil, author.
Title: Draft animals : living the pro cycling dream (once in a while) / Phil Gaimon.
Description: New York, New York : Penguin Books an imprint of
    Penguin Random House, LLC, [2018]
Identifiers: LCCN 2017015784 (print) | LCCN 2017029915 (ebook) |
    ISBN 9781524705008 (ebook) | ISBN 9780143131243
Subjects: LCSH: Gaimon, Phil. | Cyclists—United States—Biography. |
    Bicycle Racing—Europe.
Classification: LCC GV1051.G35 (ebook) | LCC GV1051.G35 A3 2018 (print) |
DDC 796.6/2092 [B]—dc23
LC record available at https://lccn.loc.gov/2017015784

Printed in the United States of America
10   9   8   7   6   5

Set in Minion Pro

To Dad

INTRODUCTION

I AWOKE IN THE middle of the afternoon on a sidewalk in Trinidad, wrapped in a strip of dusty carpet I'd torn from a roll in a stranger's garage. My left arm was numb from its role as a pillow, so I shook it out, using my right hand to brush away the flies buzzing around my eyes, before I dug through my backpack to find the jersey of whatever team I was sweating for that week, with riders I'd never heard of and sponsor names I couldn't pronounce. At twenty-six years old, I'd won some big races that season, finally clawing my way to a real pro contract after years of hard work and sacrifice. I thought that meant that the tough times were behind me, but now I knew that was wrong. *Will this ever end? When do I get to feel like I've made it?*

When I was a kid, celebrities and athletes told my generation to never give up on our dreams, promising that if we dug deep and believed in ourselves, we could also achieve great things. It sounds nice, but they left out that for every big winner, there were thousands who put in the same effort, but just weren't good enough. The losers don't get a microphone to tell their story, so you don't realize how much failure is out there and your perspective is skewed. I guess I was lucky to land somewhere in the middle.

I was born the day of the *Challenger* Space Shuttle disaster, so I saw myself as an astronaut eventually, but I wouldn't have ruled out the next Michael Jordan—dreams that must have worried my parents. Mom was raised in Brooklyn. By twenty-four, she'd finished a PhD in management at Carnegie Mellon University, where she met my dad. He grew up in post–World War II Germany and came to the United States on a Fulbright scholarship to study computer science. They both earned tenure as professors at Georgia Tech, so while Jordan told me to "just do it,"* my parents reminded me of a guy who once laced my Nikes at Stride Rite and talked about his years playing pro basketball in Europe—a cautionary tale to show me and my sister the value of practical goals, security, and stability. Mom and Dad made good money, but they cut coupons from the newspaper and drove Toyotas with roll-down windows, saving up for our college funds or a rainy day.

We lived in Tucker, Georgia, an old railroad-town-turned-suburb near Atlanta, where the shops on Main Street all had names like "Grandma's Attic" and never lasted more than a year or two. Bikeways of Tucker was across the tracks past the hardware store, and rumor has it, before it was filled with spokes and sprockets, the building was a meeting place for the KKK.

When the Olympics came to Atlanta in 1996, we went to the track and field finals. I was ten years old, in awe, imagining what it would be like to join that club, to be one of the best athletes in the world. I could see that nothing on Earth was more coveted or harder earned than a gold medal. Dad always thought sports were silly, but he humored me on my birthday, spending $299 at Sports Authority and mixing cement in a wheelbarrow to install a basketball hoop in our driveway (it came out a little crooked, but I never said a word).

The closest thing my family did to sports or exercise was

---

* Are any lawyers reading this? Can we sue Nike?

riding bikes together. One of my earliest memories is visiting my dad's relatives in Germany, where we took a day trip to the Netherlands, exploring local paths on borrowed cruisers. I remember having lunch at a restaurant by a river, with a waterwheel at the entrance. Dutch pancakes are yellow and the size of a manhole cover, so I shared one with my sister, and on the way home, Dad had to push me into the headwind or we'd never have made it back.

Every summer, my parents would load up the minivan and rent a house on Jekyll Island, Georgia, for a week. Dad and I got up early to ride our Huffys to the café in the courtyard of the Jekyll Island Club Hotel. He'd buy a coffee and a newspaper, and I'd have a Fudge Brownie Chip cookie, which was the greatest thing I'd ever tasted. I teased my dad for always carrying a backpack when we were on vacation, but he liked to stop at the market for groceries on the way home. I remember once when the express lane was "15 items or less," he counted sixteen in our basket and waited in the longer line, refusing to put back the flowers he'd bought for my mom. Dad followed the rules, and he stuck to his principles.

Me, Dad, and my sister Valerie, Jekyll Island, GA.

At seventeen, I thought I was too old to do the Jekyll trip with my parents, so I'd get the cookie with my dad, ride an angst-fueled lap of the island by myself, and watch TV at the rental house while they went to the beach. At first, I was annoyed that there was nothing on other than the Tour de France,* but then Tyler Hamilton won a stage with a broken collarbone, and Lance Armstrong crashed but still beat Jan Ullrich up the mountains on the way to his fifth win.†

Dad said I was wasting my vacation.

"Why would anyone care who wins a bike race?" he asked.

But I had to see if Lance's Discovery Channel team would catch the breakaway, "pulling" in the wind while Armstrong hid in their draft to save energy for his next devastating attack.‡ There were all sorts of prizes and races within the race that affected teams' strategies, from stage victories and sprints to the "king of the mountain" jersey for the best climber. Sweeping around castles and coastlines, the "peloton" was a symphony, and bike racing was a magical combination of a fistfight and a chess match.

The city of Atlanta is basically owned by the Coca-Cola Company, so our school had vending machines filled with soda and I don't remember ever drinking water as a kid. I spent most of my teens obese and depressed, never a fan of exercise, but when we got back from Jekyll, I headed straight to Bikeways, where the owner sold me a used Trek 1200 hybrid. It was two sizes too small, so I can confirm that he was a jerk (if not a KKK member) but I loved the freedom it brought me. Riding with my friends, I was an explorer, seeing the world for the first time. When I got home, I'd catch myself smiling and singing as I leaned my bike against the wall in the garage, and I could tell it was good for my soul.

---

* And *The Price Is Right.*
† Not to be confused with some guy who won . . . *a NEW CAR!*
‡ Bike racers draft just like in NASCAR. Riding inches behind someone is about 70 percent easier than being in the wind.

I'd lost forty-five pounds by the time I arrived at the University of Florida for college, so I was known as "Skinny Phil" to the UF Cycling Club, and I was more interested in learning how to draft than in doing my homework. I bought a racing bike on eBay and came back to Tucker for Christmas with shaved legs and tights (Dad shook his head, in a scene right out of *Breaking Away*).

Bikeways went out of business, and I noticed a sign on Main Street announcing a "beautification project." Tucker planned to remove a lane of traffic to make room for more parking, and they'd already added raised cement areas filled with soil and gray, foot-high twigs. I pictured the meeting where officials delegated funds for the project and wondered if anybody had addressed the elephant in the room: Tucker has its charm like any other antique, but it's old, dirty, and full of proud history. You can't fix it. As I crossed the railroad tracks, a pickup truck slowed down next to me and rolled down the window. "Get off the road, faggot!"

I trained hard that winter, and my brain released some great chemicals when I won my first race. I was addicted, and nothing else mattered for the next ten years of my life. I felt more alive when I was racing, and it was the first thing I'd ever done that I was immediately good at. When a friend brought me to a sports lab, I scored an off-the-charts VO_2 max of 88 and it felt like I'd discovered a superpower.*

Lacking in fast-twitch muscles, I lost every sprint, but I was always fastest up a hill, and I usually won time trials (known as TTs)—a discipline where riders compete against the clock on special bikes. In the summers, friends would go off to internships and think about silly things like careers, while I roamed the east coast, rocketing up the amateur categories. Like a crooked itinerant preacher, I'd show up in your town, do a little damage at the

---

* VO_2 max is a measurement of oxygen uptake—considered one of the most important genetic factors in endurance sports.

"local race," and leave. Often I'd barely make enough to cover gas and a burrito on the way home, but sometimes I'd walk away with $1,000, and by twenty years old, I'd won enough to join an elite amateur team, attending the biggest events on the National Racing Calendar.

Pro athletes seem to dwell on their doubters. Michael Jordan always mentioned the high school coach who cut him from the team, but the only doubter I remember coming across in those years was the director of the USA Cycling National Development Program, which grooms young Americans for the UCI WorldTour—the top level of pro cycling. I was a college sophomore when he said I was too old to join them in Belgium, that I should stay in school. *Whatever. Who wants to hang out in Belgium? I'm sure I'd get sick of waffles after a few weeks.*

My parents would have killed me if I dropped out, anyway. Dad thought I was wasting my time riding my bike so much, but I wouldn't call him a doubter—he just wanted what was best for me. To him, the WorldTour was men wearing tights, playing a game, with legs shaved for no reason, but to me, Lance and his colleagues were gladiators: the peak of human potential in strength and endurance and teamwork, carved out of granite. Okay, fine: wearing tights, with legs shaved for no reason.

Believers were much louder than doubters in those years. When I considered law school, all I heard from older guys on the group ride was how miserable it was to have a "regular" job. They promised that I had talent, that I could be a "professional athlete" and "live the dream."

I thought they were being encouraging, but I know the truth now: those men weren't thinking about my future at all. They were remembering a time when they'd given up themselves—not necessarily on bike racing, but at some point they'd set a dream aside. Now, maybe they had a career, a happy family, and a $5,000 bicycle, but there were still ups and downs. It was easy to think that if only they'd *gone for it*, life would be perfect.*

Lance Armstrong's inspirational story made him a household name, and when my dad was diagnosed with cancer, my mom found strength from his book. Dad beat it after months of radiation and chemo, and Mom emerged a cycling fan.

When Lance came back from retirement in 2009, corporate sponsors were plentiful, so established teams had real money, and it was easy for young riders to find jobs on "Continental" programs—considered the minor leagues of professional cycling. At twenty-two, I joined one sponsored by Jelly Belly, so I got a bike custom-painted with jelly beans, jerseys covered in candy, and luggage with the team logo and my name printed on it. It sounds ridiculous, but I'd never felt more proud.

When you hear "pro athlete," you might picture trashed hotel rooms and fancy cars, but that wasn't my experience on Jelly Belly exactly. Top guys at our level were making six figures, but the median salary was more like $15,000 a year and mine was $167 a month. I crisscrossed America in a Toyota Matrix with roll-down windows, meeting my teammates at untelevised races with meager prize money in towns you've never heard of. We stayed with host families, who often learned the hard way to never say "help yourself to the pantry."

When Jelly Belly only offered me $6,000 to stay another year, I moved to a smaller team sponsored by Kenda tires. They paid me a life-changing $15,000, but we weren't good enough to be invited to the Tours of California, Utah, and Colorado—the only events where Continental riders could show our ability to the top teams. Instead, we went to any low-level stage race that would pay our travel expenses, or criteriums—fast races through city streets,

---

* I can't count the number of times I've heard the phrase, "I could have been a pro, but . . ."

with hay bales stacked on the sidewalk by the sharper corners, because they *know* someone will crash there. I finished second overall at the five-day Tour of Taiwan (behind a guy who'd served a two-year EPO suspension), but I tore my chin open when the lead motorcycle crashed at the Tour of the Demilitarized Zone in Korea.* If there was a Tour of Somalia with a free buffet, I'd have been there.

The UCI (Union Cycliste Internationale, cycling's governing body) requires pros to have health insurance, but teams rarely provide it. On my salary, I signed up, showed them the card to get my racing license, and then canceled the policy. My parents feared that I was throwing away the money they'd spent on my education (I was), but they still cared, so they made me renew the insurance and paid for it themselves. I thought I'd be living the dream when I turned pro, but I was far from independent, secure, or stable. *I just did it, MJ. So now what?*

Continental riders all hoped to move up to the WorldTour. Sprinters craved a pounding from the legendary "cobbled classics" like Paris–Roubaix, while climbers dreamed of competing in a three-week "Grand Tour," but out of over a hundred guys on the circuit with the same goal, maybe one made it to Europe every couple of years. Those were bad odds, but the short season left plenty of time to try other things to pay the bills. I worked with private coaching clients, got published as a freelance writer for magazines,† and started a business that sold cycling clothes

---

* You think I'm making up the Tour of the DMZ, but we raced along barbed wire for three days, and the only spectators were soldiers with M16s. The race guide warned us not to pull off the road if we had to pee, because there were live land mines, and the motorcycle official—whose job is to guide the riders and block traffic ahead of us—misjudged a tight corner on a descent, slid out on his Harley, and the entire front group ran into him.

† I'd tell *Bicycling* magazine that I wanted to write a review on floor pumps, for example. They'd send me six new pumps, I'd try them out, write five hundred words for $500, and then sell them all on eBay.

online. Some of that did pretty well, but I still lived cheap, saving money, sure that every dollar I made would be my last.

I tried dating during those years, but couldn't make anything work, too busy supporting my dream like a responsible person might support a family. When a girlfriend said she wanted to spend more quality time, I made some popcorn, turned on a movie, and did crunches on the carpet, sending e-mails for my business between sets. For some reason she still wanted to get married, but we split up when she said she wanted kids someday. I was having so much trouble taking care of myself, I couldn't imagine that kind of responsibility.

I haven't painted a pretty picture of the Continental lifestyle, but when you've convinced yourself that the future will be better, it justifies the present, and being a pro athlete was a privilege. Besides, if I was struggling those years, I had too much fun to notice. During a long race, for example, there's a lot of downtime, so once the early break is established you can talk with your friends and screw around. If you have to pee, usually you go to the edge of the road on a downhill and get a teammate to push you while you relieve yourself at thirty miles an hour. I'd have someone push me so it *looked* like I was peeing, but I'd hold my water bottle waist-high and squirt half the pack, who'd scream in horror until they saw where it came from. A quick water fight would ensue, the breakaway would get caught, and we'd pay attention again. At the end, if my team won, we'd drink champagne, and if we lost we'd drink beer, but either way it was a party.

Every year, one or two of my teammates would become lifelong friends. I've had a running joke with Brad Huff and Jeremy Powers since 2009, where we send each other photos with captions like "Hey, guys, do these shorts fit?" and my testicles are hanging out of one side, for example. Once, at a bar with people I'd just met, a girl laughed at a video her boyfriend sent of a penis flopping around, and then showed it to the table.

"How the hell do you know Jeremy Powers?" I asked.

She was confused, because the picture was just from the upper thigh to the belly button, but I'd recognize that dick anywhere. Turns out her boyfriend was on Powers's team.

My phone still has a mile of my friends' genitals on it, and I never stopped laughing those years, piling up great relationships and once-in-a-lifetime experiences. By twenty-five, counting a family trip to Hawaii when I was a kid, I'd been to forty-nine states (Alaska—get your shit together and put on a bike race) and competed on three continents—just not the one that mattered. Sometimes I'd even win, and no matter how bleak my prospects looked, for that moment when those victory chemicals rushed through me, I was living the dream.

We finally caught on that cheating was rampant in the WorldTour. Lots of sports had drug problems, but doping was particularly effective for time trials and Alps, so in cycling, the most corrupt rose to the top. Even at the Continental level, I had to report my whereabouts to the U.S. Anti-Doping Agency (USADA). Roommates would get home to find me with a USADA representative and a chaperone, signing forms and sealing up bottles of urine at the kitchen table (the last place you want to see bodily fluids).

The biggest drug scandal so far was called Operación Puerto, in which authorities found 211 bags of blood and plasma in possession of a shady doctor. The bags were labeled with code names corresponding to the rider who gave them, so, while a legal battle made it impossible to confirm, you could figure out who was who.

For example, he denied it, but twenty bags were attributed to a Spaniard named Francisco Mancebo. Mancebo couldn't find a job in the shrinking European peloton, so he made a living on an American Continental team instead. I doubt if he was doping anymore, but Mancebo's engine was bored out from years of dirty Grand

Suffering to hang with Mancebo, Redlands, 2012.

Tours, so in low-level races, he was unstoppable. Like a boss in a video game, I finally got past everyone else, and then I had to find a way to beat *him*.

As more scandals broke, sponsors saw cycling as a risk and big teams folded. I was young and still improving, but with fewer jobs available, every year was a "bad year." Talented up-and-comers went back to school at twenty-five or retired at thirty, and a teammate named Pat Lemieux was living with me when he started dating a pro triathlete named Gwen Jorgensen. When she won a few races and decided to quit her day job as an accountant to chase her Olympic dreams, we all agreed that it made more sense for Pat to follow her around, fix her bike, and cook her meals than it did to cram into my Toyota for another criterium. I thought that every season might be my last, but I'd always get a contract that was sort of enough to get by on if I hustled on the side, and there was always one win, one moment of hope I could cling to. That was all it took to sign on the dotted line, and with every rider who gave up or moved on, I got a little closer to the top.

Bitter at twenty-five, I got a tattoo that says CLEAN on my right biceps, where you couldn't miss it when I raised my arm on a podium. People thought it was because I hated dopers, and I admit I ran my mouth at those guys every chance I got, but here's the real reason: I understood why someone might cheat. I wanted it so bad it scared me, and the tattoo was meant to give me resolve in case I was tempted. Pros Nick Waite, Adam Myerson, Isaac Howe, and Brad Huff got similar designs, and we made a pact: if you dope, the rest of us will come find you, and we'll scrape it off with a cheese grater.

It finally came out that Armstrong—the face of our sport—wasn't just cheating like everyone else. He was a mastermind, hiring top doctors and innovating new methods to win at all costs. While his rivals got caught, Lance used his power and money to go after anyone who got in his way, suing a former soigneur who spoke out,* and leaving threatening voice mails that made his enemies fear for their families. Frankie Andreu was one of the first to confess, and he was blacklisted in the industry for years, finally returning as director of my Kenda team.

I try to empathize and understand the gray areas, but my former hero seemed to be a sociopath—comic-book evil. I feared that Dad was right and I was wasting my time, but things seemed to be changing in the WorldTour. Jonathan Vaughters—who'd also been teammates with Lance—built a new team that focused on antidoping and hired a bunch of Americans to race clean in Europe, like David taking on Goliath. With his huge sideburns, tiny budget, and riders wearing argyle, it was hard to tell if "JV" was serious, but when he picked up Garmin as a title sponsor, other teams pushed away their needles, and the era of widespread doping began to fizzle out.

I was just a dumb kid living out of his car and spending prize money on a tattoo, but watching Team Garmin race the Tour de

---

* Soigneurs are pro cycling's specialized massage therapists, who also handle food, drinks, and logistics at races.

France, I didn't feel so lost. I flew to China to finalize patterns for my clothing business and took on a partner to handle the day-to-day jobs so I could train more and work part-time for a small monthly check. Then I spent my savings on an $80,000 foreclosed house in Athens, Georgia, tore out the dogfighting room the previous owner had built behind the garage (you read that right), and converted it to a 1/1 apartment with a small kitchen. The new bedroom had a solid-core door and no window to the outside (perfect for sleep and recovery). I filled the garage with bikes, and upstairs were three bedrooms and two bathrooms I could rent out for income.

Athens is a great town for a pro cyclist on a budget. A parking ticket was $4, and one of my training routes included two covered bridges and a gas station where a generous square of corn bread was 25¢. Between the business and the house, I had a pirate ship: bills were paid, and bike racing went from a hobby to a job. I bought a juicer, got a weekly massage, and hired a coach to oversee my training. (My parents still paid for my health insurance.)

The Pirate Ship in Athens, GA.

Thanks to my pirate ship, I won the opening stage at the Redlands Classic, a legendary five-day stage race near Los Angeles, considered a stepping-stone to the WorldTour. I nearly fell apart on the final day when Mancebo attacked, but I ripped through corners in the pouring rain, dug so deep I couldn't walk the next day, and caught him to take my first overall win (also known as the General Classification, or GC). The margin of victory: two seconds. That's what put me on the map, but it's also how close I was to failure—to having nothing to show for those years. I remembered watching Redlands as an amateur, and then being pack fodder my first time racing it, dreaming that I could win someday. Swinging from despair to hope, I cried on that podium, feeling for the first time that it was all going to be okay as I lifted my CLEAN tattoo over Mancebo. I cried again typing this, just thinking about that moment. I'm pathetic.

The six-figure salaries that went to previous Redlands winners were out of the question after all the scandal, so I was ecstatic to sign a $45,000 contract for 2013 with a well-funded Continental team called BISSELL. It was still the minor leagues, but BISSELL was always invited to the big American races, so I'd have a chance to compete against WorldTour teams, and I'd be flying there and staying at a hotel instead of driving and sleeping on an air mattress. And yes: the sponsorship included free vacuums. My floors in Athens were immaculate. Excuse me—I mean my *deck*.

Things were looking up, but there was one problem: I was twenty-five years old, and only one guy had ever made it to the WorldTour after a late start and a college degree. His name was Ted King. Ted realized that contracts don't always come with results, so he had to sell himself to teams and be marketable to sponsors. Pros made fun of Ted for writing a blog and using social media, but his relationship with Speedplay pedals got his foot in the door with the WorldTour, and he eventually became the token American on an

Italian squad sponsored by Cannondale. Following his example, I made an effort to be worth more to teams than just race results, and I began promoting sponsors on social media and writing reviews in magazines. Folks would tweet me what kinds of floors and pets they had, and I'd recommend an appropriate BISSELL. (I still get free vacuums. Mark Bissell is a nice guy.)

With all the pieces in place, starting in January 2013 I'd finally have a living wage and a shot at the big leagues, but when Kenda Pro Cycling ran out of money and folded in the middle of the season, I needed prize money and racing to stay in shape, so I accepted an invitation to be a guest rider (basically a hired gun) for an amateur team at the Tour of Trinidad, a ten-day stage race in the Caribbean in August, where the winner would take home a car. I was so desperate, I didn't even ask what kind.

A hundred riders piled into school buses at five a.m. in Port of Spain, Trinidad, for a two-hour drive to the opening time trial, and the second stage was that evening in the same town, so instead of driving us back and forth to the hotel, they dropped us off at someone's house. After a meager lunch of white bread and baked beans, I rode into town in search of roti—a specialty in Trinidad—curried chicken, potatoes, and hot sauce wrapped in dough.* When my stomach was satisfied, exhaustion set in, but the closest I found to a bed was an old roll of carpet, so I tore off a strip and fell asleep on the sidewalk—wrapped up like a roti.

My teammate had the overall lead, so I was on the front when the police car that was assigned to stop traffic pulled into a gas station, leaving me to lead the pack through traffic with trucks zooming by at sixty miles an hour on both sides. The race offered a "king of the mountain" prize for the first rider to the top of its biggest climbs, but summits were unmarked, so I laughed when

---

* My mouth is watering. Why hasn't roti made it to America?

they presented me with the traditional polka-dot jersey worn by the KOM leader. Someone said that I also won a bull as a prize, but I never saw it, so that might have been bullsh—I mean, a joke. After the stage, I bought a six-pack of Coronas for my teammates and took the next flight home. They were angry to lose their ringer, but when two stages were canceled due to heavy rain and flooding, I tried to avoid schadenfreude, a German word for taking pleasure in someone else's misfortune. By the end of the race, some of the riders suffered from a virus, with fever and stomach problems, and I tried to avoid scheissenfreude, a word I just made up for taking pleasure in someone else's diarrhea. I never found out what kind of car went to the winner. I bet it was used. Or Hot Wheels. And someone there owes me a bull.

Back in Georgia, I took a few weeks off to rest after a long season, using the time to work on a book about my journey through cycling. Comfortable in my house in Georgia, with my first real paycheck as a pro athlete on the way, I thought that my story was over, that it was "happily ever after." But when I showed my draft to a publisher, they said I didn't have enough of an ending,* which was true, but sort of sad and insulting. By then, I'd found writing was like scratching an itch, so that fall and winter, every minute I wasn't on the bike, I was staring at my laptop. When I finally reemerged, friends said I'd disappeared for months; but trying to explain things to imaginary readers had helped me understand them myself, forcing me to process emotions I'd been too busy to feel. I made apologetic phone calls to friends whose weddings I'd missed, and I contacted former teammates to thank them for something encouraging they'd said, which they usually didn't remember. I resolved to find balance and be a better person, and then I went to "wine night" at a bar with my buddies,

---

* Translation: "You're still a loser. Keep training."

where a glass of Cabernet and a slice of pizza was $4.50, and I went home with the bartender. She had blue hair.

I didn't think it would ever leave my laptop, but it still felt good to finish my book. The theme of *Pro Cycling on $10 a Day:** follow your dreams, but play it safe, stay in school, don't make too many sacrifices. You get the idea, but I don't know how I feel about that anymore.

---

* The title was a spoof on the famous travel book *Europe on 5 Dollars a Day*, but no one got the joke.

DRAFT ANIMALS

PART 1

*Life in
the Post-Dopocalypse*

CHAPTER 1

P RO CYCLING HAD tickled the mainstream for a year or two, but 2013 was an era that I like to call the "post-dopocalypse." When mainstream sponsors threw in the towel,* managers had to make do with whatever money they could squeeze out of the bike industry. More teams folded, and the sport was a barren wasteland of the one I'd watched as a teenager.

In most sports, when someone gets caught doping, they're outcast and often don't come back, but in cycling, drugs were too widespread and too entrenched. Guys like Lance's former coach Chris Carmichael had probably made his name on the wrong side of the rules, for example, but he rode the wave into a successful coaching business, which remains to this day. Of the teams that managed to stay afloat, most of the directors and managers were former dopers, and races were won by guys who'd either served suspensions or gotten away with it. The pack was filled with prominent jaws and foreheads—side effects from human growth hormone—and nearly a third of the WorldTour racers had

---

* Nike put a lot of money behind Lance, and they haven't touched cycling since.

prescriptions for asthma inhalers, a semilegal performance enhancer. I loved Alberto Contador's toughness and racing style, but then I'd see old footage of him attacking Lance on climbs. *He must have been cheating back then, so is he still doing it? Is he only winning because of the drugs he did before?* Then Contador tested positive for Clenbuterol and blamed it on contaminated steak. His team manager was Bjarne Riis, known as "Mr. 58" for his off-the-charts hematocrit from EPO abuse back when he was a racer.*

One WorldTour team was sponsored by "Katusha"—a Soviet artillery manufacturer. The marketing was so effective, when my old rocket launcher broke, I went right out and bought a Katusha.

Another big team was owned by Alexander Vinokourov. It sure looked like he'd bribed a Colombian rider to let him win the 2012 Olympic road race. They both deny it, but the Olympics are supposed to be sacred, and it didn't feel right when "Vino" became the boss of Team Astana, funded by the Kazakhstani government.

In the dopocalypse, every time I thought the sport was cleaned up, someone I'd raced against or looked up to would test positive. Young pros would never see drugs, but it was hard to know who to cheer for, and spectators were skeptical of every performance, talking about EPO like basketball fans might debate whether Jordan in his prime would beat LeBron—endless hypotheticals of who's doing it, who's not, and who stopped but definitely used to. They trusted guys with CLEAN tattoos, but we didn't win very often.

American cycling was littered with former dopers like Jonathan Vaughters (whose clean argyle team was now called Garmin-Sharp after securing another new sponsor); George Hincapie, who was reportedly making $1 million a year for Swiss team

---

* Hematocrit measures how much oxygen is in your blood—a big factor in a stage race, and anything over 50 is considered suspect. Even among nondopers, any decent bike racer knows how to read a blood test.

BMC; and Levi Leipheimer, who'd been a leader on Rabobank (one of the dirtiest teams of that era) and was signed to Quick-Step when he came clean about his past. Quick-Step must have known his history, but when it went public they acted shocked and fired him—punishment for breaking the code of silence. Forced to retire, Levi puts on an annual "Gran Fondo" in Santa Rosa, California, where thousands of recreational cyclists pay an entry fee to ride a doper's old training routes. Is that wrong? Did he serve a punishment? Beats me. He seems nice when I talk to him.

Then there was Tom Danielson. One of the best in the world at riding uphill, he'd signed with Vaughters, cleaned up his act, and was serving a reduced suspension after giving testimony against Lance. Continental pros hated dopers, and of that generation, for some reason Danielson was the most despised—half of us couldn't stand the guy, and the other half wanted to punch him in the face. Not knowing any better, I'd cheered for him when the 2005 Tour de Georgia raced through Tucker, but I was livid when he showed up at a charity ride I was doing seven years later, so when the gun went off, I made a point to rip that doper's legs off. It backfired when Danielson told me how impressed he was, that I was a big talent and he could help me reach the WorldTour if I trained with him in Tucson over the winter. I hated that cheating bastard, but I was flattered. Old men on the group ride had told me I could make it to Europe, but Danielson was first to say it who really knew anything.

My coach at the time was named Matt Koschara. He had a long, clean career as a professional, beating himself up for a decade, competing against dopers and barely getting by, later realizing that he'd made sacrifices that he shouldn't have. Koschara was a counselor as much as a coach.

"The way the sport is right now, if you can't be friends with dopers, you might as well quit," he said. "No WorldTour team will hire a guy with a CLEAN tattoo if they think you hate their managers and half their riders."

He said I could be the link between the clean and dirty generations—the first cyclist to speak out against doping, but still integrate with the old guard. Besides, looking at the ride I'd done with Danielson in Florida—knocking out one hundred miles in well under four hours—I couldn't deny the potential training value.

"There's no better workout than having someone kick your fucking teeth in," Koschara concluded. He's also a writer. Really has a way with words. A friend and former team sponsor was trying to sell his house in Tucson, and he said I could stay there as long as I kept it clean for the parade of Realtors, so I filled my car and headed west.

I expected to hate Danielson, but I was surprised at how encouraging and positive he was (no pun intended), always asking questions and teaching me about training. Lance did everything to win, which included lots of drugs, but also the best coaching, nutrition, drugs, equipment, and drugs. Danielson had learned a lot and was eager to share the legal parts, like how to train with a power meter, a high-tech device that measured how many watts I produced. His message was "we used to do it another way, but this is better."

We'd begin with an easy 200-watt cruise to the base of Mt. Lemmon, which was basically a commute, because that was where we went to work, on a six-day training cycle:

DAY 1: three sets of twenty minutes at 400 watts, followed by endurance riding, for a total of four hours

DAY 2: three sets of forty minutes at 370 watts, with added endurance, for a total of five hours

DAY 3: six hours, all-endurance pace, with no breakfast and no carbs, to "increase fat-burning metabolism," whatever that meant

DAY 4: repeat day 1, but add 5 watts
DAY 5: repeat day 2, but add 5 watts
DAY 6: don't leave the sofa, but I couldn't if I tried

It's funny how simple it sounds to follow the numbers, but how incredibly tough it was to do. Danielson finished each effort coughing and spitting, slumped over his handlebars. I thought I'd trained hard before, but I didn't know what training meant until I was on his wheel, pelted with WorldTour sweat. I slept ten hours every night, barely able to walk up the stairs to my bedroom. I ate so much oatmeal. You wouldn't believe the amount of oatmeal.

Far from the evil doper I expected, Danielson came off as generous and eager to please. At the end of one ride, I got a flat tire just a mile from where I was staying. I told him to go ahead and cruise home, but he waited with me while I changed it. When he mentioned that he was sick of the apartment he was renting, I said, "You know what, dude? You should have a look at my friend Billy's house."

The asking price was $520,000, and Danielson bought it. The first time he doped, I don't think he was conspiring to cheat and screw over clean cyclists. He was probably with his teammates, and someone said, "You know what, dude? You should inject this EPO."

When I finally asked about doping, Danielson said that it didn't feel wrong when everyone was doing it around him, like speeding on the highway. I knew he'd made mistakes, but he seemed like a guy trying to be better than his past, and helping me was a way to give back. If you want to hate someone, whatever you do, don't get to know them.

Americans remember where they were when they heard about the Kennedy assassination or the 9/11 attacks, and cyclists are the same with Lance Armstrong's confession to Oprah Winfrey. I was at the house in Tucson with my former teammate Isaac Howe, sinking into the sofa with our CLEAN tattoos, stunned.

I didn't feel much better falling behind at the end of Danielson's intervals the next day.

"You climb like an animal," I told him, sitting on the guardrail at Mt. Lemmon's Windy Point overlook with a mouthful of energy bar.

"Yeah, an elephant," he laughed. "You're closer every time. You'll get there."

He was right. After a few weeks, I could stay with him, and once, I even dropped him. Once.

CHAPTER 2

I N THE POST-EPO era, top riders used altitude training to legally stimulate red blood cell production and
improve endurance. Since power output is better at sea level, the
trend was to "live high, train low," so I went from Tucson to Big
Bear, California, which was high enough for adaptation but only
an hour's drive from Redlands, so I could train at low elevation on
roads I knew well. I stayed rent free at another friend's house
whose parents kept it as a winter ski getaway, but after a break-in
the previous year (among other things, their Springsteen CDs
were stolen), they were glad to have it occupied for the summer.

Fit from training with Danielson, I rode circles around the
competition at the season opener in Merced, California, and
when I finished the uphill time trial at the San Dimas Stage Race
a couple weeks later, half of the riders hadn't even gone yet, but I
knew I'd won. Before results are posted at TTs, riders walk around
the parking lot, discreetly asking each other their times. I sat with
my feet up by the BISSELL van, telling everyone that I'd finished
in 14:03—a time so fast, they thought I was messing with them.

Danielson was in Europe, but I sent him my power data from
the race, and he told Vaughters to sign me for 2014. JV thought

that the numbers must have been off, but at Koschara's urging, he offered to let me do a physiological test at a lab in Denver, and I booked a trip for the end of April, when I'd be peaking for the Tour of California.

With good legs and a strong team to support my leader's jersey, I'd never felt more confident than at the start of the second stage in San Dimas. I joked with friends in the pack and floated up the climb on the first few laps, but halfway through, I looked over my shoulder for my teammates and my handlebar clipped a fence on the side of the road. It had taken a decade to get close to the WorldTour, but one mistake, one lapse of concentration at thirty-five miles an hour, and I went from race leader to unconscious in a puddle of blood, my face shredded by pavement. The race went on, except for me and Ben Jacques-Maynes, who was caught behind me when I crashed. I barely knew him and we were rivals on the bike, but he stopped to help, afraid he was watching me die as paramedics crowded around.

I still don't remember the crash or the minutes leading up to it, but I'll never forget my thoughts when I woke up, trying to push through the fog.

*I'm dead.**

Hang on, don't panic! I can see, so I'm not dead.

But I can't turn my head. I must be paralyzed. I'll never walk again.

What's my name?

Joanna.

That's not my name. Fuck. I don't remember my name! Who's Joanna?

She must be my wife.

Where am I? What's that noise?

I figured my neck was broken, so I grabbed a handful of hair

---

* What would happen to my airline miles?

with my left hand and lifted my head manually to look around. The noise I was hearing was the motor of giant blades spinning through the air, because I was in a helicopter on the way to a hospital. I'd never been so afraid, but the morphine hit fast and my neck muscles cooperated later, so I wasn't paralyzed after all. I eventually remembered that my name was Phil and Joanna was not my wife. She was a girl I'd just met, and she had a boyfriend. This also reminded me that I'm a loser.

Omer Kem, BISSELL's team director, bought me an In-N-Out burger on the way home from the hospital. The milk shake soothed my sore jaw, but halfway through a Double-Double, I spit two molars into my hand. My health insurance didn't cover teeth, so if not for a dentist/cycling fan/hero who found me through Twitter and happened to live in Redlands, I'd have had to replace them with Chicklets.

Pain meds don't mix with operating a motor vehicle, so my teammate Pat McCarty drove me back up to Big Bear. Pat was another former Euro pro—one of the rare ones who didn't take drugs (which is probably why he didn't win much and ended up on BISSELL). The rumor is that he didn't want to go on a "program" when he was on Lance's team, and when the managers found out, Pat barely went to any races and was fired at the end of the year. He'd planned a trip to Big Bear to train with me, but I was in bed for two weeks, and Pat found himself acting as my live-in nurse. I'd never liked red meat, but I think my healing flesh gave me sudden cravings for beef, so he took me to Get the Burger, a Hollywood-themed diner near the ski resorts. I sat facing the wall, where no one could see the bruises and Frankenstein stitches on my face.

My wrist was fractured and I was sore all over, but I suffered most from the concussion. For weeks, I'd forget names and where I put my keys, and I was moody and depressed. I sent hateful e-mails to anyone who'd ever wronged me and confronted a friend for sponsoring Mancebo's team, which led to a shouting match in an alley with the team's manager (he'd have given me a black eye, but it would have been redundant). Joanna said she was going through a rocky period with her boyfriend, so I made her promise to have dinner with me after I healed. Can I blame the concussion for that? Maybe it was a different part of my body. Pro athletes are supposed to be douchebags, right?

Our team doctor had us take a baseline concussion test in the off-season, so when I hit the same score on the series of memory and word puzzles, it meant my brain was recovered enough to ride again.* The Tour of California was a few weeks away, so I put in some of the hardest rides of my life, doing repeats of the eight-thousand-foot climb from Redlands to Big Bear. I remember sitting on the floor in the shower those days, unable to stand.

My form had evaporated, but I was too cheap to throw away the plane ticket I'd bought before the crash, so I still went to Denver for Vaughters's lab test. Dr. Iñigo San Millán hooked me up to an oxygen mask and slowly increased the resistance on a $40,000 stationary bike, pricking me with a needle every few minutes to measure the level of lactic acid in my blood. He'd tested dozens of WorldTour riders, and he said that my twenty-minute power-to-weight ratio was probably among the top fifty in the world.

As cycling got more scientific with lactate tests and power-to-weight metrics, it also got more anorexic. I'd eaten a lot of salad that spring, so my reflection in the mirror was all skin, veins, and bones, but Dr. San Millán said I could lose two pounds.

"I could cut off half my penis," I offered.

He didn't laugh. Some of the WorldTour teams were known for "starvation camps," where they sent riders out on long rides, with maybe an apple for fuel if they were lucky, and I'd heard of pros who ate "negative-calorie soup": diluted beef broth with

---

* Or it meant I took the test twice a day and got better at it.

celery and other high-fiber veggies.* I made one bowl, and decided I'd rather get dropped.† I also once saw a pro buy a bar of dark chocolate at the airport, smell it, and then throw it away.

Vaughters was impressed at the test results, and so began a weeks-long interview process, all via e-mail. He'd ask a question—like how did I come out of nowhere to win Redlands in 2012—and I'd spend hours crafting the perfect two-sentence response. Our conversation continued through the Tour of the Gila in New Mexico, where I tore the race apart on the final "Gila Monster" stage, finishing second overall, only caught by Mancebo in the last kilometer.

On the way to the airport after Gila, Vaughters criticized my tactics but complimented my effort, and then asked if I get homesick—if I could handle moving to Europe. I remember wondering if anyone had ever screwed up the interview on that question. ("Wait. It's in Europe? Never mind.")

I told him I'd taken two semesters of Spanish and I love paella.

I landed in San Diego, still thinking I needed a result at the Tour of California the following week. My friend JC had borrowed my car while I was racing, so I was sitting on the hot metal bench at the airport, waiting for him to pick me up, when I heard the "new e-mail" notification on my phone, with a contract from Vaughters in my in-box. He knew I was going well and wanted to sign me before I got the big result. The offer I'd been chasing for a decade, which I'd flown to Denver and endured a three-week interview for: $50,000—the WorldTour minimum—take it or leave it.

What was Vaughters thinking, sending that shitty offer? That his team was some kind of elite fraternity that would change my fate forever? That I would uproot my life, drag myself to Europe,

---

* Somebody's going to read this and try it. Please don't.
† I don't think I ever had an eating disorder, but it wouldn't surprise me. My job was a power-to-weight ratio, and I never got weak or sick from going overboard, but feel free to diagnose me.

and start from scratch for less than his trash guy makes? That I'd do twice the work for $5,000 more than I got from BISSELL? He did think that, and he was right.

I'd been aiming for the WorldTour, but I never really thought it would happen. When I looked into the future, I saw an abyss—I figured I'd have to go back to school or park cars for a living, or lie in the dirt somewhere, soaked in urine and yelling at strangers. This contract would save me from that, but more importantly, it came with glory, which was worth all the intervals, all the times I'd raced in the rain and had to fly home with a muddy bike and a suitcase full of wet clothes. It was even worth the crashes. I was an orphan, and JV was adopting me: he found me in this impoverished world of Continental racing and he plucked me out, trusting that I could adapt to his fancy WorldTour home on the other side of the tracks. He could have signed anyone he wanted, but he chose me, and I loved him for it.

Danielson said that minimum salary was standard for the first year, which was even less on middle-tier teams (there are guys racing the Tour de France on $35,000), but if you prove yourself as a solid team member, you get multiyear contracts and you're bumped up to $150,000–$200,000. If you can win, it's $400,000, and if you win big, a handful of guys take home seven figures. Once again, I found out I'd only clawed my way to the middle. Living the dream was up just one more switchback.

I could have sent my contract from the FedEx Ship Center next to the Tour of California's first hotel, but there were nosy team managers and media everywhere, so I went on a secret mission—to a different FedEx store four miles away. I was so excited, I got pulled over for speeding (88 in a 65 mph zone), but he let me off when I told him why I was in town. Cops love the Tour of California. They get paid overtime for special events and all they have to do is stand around.

I sprinted into the FedEx office and left with the swagger of a man who'd just hit it big. Then I fell into my Toyota, bawled my eyes out for a few minutes, and headed back to meet my team, driving exactly sixty-four miles per hour.

My new job wouldn't start until January, and I was supposed to keep the news hush-hush until Vaughters made the announcement, which meant that I told everyone I knew, but made *them* promise not to tell. I also e-mailed the publisher that night with an idea for a new ending: Vaughters and Danielson are unlikely heroes, and I join the WorldTour with Garmin-Sharp. They gave me a $10,000 advance and, just like that, two dreams came true.

Vaughters expected me to finish on the podium at the Tour of Cali, but I had horrible legs and dropped out after a few days. I chalked it up to a cold or allergies at first, but now I think it was more emotional. I'd put myself through a lot for that contract, and when I finally got it, my body just shut down. It was as if my nervous system was complimenting my work ethic, proof that I gave it absolutely 100 percent. Or it was just a cold and I'm being dramatic.

I bounced back at the national championship road race a week later, where the winner gets to wear a stars-and-stripes jersey for the year. I attacked at the perfect time, and it looked like I had it in the bag until a half mile from the finish, when WorldTour rider Matt Busche sacrificed his own result to catch me, probably as a favor to a friend on a different team. Collusion is against the rules, but it's also pretty common, and it backfired when Jelly Belly's notorious sprinter Freddie Rodriguez took the win. Spectators reported seeing Freddie take a "sticky bottle" up the mountain on the last lap, so he should have been disqualified, but officials fined him $2,000 instead—a bargain for a national championship.*

Vaughters said that I should fuck Busche's wife as revenge,

---

* A "sticky bottle" is when the team car holds a water bottle out the window, but instead of taking it, the rider holds on and takes a tow. I got many sticky bottles the year I rode for Jelly Belly, until it got me kicked out of a race in China, and I never did it again.

which wasn't great to hear from my future boss, but I couldn't judge. I was too busy trying to fuck someone else's girlfriend.

When Garmin-Sharp finally announced my contract, within hours I'd doubled my Twitter followers and had interview requests from every cycling publication, along with hundreds of congratulatory e-mails, texts, and Facebook messages. During my ride that day, a series of smoke signals lit the hills outside of Redlands, which I assumed said "Congratulations, Phil!" But it turned out to be a forest fire, forcing a detour that brought my ride from a nice six hours to a painful seven. (Pros talk about seven-hour training rides, but they rarely do it on purpose.)

I appreciated the support, but it was scary that people liked me more all of a sudden. Did that mean they'd like me less on the way down? I usually communicated with my friend Jeremy Powers via dick pics, but he was a few years ahead of me on the success curve,* so I also called him for advice.

"That's why we move in closer with our real friends, Phil. Now you have to be more careful about who you let into the circle. Remember who returned your calls before you were in the World-Tour, and you don't want to date the girl who likes you because you're fast."

"Got it. Only date girls who like me because I'm so handsome."

"Exactly. Then you're fine as long as you can afford kibble for her Seeing Eye dog."

It was sound advice, which I couldn't take because it was time to hire an agent. Now that I had my foot in the door, guys who'd ignored me in the past were offering to help with my next contract, including the top dog: Andrew McQuaid. Andrew's father, Pat McQuaid, was the head of the UCI, who'd supported Lance and somehow had no idea that everyone was doping as long as his paychecks showed up. For his son to represent riders sure seemed

---

* Until now, bitch! I wrote a book!

like a conflict of interest, but with some of the top cyclists in the world as Andrew's clients, I felt like a big shot when I signed on. He wouldn't take anything from my 2014 deal with Garmin-Sharp, but he'd get 10 percent of my next one, when the real money would roll in.

CHAPTER 3

THE REST OF the summer didn't go well for me or my BISSELL team. I'd get the occasional "good luck" or "nice job" from Mark Bissell, but his board of directors was sick of sponsoring cycling. At our first meeting at the Tour de Beauce in Quebec, Omer announced that they needed a $500,000 cosponsor to appear beside BISSELL's logo on the jersey the next year, or the team would fold.

"How about Dyson?" I suggested. "Or maybe Hoover?"

Everyone laughed, but only for a second. You can't laugh too much at your own unemployment.

Since I was the only one with a contract, I understood that guys didn't feel like working for me anymore, but as teamwork took a backseat, we didn't have as much fun as we did in the spring. Some guys were bitter that I was moving up, watching me pose for pictures with fans (I had fans all of a sudden). I'd mentioned in a blog that I liked cookies, and people were baking and delivering them to me at races. It was bizarre and wonderful (and of course I shared), but I think even Omer was jealous. A failed Continental racer-turned-director, he gave me a lecture because I forgot to pack my team-logo polo shirt to the Tour de Beauce in Quebec.

"When you're in the WorldTour next year, never forget your polo," he warned.

What the hell do you know about the WorldTour? I didn't ask.

I caught a cold that week, and it wasn't emotional this time: with a fever and a bad cough, I fell behind on every climb and finally dropped out during the third stage, along with teammate Carter Jones, who shared my hotel room and caught my disease. Too embarrassed to show our faces at the race buffet that night, Carter and I borrowed the team car and went to a restaurant for poutine: Quebec's greasy specialty of French fries covered in gravy and cheese. Omer gave us the car keys, but disciplined us the next morning for using them. He said that Chris Baldwin, one of the older guys on the team, complained that we were being unprofessional by "quitting the race," and then "going out." Omer was kind of a worm. I'd heard him brag about how he played riders against each other to make us more competitive, because what a folding Continental cycling team really needs is a Machiavelli.

The old men who told me to chase my dreams often followed it up with a story about annoying coworkers or shitty bosses, but pro cyclists have it, too. A bad teammate can ruin your day, and directors have a say in who's hired, what races you do, and your role in each stage. If he doesn't like you, he'll leave you at home, put you on bottle duty, or worse: send you to criteriums.

Most directors are retired racers, but it's crazy how fast they forget what it's like. I was still dunking my hand in ice after bumpy rides, sore from the wrist I'd fractured in March, and now I was expected to race sick and disciplined like a child. Being a pro cyclist reminded me of Oregon Trail, a computer game I'd played as a kid based on pioneers moving west in the 1800s. In the game, you'd purchase "draft animals," like oxen or horses, to pull your covered wagons. You could sell or trade them, but more often, you'd just use them up and buy a new one when they died.

Carter apologized to Omer, but I couldn't swallow my pride anymore and I had nothing to lose, so for the first time, I talked back to my director. Standing up for myself was so much fun, I kept it up the rest of the year, laughing in Omer's face every chance I got. What could he do? Not race his best guy?

CHAPTER 4

I HAD A GOOD month of training when I got back to Big Bear. Blood tests showed an increased hematocrit, but living alone in an empty ski town was a steep price to pay, so I was excited to see my teammates again at the five-day Cascade Classic, which would be my final preparation for Utah and Colorado. I told anyone who'd listen that I was going to attack with 5k to go and win Cascade's first mountaintop stage. They laughed, and then they watched me do it, like Babe Ruth when he pointed at the stands and hit a home run. Babe Ruth, but skinnier, although I think our pants were equally tight. Mancebo finished second, after pouring what looked like a thousand milligrams of caffeine pills into his mouth on the first climb. There's an old-school Euro racer logic: find out how much will kill you, and take one less.

I enjoyed a brief podium ceremony on top of the mountain, followed by a longer ceremony of peeing into a cup for authorities. Normally, I took pride in how fast I got through the steps of a drug test: filling out the forms, matching the number on the packaging to the vial, opening the official seals, etc. It's always the same routine and you don't want USADA to walk you through it like a rookie, but I was dehydrated that day, so my first attempt was less than ninety milliliters, requiring extra paperwork.

Weeks later, you get an e-mail that test results are ready, so you log in to USADA's website and download the official letter (it starts with "Congratulations!"). Of course I'd never cheated, but my blood pressure would go up every time I waited for that letter to download, like you might get nervous when a police dog sniffs your bag at the airport. I'd think about Contador's "contaminated meat" excuse, and the tacos I ate out of a food truck. *Could a taco be tainted?*

If you've read any other books by professional cyclists, you know that they all have a doping revelation of some sort, so I'll get that out of the way here. USADA, remember this day at Cascade where you made me sit in a camp chair by the finish line, chugging water for over an hour until I could fill the pee cup? And remember all those times that you came to my house to take my blood? I wasn't always being completely honest with you, USADA. The truth is, from 2008 to 2013, I stole several of your pens (I like to think that I'm the reason they switched to iPads).

My lead slipped after the first stage, so I only finished sixth overall at Cascade, and every time the road went uphill in Utah and Colorado the next month, I'd be in the second or third group. I'd proven the best climber in the Continental races, but against the top guys and big teams, I was climbing like an elephant.

On BISSELL, we worked together, but our strategy at big events was scattered: Carter and I hoped to finish in the top ten overall, while others would go for the sprint or try to make it into a breakaway. I noticed that WorldTour teams were different, with eight guys all focused on one goal. In a pack of 150, only ten have a shot at a good result, and their teammates all have a task to make it happen: ride on the front to catch the breakaway, get bottles for the leader from the car, help the sprinter catch up if he gets dropped on the climb. These role players are known as "domestiques." They're the working class. That would probably be me next year.

For most cycling fans, when domestiques are at work, the TV is only on in the background. They pay attention near the end, when the climbers start attacking each other or the "leadout" riders help sprinters fight for position. That's when you find the drama. The glory. The crashes.

Domestiques don't have to worry about that mess. When the big names start racing, they fade to the back, and someone yells, "Groupetto!": the cue for half of the pack to call a truce, riding slow to the finish together, chatting and joking around. Destined for the WorldTour at twenty-six, I was supposed to lead my team to a GC podium in Utah, but I experienced my first groupetto instead, while twenty-one-year-old Lachlan Morton won the Mt. Nebo stage for Garmin-Sharp. I was in the groupetto again on Snowbird when Danielson took the lead, and I stayed there for most of the Tour of Colorado.

Groupetto residents are usually anonymous, but there was one exception those weeks: Jens Voigt. Jens was known for the early breakaway—putting on a great "suffer face" as he hopelessly tried to steal victory from a charging pack of sprinters. European fans didn't think much of Jens, but a culture that tells everyone to chase their dreams loves a guy who goes for the win, tries really hard, and fails, so Jens was a hero when he raced in the States, soaking up applause as he finished minutes behind the leaders. I respected his determination, but I had one little problem with Jens: he'd raced through the dirtiest decade on some questionable teams, and still insisted that he'd never doped, or even seen anything suspicious.

Either Jens needed an eye exam or he was full of shit, but when he asked if I wanted to hear a joke, part of me was honored that such a big name would acknowledge my existence.

"Three men were at the *Guinness Book of World Records*," he began. "One said, 'I want the record for world's smallest hands.' So the other two wait, and he comes out all excited with a certificate for his new world record. The second guy goes in for the record for smallest feet, and he comes out with a certificate, too. Then the third guy says, 'I'm going in for the smallest penis record.' They wait and wait, and finally, he comes out with his world record. 'Congratulations, Jens!' they said."

"If you tell that joke, you can use any name that you want!" Jens explained, in his thick German accent. "You can use your name, or the person you're telling the joke to, or even mine if you'd like."

"I understand. Thanks, Jens."

I told him the one about my cousin Mike, who came to stay at my house.

"I forgot to knock and just walked into his room, and, well, he's thirteen, so you know what he was doing. I said, 'Mike, if you keep that up, you're going to go blind.'

"Mike said, 'Phil, I'm over *here*.'"

Jens didn't get it.

I remember the dick jokes verbatim, but don't ask who won the stages in Colorado, because I couldn't see from ten minutes behind. There's a good chance it was Peter Sagan, a young Slovakian all-rounder. Sagan had won some big races, but he was most known for grabbing the butt of a "podium girl" at the Tour of Flanders in 2012. I'd hoped that the incident would bring an end to the misogynistic idea that the winner gets a kiss from a pretty girl, but race organizers insisted that hiring models to stand around in short skirts is tradition, and they're not primitive sexual prizes—they're professionals, who should never be objectified. Fair enough, but from what I've seen, most of them end up in someone's hotel room by the end of the race.

I was selected for a random drug test after a stage in Colorado, which proves that it is truly random if you consider my eightieth place overall. During the testing process, you list your vitamins and therapeutic use exemptions (TUEs), which allow you to take certain substances if a doctor can make a case for it. All I had to declare was a multivitamin, while one of the WorldTour riders detailed his regimen on the other side of the room. Aside from a variety of innocent supplements your mom probably takes, he had TUEs for asthma medication, the legal limit of cortisone, a painkiller called tramadol, way too much caffeine, and a long list of other things I've never heard of. Basically, if Hunter S. Thompson decided to take on a marathon, this would be his shopping list. *Is that normal? Is this what I'll be up against in Europe?*

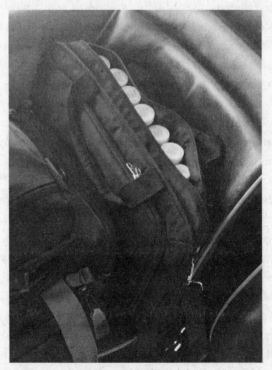

WorldTour team doctor's bag.

Unprepared for longer stages, tougher competition, and with not nearly enough pills, I wasn't the only Continental rider to struggle those weeks. Pat McCarty caught Freddie Rodriguez taking a sticky bottle on a climb again, so he took a handful of Freddie's national champion jersey, yelling until the car drove away.

Tough racing always brings out the cheaters, and I noticed that when guys are in the red, they also crash more often. You know that moment when you're just sitting at your desk at work, and suddenly bikes and dudes are tumbling around you and all you can do is squeeze the brake levers on your office chair as hard as you can amidst sounds of crunching carbon, tearing flesh, and the screams of grown men in pain? Then your wheels are locked up, you're pointed the wrong direction, and at exactly the moment when the ground is sucking you down and you think it's all over, you let off the brakes, momentum sets you upright again, you find a hole through the carnage, and you're back in the office, laughing with your friends like nothing ever happened? Oh, that's not a thing at your job? Lucky.

With no luck finding a cosponsor, the mood on our team was dismal by the end of the summer. Chris Baldwin announced his retirement, so Colorado would be his bittersweet farewell race, which made it even more tragic when he stuck his finger in his wheel and didn't finish. I'd always looked up to Chris, but he'd been difficult since I signed my WorldTour contract, arguing at meetings, even chasing me down when I might have won a second stage at the Cascade Classic. He'd started a fight about water bottles that day in Colorado, and I told him I was going to kick his ass when we got to the bus after the stage. Then Chris tried to adjust his speed sensor "on the fly" and ended up in a hospital. Baldwin was a solid bike handler, but one mistake, one lapse of concentration at thirty-five miles an hour, and he's sitting in the dirt outside of Steamboat Springs, hoping someone can sew his pointer back on.

Chris returned to the race the next day and as a commentator the year after, but he always avoided me. A friend suggested that subconsciously, Baldwin broke his finger on purpose, just to avoid the ass kicking I'd promised him. Both of us were six foot one and 148 pounds, with no upper-body muscle, world-class endurance, and a stubborn willingness to suffer, so it would have been a great fight, but Chris, if you're reading this: I was just going to yell at you.

With Baldwin out, BISSELL had a high attrition rate. We started with eight, but I found myself at breakfast one morning with just Carter Jones, Pat McCarty, and Jason McCartney. Jason said that he did the Vuelta a España once and his team only finished three. He was yet another former WorldTour rider and teammate of Lance's, so when I told him I'd be based in Spain the next season, he had lots of good advice, and a three-year-old flip phone with a Spanish SIM card that he wanted to sell me, for the bargain price of $40.

Pat and Jason knew Danielson when he was dirty, so I asked what they thought of my new friend and benefactor.

"Man, when we were teammates, even the Spaniards thought that Tom was 'abusing the medicine,'" Pat said, frowning (if the Spaniards said it, you know it was true).

"What about now, though? You don't think he can change?"

"You know me pretty well, right, Phil? You know I'm a good guy?"

"Sure, Pat. The best," I said, remembering all those times he took me for burgers in Big Bear when my face was busted.

"So sometime when you're hanging out with Tom, ask him about me and see what he says. That's how you'll know if he's okay."

I liked that answer (it was very *Godfather*), but I already knew that Danielson didn't like McCarty. Maybe I could have friends on both sides, but I'd never be able to cut through the anger from those years. Pat had also decided to retire when BISSELL folded, and joked about how fat he would get when he stopped racing. The Christmas card he sent that year was a photo of himself and his girlfriend, with digitally enlarged bellies and double chins. Pat wrote a note on the back that said, "Keep chasing your dreams, Phil." I'm pretty sure he was fucking with me.

Jason didn't offer an opinion on dopers. I doubt if he saw any notorious doctors, but a lot of guys from his era drove to Mexico to buy EPO or ordered drugs off the Internet, hoping they wouldn't die when they injected it alone in a bathroom somewhere, doing what they felt was necessary to keep their jobs.

Pat and Jason taught me how to pack a WorldTour "rain bag." BISSELL gave each rider space in the team car for spare shoes and arm warmers if we needed them during a race, but in Europe, every rider has a bag in the trunk filled with jackets, vests, gloves, and shoe covers to race in any conditions.

Omer overheard the rain bag conversation and reiterated that I should always have a team-logo polo in my suitcase.

"You can get away with that sort of thing here, but not in the WorldTour," he said.

"If I can get away with it, why do you keep bringing it up?" I asked.

"What the fuck does that guy know about the WorldTour?" Pat laughed, when Omer was out of earshot.

The final stage was laps through downtown Denver, with Ted King controlling the pace for Peter Sagan. Just for something to do, I went to the front and traded pulls with Ted, until Jason came up and whispered to me.

"Phil, are they paying you to ride the front?"

I'd heard of tired teams making that sort of deal, but obviously it wasn't the case here. "Yeah, Cannondale really needed more horsepower. They were begging me all day so I told them to bust out their checkbooks. Next week I'll put in a swimming pool at my house."

"Then get the fuck off the front, Phil. You don't do another team's work for free."

"What do guys get paid to chase for another team?" I asked, as we coasted back into the group.

"I've known dudes who got $1,000 a day if a team was desperate enough," Jason said.

After the finish, I should have tracked down Ted or Sagan and demanded a dollar for my three pulls, but my main focus was on the boogers that built up from the dry, dirty Denver air. My mom spent half my childhood trying to convince me to stop picking my nose, until my grandfather gave me honest advice that adults should give children more often (instead of that garbage about following dreams):

"Just make sure nobody's looking," he said.

Grandpa has a huge nose, so if there's anyone I could trust when it came to boogers, it was him. I found a seat in the back of the RV and got to work on my nostrils.

Colorado was the last race of the season, so it was time for good-byes. Pat was just getting out of the shower, so he got a big, wet hug, but when I reached for Jason's hand, he left me hanging.

"Good luck in Europe, Phil. It was nice working with you this year, but I'm not gonna shake your hand because I just saw you pick your nose."

Don't tell my grandpa.

Tejay van Garderen won the Tour of Colorado, but all eyes were on Chris Horner, who'd finished second overall in Utah and won the Vuelta a España a few weeks later. A four-time Redlands winner before I'd ever pinned on a number, and a career domestique in Europe, fans loved the story of Horner getting his big chance at forty-one, but if something seems too good to be true, in cycling, it usually is. While Danielson and others made their confessions public, some guys chose to have their names removed in the testimony. Horner always denies it, but it's generally assumed that he's "Rider 15." I bet he was off the good stuff by 2013, but the antidoping system still had some loopholes, and the rumor is that he spent the first half of the year "injured," pumping himself full of cortisone. An effective treatment for bad joints and inflammation, cortisone is legal out of competition, so it's common to abuse the steroid between events, raising your power while body fat falls off. Chris wouldn't test positive, but all the teams were suspicious, and it says a lot that after winning a Grand Tour, he barely managed a contract for the following year. It was frustrating to see the outpouring of support for guys like Horner and Voigt, but if I could barely figure out who to trust, how could fans be expected to get it right?

CHAPTER 5

WITH THE SEASON over, I was looking forward to Europe, my book was almost finished, and my business was nearly on autopilot. I should have been happy, but there was a hole in my life: I was tired of doing it alone, and fixated on Joanna, who'd finally broken up with her boyfriend.

When I was living in Athens, whenever I brought a girl home, she had two questions the first time she saw me naked:

1. "What are those tan lines from?"
2. "How many times have you crashed?"

So I'd given up dating girls who didn't ride bikes. Joanna raced on weekends and dreamed of being a pro cyclist (or an actress), but she had a social life and a day job in TV production in Hollywood. Some might argue that the early stage of a concussion is the last time to trust your instincts, but I took it as a sign that I'd thought of her name in the helicopter when I still couldn't remember my own. She said she wanted to be single for a while, but instead of driving back to Georgia, I convinced her to let me join her in L.A.

I was excited to take the usual end-of-season break and spend time with my new girlfriend, but Vaughters had another idea. My training had always focused on short, uphill efforts like I'd encounter at Redlands and Cascade, but seeing how bad I was in Utah and Colorado, he wanted to improve my endurance by simulating the length and intensity of a Grand Tour: five-hour rides every day for three weeks at 300–350 watts (that's a lot), with two rest days in the middle, dubbed the "Tour de Phil."* Friends said that my new boss was hazing me, or maybe it was some sort of test, but in a twisted, masochistic way, it sounded like fun.

The start was the hardest part. Suffering on day two, it was hard to imagine I could keep it going for three weeks, and on the third day, a car turned in front of me on my way out of town. I caught myself on the hood with my left hand, irritating the wrist I'd fractured six months before and putting a big bruise on my palm where it rested on the handlebars.

Shaken up, my first instinct was to take a few days off, let the hand heal, and restart the Tour de Phil the next week, but then I remembered that this was supposed to be a Grand Tour simulation. If I did a real Grand Tour, maybe (hopefully) I wouldn't hit a car, but there'd be some sort of adversity to push through, so I rode home for a pair of padded gloves and headed back to the hills.

I asked everyone I knew to ride with me that month, but if you ever want to make a bike racer cringe, invite him to do five hours at 325 watts (and if you want to make him hang himself, ask in September, when the season is supposed to be over). A former teammate named Stefano Barberi joined me for a few days. He was a good friend, and like any great cyclist, he also appreciates masochism. Stefano was one of the best when I was coming up (especially if you scratch the dopers out of the results), but he was another victim of a shrinking sport—a veteran rider unable to find a contract.

---

* JV is very creative.

Racing as an amateur, he'd moved to Thousand Oaks with his fiancée, Katie, where a pro named Jesse Anthony (who rode for a Continental team called Optum) showed us the roads.* Just a few minutes north of L.A., I expected car horns and traffic, but other than celebrities who live there, there are few cars on the climbs that start from the Pacific Coast Highway along the ocean, up to Mulholland Highway at the top of the ridge. Riding just minutes from a major city felt safer than the countryside in Georgia (I was once attacked by an angry redneck at a Waffle House in Athens), but I'm pretty sure I got cut off by Tom Selleck one time.

I felt better the second week, surprised at how well my legs adapted to the effort. One day, I rode inland to San Dimas, to pee on the spot where I'd seen photos of paramedics crowded around me after my crash, because who gets to piss on their own symbolic grave? My various medals and awards were buried in a box somewhere, but that night, I hung up the San Dimas leader's jersey that they'd cut off of me in the hospital, still bloody and dirty. That was the first time I'd danced the lined between life and death. I was proud that I'd overcome it, and it seemed like something I shouldn't forget.

Entering week three, my brain was confident that I could finish the Tour de Phil, but my body disagreed. Power output was still good, but my heart rate wouldn't crack 140, and every acceleration was a chore. With no team car or soigneur to hand me bottles, I'd been allowing myself a break in the middle of every ride. The first week, I stopped at gas stations, refilled my bottles, and jumped back on the road. Week two, the break got longer—often a grilled chicken wrap at Chick-fil-A in Thousand Oaks. By week three, it was the In-N-Out Burger on Ventura Boulevard in Woodland Hills, and I'd stay for an hour, giving my bike the

---

* Garmin-Sharp's Dave Zabriskie also lived there. I saw him a few times and waved, thinking we should ride together since it looked like we'd be teammates soon, but he never waved back. I'm told he didn't get along with Danielson.

middle finger if it looked at me wrong. I'd eaten everything in the fridge by then, so I'd order pizza for dinner or get take-out Thai or Mexican. Most nights, I woke up at four a.m. and ate peanut butter out of the jar, glad that Joanna was out of town at a race of her own.

When I woke up on the last day, I was trashed, and I couldn't imagine pushing myself anymore, so I decided to let the steepest climb in Malibu do it for me. I parked my car in the dirt at the base of Decker Canyon and cut the sleeves off of my jersey with the Leatherman that lives in my glove compartment. For the next seven hours, I threw my bike up switchbacks as hard as I could, made a U-turn at the top for ten minutes of blissful coasting, and went right back up again from the ocean.

After twelve laps, my tank was empty and I collapsed into my car. Still in my tights, barefoot, with three weeks of beard, and sunburned from the sleeveless jersey, I staggered into Trader Joe's, where I purchased a gallon of milk and a box of chocolate chip Dunkers (cookies shaped long and narrow for dipping). Most Grand Tours end with champagne at a lavish after party, but the Tour de Phil closed with me eating an entire tub of cookies, chugging whole milk from the jug on a curb in Westlake Village.

I don't think Vaughters ever sent anyone else on a Tour de [your name here], so maybe it was hazing, but I was glad I did it. I'd been scared shitless that I wouldn't be ready for the World-Tour, sure that he'd made a mistake in signing me. Now, instead of ending the season with a whimper, I'd accomplished something that I wouldn't have thought was possible. I felt empowered and prepared for the next season, having earned my time off—and my Dunkers.

While I was training, Pat McQuaid was finally ousted as head of the UCI, in an election that seemed like a lot of campaigning for not much of a contest, considering all the scandal around him. If you're commissioned to build a bridge, you're an architect, but if you built it out of shit and it falls apart, you're a crook. "Good riddance to that asshole," I couldn't say, because his son was my agent.

Despite the cookie binge, I finished the Tour de Phil five pounds lighter than I'd started, so I made an appointment with a nutritionist the following week. Dr. Phil Goglia had worked with all kinds of athletes and movie stars, but most importantly, he was a cycling fan, so he waived the $250 fee for a first visit. A former bodybuilder, Goglia had suffered from side effects of steroids, so he'd dedicated his life to nutrition and safe ways to get the most out of his clients. When actors sign on to play a superhero and want to get big and ripped without killing themselves, they hire Goglia.

Starting with a blood test and body composition assessment, he wrote a meal plan designed to keep me fueled, with tons of water, good carbs, lots of veggies, more water, a variety of protein sources timed out over each day, and then some water. He made me promise to return every few weeks to repeat the tests and tweak the meals, and then he went to the back room and came out with a box of pills.

"What's all that?" I asked.

"Supplements!" He smiled.

"Nah, I don't need that stuff. I have a multivitamin already, and all the nutrients I need are right here," I said, pointing at the meal plan.

"Sure, but good luck sticking to that when you live in airports seventy-five days a year, or at races when all they feed you is pasta. Your body is in the top 0.1 percent of the world, and you put extreme demands on it. The testosterone on your blood test is like a ten-year-old girl's, and your immune system is shot."

Goglia explained the purpose for each one, checking ingredients with USADA's database and researching manufacturers to make sure nothing could be tainted. My blood was low in vitamin A and amino acids, so he gave me a pill of vitamin A and a capsule of amino acids.

"And here's some tribulus for your testosterone," he said. "Maybe now you'll stop crying at movies." *How did he know?*

High-end supplements aren't cheap, so I drove home in a $2,000 car with $800 worth of vitamins. Twenty-four-year-old Phil would have been angry if he saw the handful of pills I took twice a day, but it didn't feel wrong. I'd heard Frankie Andreu talk about how well EPO worked, how you were stronger right away, but the only difference I noticed on Goglia's plan was that all the protein kept my weight down so I didn't feel like I was starving anymore, and I woke up two or three times every night to pee.

When it was finally time to take my off-season break, I found myself restless. I'd accomplished my goals and I had some money in the bank, but it's hard to go out for a nice dinner, for example, when you're only a couple years removed from living out of your car, sprinting for gas money to get to the next one. There was this feeling that I didn't have the right to relax, because everything could slip away at any moment. I still feel that way sometimes, but instead of coming up with new ideas for my business or feverishly writing like I had the year before, I made an effort to slow down and enjoy myself. I watched movies with Joanna (without multitasking), and I was minister for Stefano and Katie's wedding in Las Vegas (anyone can be a minister for $40). Then I bought two plane tickets to take Joanna to the reception Stefano's family hosted in Brazil, leaving my bike and my laptop at home.

If Joanna enabled me to act like a human being for the first time, my contribution to the relationship was long-term planning and frugality. Neither of us could really afford the place she'd been renting, so we moved into a tiny apartment in the San Fernando Valley. We had a roommate, a hostile downstairs neighbor, a living room full of bikes, and a coin-op washer downstairs, but we were saving money every month, and Joanna's dad lived in a house around the corner. A cyclist himself, he didn't mind when I overflowed my fancy bikes into his garage.

I was sure I'd hate living in L.A., but it was great once I learned the roads. If my workout called for a longer climb, Mt. Wilson was only a few miles to the east. For intervals, a bike path took me to Griffith Park—home of the "Hollywood" sign, a four-mile flat loop with a bike lane and several short climbs, mostly closed to cars unless they're shooting a commercial.*

On Friday mornings, I'd meet a group of cyclists at a restaurant called Sweetsalt in Toluca Lake, a quiet corner of Hollywood where the streets are clean, the Trader Joe's is filled with celebrities, but there's no paparazzi and parking is plentiful. Riverside Drive feels like a small town, with Sweetsalt right in the middle, where the owner is a cyclist. He was kicked off of *Top Chef* for botching a crème brûlée, but his cookies are excellent.

Group rides are usually competitive and obnoxious, but the "Sweet Ride" would always pause if anyone got a flat tire. I'd do my intervals on the climbs, and we'd all wait at the top to regroup, take pictures, and enjoy the views of the city. It only got intense if the pack was running late, because Sweetsalt stops serving breakfast at eleven, and it's every man for himself when bacon's at stake. It's usually scary to move somewhere new, but I made friends quickly and felt right at home.

---

* Anytime you see a car ad, the twisty part is Mulholland Highway in Malibu or Calabasas, and the narrow road with a city view is Griffith Park. I always asked if they needed a cyclist when I passed a set. One guy said yes, so I stopped, but he decided that I was too skinny.

CHAPTER 6

MY FIRST TASTE of the WorldTour was at Garmin-Sharp's orientation camp for the twelve new guys on the team. BISSELL had at most two mechanics and two soigneurs at our biggest races, but there were twenty-five staff on the list taped to my hotel room door in Boulder, which meant marathon appointments with doctors, chiropractors, and physiologists. Then I sat at an intimidating, long, wood table like you might see at a business meeting in an old movie, with what felt like a hundred team directors to discuss my goals and race schedule.

With eight guys in each race and a total of thirty on the roster, the calendar is a puzzle. Different riders specialize in different terrain, and team leaders use low-level UCI races to train for prestigious WorldTour-classification events. For some races—like the Tour de France—a "long list" was already made, and even the best riders would have to fight for their spot.

I had no shot at a Grand Tour. My job was to keep my form consistent, so I could support the GC leaders year-round as a domestique, starting at the Tour de San Luis in Argentina in January, followed by a handful of races in Europe I'd never heard of, building up to my first WorldTour event: the Volta a Catalunya in March. Then they explained that the calendar could change completely, so I shouldn't put any faith in it.

Riders compared our race schedules at dinner. I knew the Americans on the team already, but there were a handful of European kids I'd never heard of, and I'm always jealous when I see a young guy on a WorldTour team. One of them looked chubby and couldn't have been more than twenty years old. *What's he done to deserve it? He never paid his dues. He never lived out of his car.* All week, I wondered how he got there, and then I finally Googled him: Lasse Hansen had an *Olympic gold medal* in the track omnium. Some riders don't have to pay dues, and he was probably just big-boned.

One of the young guys noticed that a pretty girl had gone through and liked dozens of his old photos on Instagram—a form of flirting in 2013. He told me her name and was sad to learn that she'd also done it to me. Athletes have the same problem as attractive women: sometimes, people don't appreciate us for who we really are. Mark Cavendish could post a picture with Gandhi, but he'd get more likes on a shot of his bike leaning against a fence.

I was new to the WorldTour, but here was a situation where I could teach something. Pro cyclists don't get out much, so if you have a decent audience, social media is a great way to meet women. I went through his followers, scrolling past thousands of middle-aged men until I found a woman who wasn't following any other pro cyclists.

"Oh yeah! I noticed her!" he said.

"Follow her back, and like a selfie that's a few weeks old," I told him. "That says you're checking her out. Then the next time she comments on one of your pictures, respond in a private message so you're chatting. You talk there for a while, and then you ask for her cell."

When I was single and driving around the United States, if a pretty girl liked enough of my posts, I crept through her pictures, imagining what our lives would be like together, and if she was nearby, we'd be having dinner before she knew it. I didn't invent this, of course. I know a girl who said that Lance Armstrong messaged her on Twitter and then drove more than two hours to have sex with her.

Vaughters lived nearby in Denver, but we didn't see much of him that trip. He was taking business classes for an MBA, which was odd because JV already had a job at a multimillion-dollar company that he'd started himself, and now he didn't seem to have much time to manage it.

Another reason for JV's absence that week was a media shitstorm, because Ryder Hesjedal had been outed as an EPO user in the years before he signed with Garmin. Vaughters had endured plenty of criticism for hiring former dopers to his "clean" team, so fans were pretty pissed that while Danielson and others confessed and took lenient suspensions, Ryder kept quiet and won the Giro.

When it came to the antidoping mission, it did seem like Vaughters was sincere. In a closed-door meeting, he looked us all in the eye and said he'd rather lose than cheat, and if there was ever a positive test, his experiment had failed and the team would dissolve.

The next meeting was with Cervélo, our bike sponsor, who gave a presentation about their products. We'd all have three frames to choose from at every race: a climbing bike; a stiffer, aerodynamic bike for flat races; and one that was in between. Each had impressive features and engineering, but nobody paid attention to the lecture. If we could handle meetings and Power-Points, we'd have real jobs (Tyler Farrar folded a paper airplane, but he didn't throw it), and since we get them for free, pro cyclists don't give a shit about bikes. Talk to a guy who saved up to buy a Cervélo, and he knows all the specs and the science behind it, but pros get something different every year, contracts don't allow us to keep them, and we're probably going to crash it into little pieces, so why would we get attached? I did notice that when they got to the slide with Hesjedal's picture, they hit "next" real fast.

I met the team's PR manager after the meeting. She said she was glad to have a guy with a CLEAN tattoo on the team, so when Castelli, our clothing sponsor, fit me for jerseys that afternoon, I made sure to ask for the shorter sleeves so it wouldn't be covered up.

Mavic, the team's wheel sponsor, was also at camp. They noticed the effort I put into social media and offered me $5,000 to race in their bright yellow shoes.

Five thousand dollars.

To wear shoes.

Mavic's contract also included bonuses for all sorts of results that I had no hope of achieving: $15,000 to win the Tour de France overall, $8,000 for second, all the way down to $2,500 for a stage win at a UCI 2.1 race. It was hard to keep a straight face when they explained that they'd have to cap my bonuses at $5,000.

Dinner at training camp was always a nice restaurant on Pearl Street—downtown Boulder's outdoor mall—with all the staff and lots of new names to memorize. I sat next to a man in a nice suit one evening, who thought I was a mechanic.

"What do *you* do for the team?" I asked, after we straightened that out.

"Oh, I burn money," he said, sipping wine.

The WorldTour's big, dirty secret in the post-dopocalypse is that it isn't really run on sponsorships. Sponsors help, but most teams have a wealthy backer—someone who's passionate about cycling and doesn't mind spending ten million a year to feel like he's part of the glory. In Garmin-Sharp's case, a handful of smaller "investors" kept the team afloat, and now I'd met one in his natural habitat. I wondered how Vaughters sold him on it,* but we talked about books instead (English degree, very slowly paying off). He recommended an author that I promised to read and never got around to, so if I ever run into him again, I'll grab a cigarette and start washing a bike so he doesn't recognize me.

A few of the guys went out to bars after dinner, but I mostly stayed in, afraid of making a bad impression. I regretted that later, because it turned out that the team expected partying that week. The annual fall trip was informally called "drinking camp," and years before he won the Tour de France for Team Sky, Bradley Wiggins took off his argyle and streaked Pearl Street on a dare.†

I flew out of Denver with a shiny $10,000 Cervélo R5, a laundry bag from the team with my name misspelled (Philip), a new Garmin computer (set to metric units‡), and a ton of argyle clothing, but I respected my contract, still wearing the BISSELL gear until January 1. I will admit that I modeled the argyle in a mirror at home a couple times, with a big smile on my face.

My old team probably wouldn't have noticed if I breached my contract. Omer was busy finalizing a deal that must have been brewing under our noses all summer: instead of finding new sponsors for their respective programs, Axel Merckx offered Omer a job if he could convince BISSELL to sponsor his Bontrager/LiveStrong development team. I was mad at Omer for saving himself while

---

* I later met a TV/movie screenwriter named Paul Guyot. Paul had taken his eight-year-old son to a team "meet and greet" ride, and the kid was devastated when he couldn't hold the pace. Paul teared up when he told me how Danielson turned around to chat with them, introducing Paul to Vaughters that afternoon. JV smelled money, and they were best friends for weeks. "How would your son like to be in the team car at Paris–Roubaix?" he finally asked, offering access to the team for $1 million a year. Paul said he was between jobs, "but would you take $250,000 for this year?" That's a quarter million for basically nothing in return, but Vaughters stopped returning his messages.

† The Sundown Saloon is the seedy bar of choice in Boulder and Bustop is the strip club. Lots of pros pass through Boulder, so a high percentage of the peloton is familiar with both of these establishments. If you take the team car, you park at the bike shop down the street or you're in trouble with sponsors.

‡ This means that you'll have to set your brain to metric units. Feel my pain.

most of the riders were forced to retire, and I resented Axel for making one call to keep his team alive by taking someone else's sponsor, instead of making a thousand calls to find a new one, but they were just doing what they had to in a shrinking sport, where a merger could prevent two struggling teams from going away completely. Continental racing wasn't a business—it was a knife fight, and I was glad to be out of it.

CHAPTER 7

MATT KOSCHARA WAS like family to me, but he'd never worked with anyone in the WorldTour, so I hired a new coach that fall, recommended by Vaughters. At the top level, margins of ability are tiny, so you have to be at your best at the right time, and through four coaches over nine years, I had a tendency to train too hard in the winter, kill everyone in the spring, and fizzle in the summer. As a role player on Garmin-Sharp, I'd need to be more consistent, so I emphasized that his main job was to make sure I didn't peak too early.

Road cycling is non-weight-bearing, so after a couple young riders were forced to retire with osteoporosis, I made an effort to hit the gym in the off-season to build bone density, but this coach put an end to that. He said that we had work to do on the bike, so long-term health would take a backseat. In other words, to be the very best at bike racing, you have to let it cripple you. Fortunately, society says it's okay to throw away the beginning and the end of your life as long as you're a professional athlete somewhere in the middle.

Before the holidays, I headed back to Athens, where Jeremy Powers came to visit between cyclocross events. He said that he was aiming to win a World Cup—the highest-level race in cyclocross.

"What's *your* long-term goal?" Jeremy asked.

"I don't know if I ever set goals beyond the next step," I realized. "I just stare at the ground and keep shoveling coal into the engine, hoping it goes forward."

"Yeah, Phil, and that's why you end up at shitty races in Trinidad. Let's set some goals."

We decided that I should try to win a UCI-level race. Given my domestique role, Jeremy admitted it would probably take a few years, but I thought it might be more like never. Then we laughed about the bonuses in my Mavic contract.

"No offense, but these guys are smoking crack," he said.

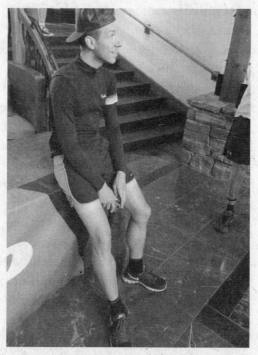

Jeremy Powers, ready for a jog.

That night, Jeremy spilled granola or goji berries or some other hippie food in my kitchen, and found an old vacuum in the hall closet to clean it up.

"Phil. A Eureka?" he asked, in disbelief after suffering through my BISSELL promotions on Twitter all year. "You've got a lot of balls!"

"It still works!" I argued. "What am I supposed to do? Throw out a perfectly decent vacuum just because I got a free one from a sponsor?"

"A lot of balls!" he yelled.

I sold the vacuum and everything else from the house on craigslist, because now that I was living in California, full-time renters would be taking over the pirate ship. Somehow, I also got through thirty-two hours of riding in seven days, with one day off in the middle to be minister at another wedding.* Not sure when I'd come back, I stayed late at the reception that night to say good-bye to my friends. They'd seen me leave parties early and come home from rides late, so they wished me luck in Europe, hoping it would all pay off.

"Of everyone over there, you had to earn it more than any of 'em," slurred one. "Now go kick their asses." He was drunk, but the words stuck with me.

When I got back to L.A. in January, I was able to really focus, and my training was perfect. Danielson complained about missing rides due to snow in Boulder and Tucson, but all I had to worry about was sunburn. My new coach prescribed strict, specific workouts—"ten minutes at 250 watts and 70 rpm, followed by five minutes at 300 watts and 120 rpm"—so complicated that I had to write it down on an index card and tape it to my handlebars. Analyzing my power output, he complained that I coasted too much in the canyons, so I should find flatter routes to eliminate descents. I

---

* That's ministering two weddings in one off-season if you're keeping track. How's that for balance? Okay, Morgan and Thomas were both pro cyclists, so it doesn't count.

like climbing, and I love coasting, but the races were about to get harder, so it made sense that training should, too, and he assured me that with longer rides at low intensity, I wouldn't peak too soon.

The "no descent" rule meant long days on the bike path or the Pacific Coast Highway, which was always heavy with cyclists, and now that I was wearing a WorldTour jersey, everyone I passed was suddenly trying out for the team. I'd catch a guy like he was standing still, and ten seconds later, he'd sprint around me so he could brag to his wife that he'd "beaten" a pro. One man sat in my draft for two hours from Oxnard to Santa Monica. I wanted to crash him into the ocean, but he finally introduced himself when I stopped at a café.

"Hey, Phil! My name is Michael. Thanks for the draft. Mind if I join you?"

"Hi, Michael. You're buying," I said.

I believe that's called symbiosis. We had a pleasant conversation. He was an architect.

Days before the Tour de San Luis, a sleek Cervélo P5 time trial bike arrived at my apartment, previously used by American Jacob Rathe (his name was on the sticker). I almost took it to an expert to be properly measured and fit, but I got lazy and did the best I could with a tape measure in my living room instead. We'd have staff in Spain to get it dialed in February, and the time trial was the fifth stage at the Tour de San Luis. I'd be sixtieth overall by then, and domestiques always ride the TT easy, saving energy to help their leader the next day.

The truth is, my focus that week was nowhere near the upcoming race. With just a couple days between my return from Argentina and a three-month trip to Europe, my relationship with Joanna was about to go long distance. We hadn't been together very long, but we got along great, and she gave me something to focus on outside of my performance, smoothing out the roller coaster of being an athlete. I didn't want to lose that, so I went to a jewelry store, and the night before I left, I asked her to marry me.

She said yes and she wore the ring, but she didn't want to set a date, which was fine with me. Bike racing had taught me that I had to earn what I wanted, but it would come with time and dedication. Racing also made me good at fooling myself.

She gave me a silver chain with a brass ring on it, and we celebrated with steak and wine at an expensive Italian restaurant, closing the evening in her dad's romantic garage, packing bikes for my first race in the WorldTour.

PART 2

We Can Do Better Than That

CHAPTER 8

THE FIRST RACE in a long season, the Tour de San Luis is considered a low-pressure event, but it would still be the biggest race I'd ever done. The team sends riders early when there's a time zone adjustment, so with two days to kill, we piled into a taxi to find a barbershop. It was too hot to be shaggy, and a haircut is a good adventure in a foreign country. I showed the barber a picture of George Clooney I found in a magazine, but it came out more "Jim Carey."

While his teammates got haircuts, Danielson stayed at the hotel with his feet up. At thirty-four years old, fifteen pounds lighter than he'd been at the Tour of Utah six months before from a strict anti-inflammation and vegan diet (which I think means he ate nothing), he was here to win. With the lofty goal of an overall podium at a Grand Tour in 2014, he'd spent another winter doing intervals on Mt. Lemmon, and I was supposed to be not peaking, so we were both confused when I dropped him on a climb the day before the first stage, doing "opener" efforts to get our legs into race mode. I chalked it up to the heat, which I was accustomed to from Los Angeles. We regrouped at the top, where Tyler Farrar crouched over a huge pile of cow shit, so it looked like it was *his* shit. I took a photo and it kills me that I can't find it for this book, so stop reading for a second and try to picture it, okay? He's grimacing.

A former pro named Chann McRae (guess whose team he was on a few years before) was director for the week. At our first meeting, he said that Danielson would be our leader, and Janier Acevedo would be protected to help on the climbs. Janier also came from an American Continental team, so we were rivals the year before, but after suffering from knee problems all winter and seeing me during my openers, he suggested that maybe I'd be better for that role.

Chann looked at me, doubtfully. "We'll see how the first stages go. For now, we save Janier."

My job was to get water bottles from the car.

"Or if you feel like it, Phil, try and sneak into the early breakaway." He shrugged. "The big teams don't know who you are, so maybe they'd let it go." I didn't mind doing the bottle thing, but I thought I had more to offer, and a breakaway would be fun.

As we headed to the venue in a rusty van, I listened to a playlist that Joanna made for my WorldTour debut. I think she included it as a joke, but I got emotional when Drake's "Started from the Bottom" came on, thinking of myself at twenty-four—just a hopeless kid driving to bike races in my car, wondering what I was doing with my life until this little team wearing argyle gave me something to shoot for. Now I'd made it. I was one of them.

Drake was still in my head at the start line when the top riders were introduced. The crowd went wild for Nairo Quintana—an inspirational young Colombian who'd climbed to second overall at the 2013 Tour de France—but they also cheered for Filippo Pozzato, an Italian with a long history of questionable doctors. Pozzato hadn't won a race in years but he was still cashing paychecks, partying, and womanizing, and if that's not enough reason to hate him, Pippo trained in Malibu one winter and went out with Joanna. On a recent trip to L.A., he was disappointed to learn that she was taken now and excited to race against me.

"We'll see who is the better man in San Luis," he'd told my fiancée. Douchebag.

The race had barely started when I found myself a minute up the road from the pack with five riders from smaller teams, in a move that seemed doomed like every other early breakaway. Teams with good sprinters would keep us within three minutes and reel us in at the end, but the Tour de Phil must have helped my endurance, because 80k into the 170k stage, the three South American riders couldn't pull with me anymore, and I was still feeling good.

"No sprint!" they promised, meaning they wouldn't contest the finish if—by some miracle—we stayed away. That left me and Marc de Maar from the UnitedHealthcare team to do the heavy lifting. I outsprinted Marc to the top of a mountain for KOM points, relieved to at least earn a polka-dot jersey on a day that would turn out to be a waste of energy, but with 60k to go, a race official came up on his motorcycle to say that our lead had increased. Sprinters' teams had argued about who should chase down the break, and the pack was twelve minutes behind.

I'd followed this pointless breakaway on a whim, but now I was guaranteed a podium finish at a UCI stage, and if they didn't hurry up, the whole GC would be between me and de Maar. Both shocked, we gave each other a look, shaking our heads, but Marc and I cooperated, digging deep to keep as much of our lead as possible.

With 40k to go, we were still eight minutes ahead, blindly following two police motorcycles down a highway through a treeless, boiling-hot plain. I was pulling when we entered a roundabout, where one of the motos went straight and the other turned left. Not sure who to follow, I looked back to see if my breakmates knew the route, but one of them wasn't paying attention. He crashed into de Maar, taking them all down in a heap.

I soft-pedaled for a minute, wondering if I should stop to let them catch up. Waiting is more sportsmanlike, and I'd go faster taking turns in the wind with de Maar, but for all we knew he'd have a trashed bike or a broken collarbone. Chann drove up next to me and told me to press on, alone.

They say that insanity is repeating the same thing and expecting different results, but perseverance doesn't look much different. When a hitter pops up the baseball and it looks like an easy out, if he wants to protect himself emotionally, he'll trudge back to the dugout and have a seat, but a real pro is taught to run full speed toward first base, because someday they'll miss the catch and he'll be safe. Over the years, I'd been in a hundred early breakaways, believing over and over that this could be the day that it "stuck," only to be disappointed, finishing sore and five minutes down. Now, on my first day with Garmin-Sharp, they'd finally dropped the ball. It was still a long way to the finish, but I was going to win one.

For the next hour, the road was so straight I could see the curvature of the Earth on the horizon, but I kept my head down and my speed up. In the final kilometers, my legs were locking up from cramps while blisters bled where my forearms leaned on the handlebars, but as those delicious victory chemicals rushed through me, I felt no pain. Capping off a day that fans would call the greatest entrance to the WorldTour in history, I crossed the line kissing the necklace that Joanna gave me, with the pack still five minutes behind. At the awards ceremony, I felt bad having podium girls kiss my cheeks when I'd just gotten engaged, and made a mental note that the next time I win a UCI race, I'll refuse the kisses to make a statement. (I'm still waiting for that.)

The sun was setting by the time I carried a trophy, flowers, and a leader's jersey—all covered in confetti—through a mob seeking autographs and photos (living the dream!). I soaked it in, but still couldn't believe it was happening to me. My phone had a thousand messages, but after a quick call to Joanna, I only had the energy for one post on Twitter:

"Pinch me."

I tried to unwind with some music on the drive back to the hotel. I never thought I'd cry to a Drake song, but "Started from the Bottom" got me good.

Pinch me. Tour of San Luis.

My teammates had gone back to the hotel while I was on the podium, so I hadn't seen them since the first five hundred meters of the stage. I wondered if they'd be jealous of my luck, or what if they didn't care? I worried that the WorldTour would lack the emotion I'd had on previous teams, now that it was a job instead of a passion, but one by one, they burst into my room with high fives and hugs. I was so happy, I only complained for half an hour that night about the beeping and ringing from the casino next to the dining area, or the buffet of beet salad, cold rice, and choice of beef, chicken, or fish, but good luck telling them apart (and be glad there's ketchup). Most of the racers were staying at the same hotel, and I was surprised to see Tom Boonen, Vincenzo Nibali, and Mark Cavendish eating the same shit. Watching them cross the line with their arms up at the Tour de France or Paris–Roubaix all those years, I'd never have guessed that this was the glamorous life of the best cyclists in the world: millionaires eating cold rice.

I'd barely put down my fork when one of the soigneurs tapped me on the shoulder. The man behind her carried a clipboard, and we all knew what that meant: another drug test. I waved good-bye to my teammates and followed him out, head down and hands crossed behind my back like I was headed to the gallows.

Before bed, we met in Chann's room to reassess the strategy after a day that no one expected.

"Phil, do you want to race for the overall?" he asked. "Or should we stick to yesterday's plan and Danielson as leader? It's a mountaintop finish tomorrow, and some of the best climbers in the world basically had a rest day while you were out there killing yourself in the wind."

The room went silent, with six sets of eyes awaiting my answer. They'd discussed this behind my back, wondering if I was ready to lead a team. I didn't know what would happen, but I'd never get a chance like this again.

"Fuck yes, I want to ride for GC. I'm not the best guy here, but they gave me a nice head start. I'll make them regret it."

Ben King gave me a shoulder massage, his Virginia smile stretching ear to ear. Bike racers love dumb courage.

"Fuck yeah!" said Danielson, pumping his first.

Nate Brown grinned. "I can't wait to suffer on the front for you, Phil."

When the meeting was over, Chann had me stay behind to talk privately. It was time to address the elephant in the room.

"Listen, Phil. I'm sure you know that a lot of guys here are dopers, so I wanted to tell you that it's January, so I bet they're not doing much yet. You'll probably be able to hang."

Gulp

On my second day in the WorldTour, I came to the start line in the leader's jersey, the last rider introduced to a roaring crowd. I lined up next to Pippo Pozzato on purpose and gave him a smile. *So who's the better man, fuckface?*

When the gun went off, it was a mixture of muscle memory and shock. I'd done hundreds of races, I'd worn lots of leader's jerseys, and I'd been in over my head many times, but it was crazy to see young talents Nate Brown and Ben King pulling more than one hundred kilometers for me in the heat. Then a voice came out of my mouth that said, "Hey, Tyler, can you get some more bottles?" While a voice in my head said, *Holy shit. Tyler Farrar is getting me bottles.*

Tyler was a rider I'd admired since my first Under-23 national championships at nineteen. I got dropped, went home early, and watched from a sidewalk in Park City as the big, freckled sprinter came in second place on a mountaintop finish against a pack of climbers. He went on to ride for a French WorldTour team and lived in Ghent, Belgium, with his girlfriend. In interviews, Tyler answered in English first, and then repeated himself in fluent Flemish.

So my day had already turned surreal, and then Danielson went to work for me on the final climb. He'd cut out gluten and meat for months to win this race—not to help my dumb ass up a mountain—but he rode the front and dropped back to help me when the attacks started, so I only lost a few seconds to the front group. Nairo Quintana was known for a poker face when he suffered at the Tour de France, but he couldn't hide his surprise when he saw me at the finish. We both thought I'd lose minutes, but now he knew he'd have to work for this win. If you were to survey

professional cyclists and ask who they'd least like to race up
mountains in South America for a week, Quintana would be the
unanimous choice.* This was as close as he'd get to a home race,
and it sent a chill down my spine to know that he wanted my
jersey.

When I'd raced against Euro pros in the past, no one ever noticed Phil Gaimon in the hallway at the hotel. They did something
that I call "big-timing": walking past with no wave and no eye
contact like you don't exist—like girls did when I was in high
school. But now, I could feel the competition sizing me up. My
sore body wanted to use the railing up the stairs, but when Julián
Arredondo was behind me on the way to breakfast, I couldn't let
him know I was hurting. I ran the steps two at a time, grinding
my teeth through the pain.

They don't tell you how much extra pressure and work is involved when you're in the lead, with doping control after every
stage, daily press conferences, and interviews in the evenings. By
the time I left the venue each day, the competition was long gone,
resting at the hotel while I still had to fight through a crowd asking for autographs. I stopped for some and hated myself for everyone I had to push past, amazed at how fast it went from a thrill to
a chore.

I was also flooded with hundreds of personal messages that
week, from friends, acquaintances, and complete strangers. One
was from a girl who'd turned me down for a date years before. She
was headed to Los Angeles soon and knew that I'd moved there.

"I want to fuck," she explained.

"Sorry, I just got engaged," I said.

"Whatever. Is she hotter than me?"

Joanna's photo was the background on my phone.

---

* Jens Voigt would be second, but only because he'd never shut up.

"Well, that's not exactly the point, but yeah, she is."

Then there was the note from Jeremy Powers:

"I guess you need to set a new goal. Took you one damn day to win a UCI race."

I was the hero who made it to the WorldTour without cheating, and now everyone wanted to congratulate me, wish me luck, or fuck. I felt like it was important to respond to all of them, so I sat in bed, copy/pasting "Thank you!" But with only a few hours from the finish until bedtime, it added up. They say you get extra strength from wearing a leader's jersey, but it also wears you down, and this was just the Tour de San Luis! Imagine the stress of leading the Tour de France. Or, like, being Ringo.

I barely slept the first night, so I asked our team doctor for sleeping pills after that.

"Whatever killed Michael Jackson, but one less," I demanded. I got temazepam instead—a muscle relaxer in a pill that looked like a tiny butterfly—and I slept like a log. I liked it so much, he downgraded me to Ambien for the rest of the week.

The fourth stage had a long, steep climb to the finish. I was pushed around by some of the big names in the fight for position, so I wasn't in the top five where I should have been when it started, but I don't think it would have mattered. Nairo's team sprinted from the base to launch him away at full speed, and I learned what happens when you try to compete with the big boys (in cycling, "big boys" are 120-pound Colombians). Danielson tried to help, and I kept thinking I could just dig deeper, but Quintana was out of sight with 7k to go. I died a million deaths to minimize my losses, with Chann in the car behind me, shouting time checks.

I blacked out when I crossed the finish line, collapsing face-down in the dirt, where I simultaneously threw up and peed in my shorts. When I came to, I yelled at a photographer not to get too close, because I was afraid he'd get a picture of my urine puddle.* I'd kept the jersey, but my lead went from four minutes to four seconds, and with a time trial and another mountaintop finish coming up, there was no way I'd win the GC anymore. I'd lived the dream for a few days, but Nairo Quintana had pinched me.

That night, I read predictions about the next stage: a 20k flat time trial. One reporter asked Tom Boonen if he thought I could keep the overall lead.

"Well, I don't hear of him until this week, but maybe he wins. He does look very skinny," Boonen said.

The consensus in the media was that Phil Gaimon would pad his lead on Nairo Quintana by twenty seconds.

"Based on what?" I asked Tyler. "All those seven-day stage races I've done? I've never cracked the top thirty in the time trial at the Tour of California, and the field here is tougher. I'm riding Jacob Rathe's bike!"

"Just because you're bigger than Nairo, they think you'll time-trial better. Don't read that shit anymore."

Tyler had learned the hard way. To fans, it might look like all the WorldTour teams are equal, but with no salary cap like in other sports, Garmin-Sharp had a budget of $5–$10 million a year, trying to compete against teams like Sky and BMC, who both spent closer to $40 million. Tyler was the best sprinter on the team, so fans and media always expected a contender at Tour stages and one-day classics. He got some great results, but every time he crossed the line sixth, they'd want to know what happened. What happened was that Vaughters couldn't afford Mark Cavendish.

Castelli had provided each of us a $500 wind-tunnel-perfected one piece "speed suit" to wear for time trials. Out of the box, it

---

* Turns out I ended up in the dirt, soaked in urine, and yelling at strangers after all. Shout-out to soigneur "Disco" Jon Adams for not letting me punch the cameraman.

was barely the length of my torso, but with stretchable, high-tech, aerodynamic fabric, it was guaranteed to save seconds. But that stayed in my suitcase, because unless I wanted to pay a $1,000 fine, I had to use the orange "race leader" skinsuit that the race provided, which was baggy on my arms and flapped in the wind. I slapped myself for neglecting that bike fit before I left L.A.

I'm sure that I gave my best effort in the time trial, because although I didn't piss myself again, my nose started bleeding with five hundred meters to go. Nairo still went thirty seconds faster and I fell to second overall.

"How disappointed are you to lose the race lead?" asked a reporter.

I laughed. "Don't you understand? I wasn't ever supposed to be here."

It was a relief to walk past the podium and the press conference, out of the spotlight, headed to the hotel for a nap.

My teammates had worked for me all week, so I knew they were worried that I'd implode on stage six—the final mountaintop finish—where bad legs like I'd had two days before would send me out of the top ten overall. This time, I fought for position as we approached the climb, putting a shoulder and hip into Vincenzo Nibali. He yelled something in Italian, and then he got dropped (a few months later, he won the Tour de France). I suffered but stayed within myself, and when I started fading back with five hundred meters to go, the front group was ten guys: some of the best climbers in the world and, somehow, me. Danielson had shepherded me up the climb, but second overall was secure, so I told him to go for it when the leaders started to attack for the stage win, sure that he could at least hit the podium.

"Leave me," I said, like I was dying in the desert. "Go win."

But he didn't care about that. I was his project. He'd trained with me, he'd put me on the team, I'd gotten lucky, and now he wanted to be beside me when I backed it up.

"Nah, man. We're crossing the line together."

When people first saw me with Danielson, they were confused that the guy with the CLEAN tattoo could be friends with the notorious doper. Some hoped that I was an undercover reporter, "Inside the Evil World of Tommy D," as if when he left the house, I'd open a secret cabinet and be covered in an avalanche of syringes and blood bags. Others thought it was some sort of Faustian bargain: he gets me to the WorldTour, and I try to convince the public that he's okay. I'd tried to not like him, but from that moment at the top of the mountain in Argentina, Tom and I were brothers. We were both crying.

With Tommy D at the top of the final climb in San Luis.

I'd already had backlash on social media from doper-haters, calling me a traitor. I ignored it at first, but after San Luis, I couldn't help but defend him. It felt good to tell the world that good people can make mistakes. It's easy to change beliefs and opinions via Twitter, so I pretty much convinced everyone and we all lived happily ever after. Wait a minute. No, actually I just pissed people off and made myself look naïve.

While most of the racers went to the after party at the governor's mansion, I stayed at the hotel, analyzing my power data. I'd broken all of my records that week, and the new coach was excited at my improvement, but I knew it meant that I was peaking in January. I was lucky it worked out, but I'd pay for this in a few months. I'd just had the best result of my life, and I had to fire my coach.

It wouldn't be fair to leave out the other factor in that decision: he charged $250 a month, and I was stressed about money. BIS-SELL's paycheck had always arrived at the beginning of the month, while Garmin-Sharp's wouldn't come until the thirtieth, and with taxes and health insurance taken out, my monthly World-Tour check was less than I'd been getting as a Continental rider. Not to mention my next credit card bill would include a very expensive rock with no intrinsic value, which I'd given to a woman to wear on her hand symbolically.

CHAPTER 9

I TURNED TWENTY-EIGHT WHEN I got back to L.A., and Joanna put together a birthday/going-away-to-Europe party, remembering what I ordered at my favorite barbecue restaurant in Georgia, with pulled pork, mac and cheese, and a cookie cake from Sweetsalt. I'd gone all over town to buy gift certificates to her favorite restaurants, coffee shops, and nail salons, and other gifts to hide around the apartment, but we were both overcompensating. It felt horrible when it was time to leave.

Fans romanticize pro cycling. They'd say I'm lucky to get paid to ride a bike, and my answer was that's not what they pay me for. Riding a bike is great, so that's on me. I get paid to be on the road for months, away from friends and family, to have dinner alone. I get paid for long training rides in cold rain, for adjusting to time zones and changing a flat tire on the side of the road on a hot day. I get paid for every cookie I don't eat.

When I landed in Barcelona, customs agents told me to wait while they went through my bags. They'd fill a security tray, take it around the corner to an X-ray machine, and return for another load. When I was finally free to go, all of my stuff was in a big pile on the floor, and a pair of sneakers and a Swiss Army knife were missing. Welcome to Spain.

The team had a taxi waiting to take me to Sant Gregori, a small town three kilometers outside of Girona. Tom rented me a room at his town house but he wouldn't arrive for another week, so I had the place to myself. Sant Gregori had a problem with strays, so the neighborhood sounded like a cat opera at night, and my room was full of toys from Tom's kids.

Girona is in the Catalunya (Catalonia) region of Spain, which wasn't known for cycling until Lance and his teammates moved there, "coincidentally" timed with France passing strict antidoping laws. With tree-lined roads, peaceful climbs, and views of castles along the Mediterranean, I could see why it became a base for so many English-speaking pros, and locals seemed to welcome us. Cars waited patiently to pass, and if they slowed down next to me, it wasn't to call me a faggot—it was to smile and wave, or take a picture.

Riding was easy, but living there took some getting used to. I'd studied Spanish in college, but many Catalunyans sought independence from Spain, and they had their own language (something I would have known *before* moving there if I wasn't an idiot). I didn't know any Catalan at first, and found that most locals would rather play charades than speak Spanish—the language of a country they saw as their oppressors.

Catalunya didn't give up the Spanish tradition of siesta, though. I'd been warned, but it was hard to believe until I saw it with my own eyes: every store was shut down from noon to four p.m., and restaurants didn't open for dinner until eight. Tom said that he once showed up at a BMW dealership ready to buy, but it was 11:45 a.m., which is almost time to head to the café for lunch and beer, so they told him to try again later. Coming from the rush of Los Angeles, a relaxed society was charming, but errands that only took a minute at home could take hours there, like mailing a letter or making a copy of a key.* We called it "getting Spained," but I'd mostly settled in before it was time to hop another plane, this time to Majorca for training camp.

---

* Was it hard to get things done because everyone was so relaxed, or did the locals become relaxed because it was hard to get things done? It's a real chicken-and-egg. Wait— it's a real *pollo*-and-*huevo*. (I'm sorry.)

CHAPTER 10

WHEN YOU JOIN a new team, it's like the first day of school: for the next year, these are your training partners, your roommates, your best friends, and your worst enemies. Someone here you'll love forever, and someone you'll cuss out in a bus after a race. I looked around as Vaughters made introductions at the first meeting, trying to guess who was who.

David Millar sat up front. He was one of the best time trialists in the world before he served a two-year suspension for EPO.* Johan Vansummeren, a Belgian who'd won Paris–Roubaix, was at the back with Thomas Dekker—another guy who'd taken an EPO "vacation," and Nick Nuyens, who'd won the Tour of Flanders for Saxo Bank.

When I introduced myself to Dan Martin, he was quiet, maybe shy—not the confidence you'd expect from the guy who'd won Liège-Bastogne-Liège—the biggest one-day race for a climber. Dan and I are the same age, and if you dig deep through the race results, knowing who's been clean their whole career versus who

---

* Millar's whole message was "doping doesn't pay," but he sure posted a lot of pictures of his new Maserati.

had to stop around 2006, Dan is often considered the best of the guys who never touched the stuff.

I was honored to be in a room with some of my heroes and consider them my peers, until I heard conversations about a $10,000-a-month apartment in Monaco and noticed all the $20,000 watches.* There's a big disparity between the top and the bottom of the WorldTour, so being teammates didn't quite make us equals. I wasn't the only one on the minimum salary, but a lot of these guys were paid more in a month than I was for the year.

I'd heard that there were doubters when I joined the team: guys who resented Vaughters when they heard that I was twenty-eight and I'd never even ridden in Europe (I didn't tell them about the bike paths in the Netherlands when I was six, because I'd have to admit that I'd needed a push in the headwind). If you want to race in the WorldTour, you're supposed to have your first road bike as a placenta, so you're comfortable in headwinds by three years old, and national champion at twelve. Your father (who was a pro cyclist himself) showed you how to clip in to your pedals before he helped with homework, and you don't waste four crucial years from eighteen to twenty-two looking at books. You joined your national development program out of high school, and you were a neo-pro with a two-year contract by twenty-three. That's how almost everyone at Garmin-Sharp had done it, from riders to management, including head director Charly Wegelius, who asked if I finished college and gave a disgusted look when I said "yes." I knew that my degree wasn't helping here, but I never thought it would be a detriment.†

David Millar heard that I had a book coming out. He had one, too, but he'd used a ghostwriter and the story was a flimsy effort

---

* I later learned that the watches were mostly gifts. If you win a big race, it's customary to buy something nice for anyone who worked for you. If you have a decent career in the WorldTour, you end up with a Rolex or two.

† Damn it, Phil! Stop using big words!

to justify his doping. Also based in Girona, Millar asked if I'd learned Catalan in the off-season.

"No," I admitted. "I was editing in my spare time all year, and it didn't make sense to learn a language with a one-year contract."

"Well, is racing your priority, or writing? Maybe if you learn Catalan, you'd get better than a one-year deal," he said, walking away.

I made sure not to talk to Millar ever again. He didn't take me seriously because I hadn't made the proper sacrifices. I would have loved a reason to drop out of school and focus on racing, but I didn't have a development team to ride for full-time when I was twenty-two, because his generation had driven those sponsors away.

I sat between Tom and Ryder Hesjedal at the next meeting.

"Man, Phil, don't put yourself in a doper sandwich," Ryder groaned.

We laughed, but I felt an insecurity behind it, which was consistent with something I'd seen earlier that day. According to social media, someone called "Rusty Woods" had broken Ryder's record on a climb I'd never heard of in Hawaii, where he spent his winters. This guy had won the Giro, but he was pissed about some kid's time up Haleakala.

I didn't fit in with everyone, but I still got plenty of congratulations for the win in Argentina, which was enough for most of them to give me a chance. I'd fired my coach for that early peak, but socially, I needed it. On BISSELL, I'd talked and joked around a lot. I was the leader there. The man. But here, I was a piece of shit—the only college graduate, and the most clueless. Before, I was guessing what might make me fast. I had to try things out and experiment. Matt Koschara sent me articles to learn about altitude training, for example, but now I was surrounded by guys who *knew* how to be fast. This would be a year to shut up, watch, and emulate, because if I copied what they did,

I could win the Tour de France. Maybe just a stage? Not that year—I meant eventually.*

Copying started with coffee. I was twenty-eight and I'd never had a cup, but getting off the bus for my first ride in Majorca, everyone took a shot of espresso and I followed suit. I can't say that I liked it, but I haven't gone a day without coffee since. Sometimes I have five. Remind me not to try cocaine.

I also paid close attention to their diets. On BISSELL, I'd judged the guys who had a drink with dinner and I'd avoided gluten and dairy, so I was surprised to watch my new teammates pass around a bottle of red wine one evening, and at breakfast, twenty-two-year-old Dylan van Baarle ate a stack of white bread with butter. I understood that bread would lead to inflammation and excess water weight, but a few hours later, a small group "motorpaced," drafting behind a team car at high speed, and I gave it everything to stay close to the bumper, while Dylan attacked the car, holding a ten-second lead in the wind for several minutes. I peeked over the roof, wondering how the hell he was doing that, and he didn't look the least bit inflamed or bloated. I later read research studies showing that the gluten thing was mostly a fad, only affecting performance for a small percentage of athletes, but I didn't need research. I had Dylan van Baarle.

In the post-EPO era, we heard a lot of talk about "marginal gains" in pro cycling: adding up lots of little improvements to achieve big results. You cut out gluten to be half a pound lighter, tire companies tested their rubber to decrease rolling resistance, and even helmets were designed to minimize weight (instead of maximizing saving your damn brain). Team Sky had perfected the process, marginally gaining Tour de France victories with Bradley Wiggins and Chris Froome in 2012 and 2013, and I knew

---

* Thanks to San Luis, I'd already maxed out the $5,000 in Mavic bonuses for 2014, so what was the point?

amateurs who spent their evenings shaving grams off their bike with a nail file. Garmin-Sharp would have plenty of that, but in February, it's okay to have wine at dinner, or break up your five-hour ride with sandwiches (bocadillos) at a café.

I tried to buy a round of coffee when it seemed like my turn, but the guys with nice watches never let me pay. Fans figured I was raking in the dough now that I'd joined the WorldTour, but my teammates could guess who was on the UCI minimum salary. These guys paid $10,000 a month for an apartment in Monaco to dodge income taxes, but at the coffee shop, they were socialists.

Unlike at drinking camp, the team expected riders to be fit in Majorca, so some laid low on the bocadillos after the doctor came around to measure our body fat. Coming from an off-season in L.A., it wasn't hard to be skinny, but I felt bad for the guys from Northern Europe. I wouldn't want to go through a real winter without a few extra kilos.

The team was also serious about sponsors. An e-mail went out explaining that photographers were everywhere, so we should remain "sponsor correct" at all times or we'd be fined.* I noticed that Lachlan Morton was still wearing a pair of dirty Vans instead of his argyle New Balance, and instead of his Garmin-Sharp T-shirt, he wore one with a picture of Lance Armstrong's face, and the words "So Dope" underneath. I liked Lachlan.

Along with fines came a schedule of sponsor and media obligations over the course of the week, which was a big inconvenience for Johan Vansummeren.

"I just want to train and race and do my job," he complained.

Maybe social media and marketing didn't matter when he started, but in 2014, this was our job. I wasn't going to explain it

---

* BISSELL had a fine in our contracts if we left our bikes on the ground drive-side down, but I don't think they ever enforced it.

to him, though. I have a policy where I don't give advice to guys who won Paris–Roubaix.

Over the ten-day camp, we all had a daily massage, and my appointment always came after my hotel-roommate's.

"How was the rub?" I asked, passing him in the hall on the way.

"It was kind of racist," he said.

I didn't have time to ask what he meant. *How could a massage be racist?*

"So where ya from, Phil?" asked a gruff British accent as I climbed onto the table.

"Atlanta," I said.

"Oh. Lotta blacks there, huh?"

Well, there ya go.

After camp, the Americans shared a taxi from the Barcelona airport, and Caleb Fairly pointed out the McDonald's and the Burger King on the way into Girona.

"That's where you go when you're cracked," he said.

Cracked? How could you "crack" on living the dream? I'd never eat McDonald's in the States, and I was sure I wouldn't start here, but I couldn't think about food anyway. Riders are taught to use hand sanitizer at every meal, but half of the team picked up a stomach bug at the hotel buffet, so I spent the night on Danielson's toilet, vomiting into the bidet. What's a bidet supposed to be for, by the way? Oh. Oops!

I ran into former Kenda teammate John Murphy that week in Girona. When I went to BISSELL, he moved up to UnitedHealthcare, which sent a squad to Europe in the spring. Both of us were on an easy day, so our main goal was a café when we arrived at a town called Banyoles. I saw one on the main street and started to go in, but John shook his head.

"I think we can do better than that," he said.

I consider myself a practical person. I don't drive around looking for the best parking spot at the mall, and I won't try on more than two shirts before I buy one, but five minutes later, we sat on a wooden deck overlooking Lake Banyoles. The edge was lined with cypress trees and the water was so still, it reflected a perfect image of the blue sky with the snow-capped Pyrenees in the distance. I ordered a hot chocolate and they brought out a mug of thick, melted chocolate, which I thought was a misunderstanding at first, but "sipping chocolate" is a common menu item in Spain— the most delicious mistake I'd ever made. The best part was it came with a sugar packet.

"We can do better than that" is something I resolved to tell myself more often, but when I needed a car to get around town, I bought the first one I could find. When Dave Zabriskie retired, instead of coming back to Girona to empty out his apartment, he sold everything he owned to Lachlan Morton for $5,000, including a 2001 Renault Laguna hatchback with 150,000 kilometers on the odometer, automatic transmission, and a side mirror attached with packing tape (on Girona's ancient, narrow streets, this is a standard look). Auto insurance for men under twenty-five is expensive in Spain, so Lachlan had to get rid of it, and since I didn't want to go used-car shopping, we agreed on 2,500 euros. Zabriskie had left Neil Young's *Harvest* in the CD player, and the glove compartment had ketchup packets from both McDonald's *and* Burger King. I guess he was cracked when he left.

I thought it was a fair deal, but after a winter in the garage, the battery was dead, then the spark plugs had to be replaced, followed by the starter. I went back and forth to the Catalan mechanic every few days, where I had to express things like "catalytic converter" through charades. For the first few weeks, the car wasn't so much a means of transportation as it was a tin shelter with a radio that ate money, but it felt good to have property in Girona, like I was there to stay.

The team recommended a lawyer, who said I should leave it registered in Zabriskie's name, so he'd be on the hook legally if I got a ticket (you can move away, Zabriskie, but you still got Spained!), which meant that I didn't worry about speed limits on the way to the airport when Joanna came to visit. Since the plan was to get a raise and bring her with me in 2015, I was excited to show her what life would be like, taking her on all the rides and introducing her to my teammates.

I was sad when she left, but Tom was a great roommate. In the middle of an ugly divorce, he still took the time to help me find routes that suited my workouts, he'd tiptoe around when I was asleep, and once, I left laundry in the washer and found it dry and folded on my bed. I hadn't seen folded underwear in ten years.

CHAPTER 11

OVING TO EUROPE was a big adjustment, but it was nothing compared to the change I faced in my first races there. As the top dog in the United States, I'd grown accustomed to riding wherever I wanted in the pack, but now I had to fight, wasting energy just to keep decent position in the group. Plus, these guys were incredible bike handlers. I survived a descent with no guardrail and algae in the corners, but my face was whiter than my knuckles when Andrew Talansky rode up to me.

"Not in Redlands anymore, huh?" he laughed, completely relaxed.

"Fuck, dude!" was all I could say.

I'd raced against Andrew in college, but he wisely dropped out to test his legs in Europe. He finished tenth overall at the 2013 Tour de France, so it seemed to be working out for him, but I felt like I was in a different sport.

Alex Howes and I were told to stay with Tyler Farrar on the last climb that day, to help him catch up to the front group for the sprint. Tyler poured sweat, gritted his teeth, and was only a few seconds behind over the top, but with 15k to go, Alex and I were pulling our asses off and still losing time to the leaders, so Tyler said we should stop. I was hurting but not empty yet, so I told him that I didn't want to quit.

"It's not giving up," he explained. "It's a long year. Sometimes you just have to accept that you're out of the race and save your bullets for the next one."

The three of us rode in with the groupetto, singing "Ninety-Nine Bottles of Beer on the Wall."

After each race, I'd compare power files with my teammates. My average was usually 25 watts higher than guys who finished beside me, showing how much energy I was wasting being a dumb rookie. I had some learning to do, so I was glad when the team signed me up for a race called Three Days of West Flanders in Belgium. There'd be cobblestones, technical courses, and bad weather that wouldn't suit my abilities at all, but I'd get an education.

Crowds were waiting by the bus at the opening time trial in West Flanders, taking photos of each rider for their collections: thick binders organized by team and dating back decades. They'd get a picture, print it out, and then ask for an autograph at the next race. I was in a rush to get my time trial bike checked by officials when someone called my name and jumped in front of me with a camera. Flattered that anyone in Belgium knew who I was, I skidded to a stop.

"Sure, real quick!" I said, pointing to an imaginary watch and smiling.

I thought he'd grab a shot so I could go on my way, but he just looked at me, rolling his eyes like I should know better. "Sir, can you take off your glasses and your helmet?"

Obviously, for Belgian collectors, photos aren't valid with sunglasses on. As I stood there, more men crowded around for their own pictures, and no one even thanked me.

"Aren't they supposed to be fans?" I asked a soigneur. "Why are they so rude and demanding? Shouldn't they admire us?"

"They're not fans," she explained. "They're 'pedalphiles.'"

I felt great in the seven-kilometer TT and I paced it perfectly: I didn't start too hard and I hit the turns fast, even catching the guy who'd started thirty seconds ahead of me. That effort would have been a good result in the United States, so when I got back to the bus, I told Nate Brown that I'd nailed it and I wouldn't be surprised at a top ten when the results were posted. It's a good thing that Nate isn't a gambling man, because I finished 110th out of 190, nearly a minute slower than the winner (and twenty seconds behind Nate).

My mom called that night, but I couldn't talk because it was almost time for my massage.

"Oh, that's nice!" she said. "Enjoy it!"

Mom gets a massage every Friday to unwind from work, with candles and classical music. I had to explain that our massages aren't like that. For a grand total of about seventy-five hours that year, someone was violently untying the knots in my tired muscles to the sounds of techno music, and this soigneur was particularly brutal—like he was trying to kill me through my hamstrings. When I asked where he'd worked in the past, he gave a long list of WorldTour teams, dropping names from the doping era. Squeezing the table legs through his pummeling, I wondered how he'd kept his job, but then I realized something: those guys didn't care what happened to their legs. They cared what was in the syringes or the IV bag hanging on the wall. His previous clients felt no pain, but I had to walk up the wheelchair ramp to dinner.

The two road race stages in West Flanders would be the real test, featuring many of the cobblestone climbs from the legendary Tour of Flanders. The course didn't go a kilometer without a turn and streets were filled with obstacles like giant cement flowerpots or speed bumps, lovingly (hatingly) referred to as "Belgian road furniture," which we'd have to dodge at high speed. The job they assigned me was to help the team's sprinters through the crosswinds, but I kept my main goal a secret: don't die.

At any race in that region, you're in constant fear that someone ahead of you could crash or get dropped in the crosswind, so it's a battle to stay near the front of the pack and ahead of trouble. However, basic physics dictates that if a road is one meter wide, and handlebars are forty-four centimeters, there isn't room for two hundred dudes at the front. Is that physics? I got a C in physics, so how about this: it was five hours of the intro gag on *The Simpsons*, where the entire family sprints for a seat on the tiny couch in front of the TV, and something crazy happens every time.

Riding six wide, we approached a turn where the road narrowed. *This isn't going to work,* I thought, my shoulder already touching someone else's. I'd never seen him before, but now I trusted my life to this guy, leaning the other way so our handlebars wouldn't get twisted, while we held each other up with elbows and hips at fifty kilometers an hour. The pileup happened to be on the other side of the pack, so we made it through, gave each other the raised-eyebrow "that was close" look and shook our heads, trying to forget about it. When I played soccer as a kid (I was the chubby goalie), if someone got hurt, we'd all take a knee until he stood up, but in Belgium, no one stops to check on fallen comrades. You keep your head down, secretly happy that there's one less guy fighting for the front. Belgium is home to dozens of big events, and locals have raced each cobblestone many times, probably before puberty. If you hit "pause" at any turn on the course, you'd see one line going the long way through a roundabout, another one shooting inside the turn between stopped traffic on the wrong side of the road, with some riders bunny-hopping the median at full speed, while volunteers, police, and spectators hold their cell phones out to take pictures or press their backs against a wall when we get too close. You could send a race through the same turn a thousand times, and each would be unique, like a snowflake—until someone crashes and ruins it. I watched one guy jump onto the sidewalk before a left turn, shooting through a café's patio furniture (with customers trying to enjoy their frites), and back onto the street at full speed. I hated him for putting the rest of us in danger, just so he could move up ten spots.

There was no time to rest until we reached a set of train tracks with the gates down,* and since we'd gone nearly two hours without the usual "nature break," spectators averted their eyes while we took the opportunity to urinate, right there in the road.

"Ahneemuls!" yelled an Italian rider, shaking his fist, pretending he was offended as he joined the pee party. Everyone laughed.

In Europe, you don't need a weather forecast. Instead, just look at a map. If it says "Belgium," or "Netherlands," it's going to rain (or worse), so the second time I peed that day, it was in my shorts for warmth. On the first lap, we smelled fertilizer in the fields, but on the last lap, with cold rain spraying up from our wheels, we could taste it. I jumped the sidewalk to take the crazy sidewalk line through the café. I didn't care anymore, and the frites smelled delicious.

With 20k to go, I chased down the breakaway for our sprinters. Vansummeren had laughed when I told him it was my first time racing on cobbles, but now he patted me on the back, impressed that I was still there after all the wind and crashes. There's an upside to low expectations.

At the finish line, soigneurs gave directions to the bus, handing us a chocolate-flavored recovery drink. Nathan Haas told me

---

* Guys are so desperate in Belgium, they actually had to make a rule that you get disqualified for jumping through the gate ahead of an oncoming train.

to slam it and give the bottle away immediately, but I didn't listen, so I was attacked by pedalphiles as I pushed through the crowd, unable to go two feet without someone tapping me on the shoulder for a souvenir.

"*Bidon, monsieur? Bidon?* Can I have your bottle and your gloves? Excuse me, can you give your helmet?"

I finally tossed my bottle to the crowd, and grown men fought over it, like crows.

CHAPTER 12

THE TEAM HELD a training camp in Girona in March to prepare for the Volta a Catalunya, which meant free meals, rides through the countryside with a support car, massage in the afternoons, and I could sleep in my own bed every night. Well, Tom's kid's bed, but it beat a hotel.

We did nine days of long rides, culminating with two timed efforts up a fifteen-minute climb from the coast. Fifteen minutes was my specialty, according to the lab tests in Denver, so I set a goal on my power meter and nailed it on both efforts. I was even faster than Ryder, who was killing himself to catch me, so at the top, he made sure I knew how heavy his water bottles were, asking Nate to lift them to verify.* Is this what it takes to win the Giro? Do you have to be a lunatic?

I collapsed into bed at Tom's house that night. I felt like I'd already raced a long year, but I realized that the season was just starting back home when I got a message from an old friend from college, asking for advice about the San Dimas Stage Race. He was the best on the University of Florida team since I'd moved away,

---

* I also had water bottles on my bike.

so now, the same guys who'd told me to follow my dreams were doing it to him. I won the time trial in San Dimas after I graduated, so maybe he expected the same, asking for my power numbers to try to match them.

There's always a young kid who's the best in the neighborhood, and someone tells him he could be the best in the world. They were sure I could make it to the WorldTour, just like the quarterback who beat their high school football team should win the Super Bowl, but they don't want to consider the other possibility: maybe your high school sucked, and when the best kid from your town goes up against the best from everywhere else, he's in trouble. I try to be encouraging around young riders, but I also make sure to drop the shit out of them at least once, to punch them in the face with reality before it's too late. I feel like I had it rough, but I know guys who dropped out of high school to train full-time and never even made it to a Continental team. I told him that I did 465 watts for fourteen minutes at 147 pounds, which is pretty much like saying I have a fifteen-inch penis. They say that knowing is half the battle, but that's not exactly true.

Tom was at a different training camp those weeks, at high altitude in Sierra Nevada—a ski resort on the other side of Spain. Fans often tease former dopers: take away the EPO, and guys like Pozzato, Thomas Dekker, and Andy and Fränk Schleck didn't show nearly the promise they had when they were young and dirty. That might suggest that the drugs gave them everything, but I think it's more complicated. I've had times where I'm tired or sore at the end of a long week or a tough race, and it's agony to keep pushing the pedals. If you went clean after years of doping, that's how you'd feel every day. Before, you could fly up the mountains, recover with a blood bag, and do it again the next morning, but now, every ride hurts, every climb is demoralizing, and no matter what, you've lost 30 watts you'll never get back. It would be tough to get past that, to relearn how your body is supposed to feel. I think some guys were never able to train as hard as they should, while others, like Tom, had a tendency to overdo it, suffering through seven-hour rides in Sierra Nevada, with hard climbs and motorpacing. He was killing himself, maybe trying to escape his family problems, like he could outclimb the e-mails from his divorce attorney.

CHAPTER 13

W HEN TOM GOT home, we rested for a couple days and then parked our cars at the team's warehouse (known as the "service course") for the Volta a Catalunya. The races I'd been doing were tough—often impossible—so I was intimidated for my first WorldTour-level race, which meant longer stages, a field of over two hundred riders, and mandatory participation from all of the top teams. The best riders show up at their peak for WorldTour events, where results mean big contracts, and if you can't perform, you don't keep your job. This was the level they said I wouldn't be ready for.

My role was to support our GC guys, Andrew Talansky and defending champ Dan Martin, helping them to the front before critical points or going back to the car for bottles and clothes, which meant riding the whole length of the peloton in the wind, over and over. They had to try to beat Alberto Contador and Chris Froome, but I found the "bottle boy" role to be difficult, as the first stages had everything I feared about racing in Europe: narrow roads, wind, bad pavement, and guys who were really strong, possibly from drugs. I was told to stay with teammates at all times.

"Even if you're just headed to sign-in, you go as a team," said one of the directors.

"Like women going to the bathroom?" I asked. No laughs. Team bus was a tough crowd.

During the race, sticking with teammates wasn't easy. I'd claw my way to Talansky's wheel, someone would bump into me, we'd fly into a roundabout, Andrew would go left, I'm forced right, and suddenly I'm three guys behind him, in trouble on the radio.

"Phil! Where are you? You need to stay with us."

I'm doing my best. I didn't say, because my best would have to get better.

Halfway through each stage, soigneurs wait in the feed zone with "musettes": thin cotton bags containing two bottles, energy bars, a miniature can of Coke, and a Snickers if they're in a good mood. We'd grab the bags as we flew past, take out what we needed, and toss the rest to the crowds.* Garmin-Sharp didn't have a food sponsor anymore, because Clif Bar pulled out after the Ryder Hesjedal fiasco, but the service course still had plenty left, so we used Clif product for most of the year. Talansky's favorite was the kids' version: Clif's Zbar, but they weren't in the bags like he'd hoped.

"Phil, can you get me a Zbar?" he asked.

Digging through my pockets, all I had was a regular Clif Bar, so I offered him that instead.

"No, I said a Zbar. They have some in the car."

I looked at Andrew to make sure he was serious, and then called Danish director Johnny Weltz on my radio. He asked race officials for permission to work his way to the front of the caravan that follows the race, while I coasted to the back of the pack.

---

* I don't know whose idea it was for guys to ride one-handed, carrying heavy bags in a tight pack. I guess we do need food, but there's always a crash.

Johnny handed me the bar through the window at the top of a climb, and I found myself on a steep, technical downhill in a pack of cars.

It seemed like Garmin-Sharp had more directors than riders, which I didn't understand until I tried to follow Weltz down that mountain. One of the first pros to move to Girona, he'd feuded with Lance when they were teammates, but kept Girona as his home after he retired. Now, Johnny knew every road in that part of Spain, and as a bonus, he was fluent in Catalan and well connected in the community—the man to talk to if you needed repairs on your house or help finding a used scooter, for example. If I found myself with a dead body to dispose of in Girona,* he'd be my first call.†

Every team needs a Johnny Weltz, but at that moment, trying to keep up on wet hairpins, I hated him. I imagined myself slamming into his window and being run over from behind by other directors, all ex–pro racers driving in tight formation, with brains half-scrambled from whatever drugs were popular in their era. From Trinidad to Korea, I'd been in plenty of danger, but this was the first time since my crash in San Dimas. I started the descent inches from his bumper, but when I wussed out around some of the blind turns, inches turned to feet, and feet turned to bike lengths.

"Phil, you need to stay on the car, eh?" said Johnny on the radio.

Stop being a wuss stop being a wuss stop being a wuss, I repeated, flying full speed into the next corners until I caught up.

I just risked my life, I thought, cruising back into the pack, *so Andrew could have seventy fewer calories, in "graham cracker" flavor. What an asshole.*

To be fair, Andrew didn't know the descent, but he did have a

---

* Hypothetically, of course. I've never murdered anyone.
† But the day is young.

reputation for being demanding and having a temper. Fans might remember an incident where announcers misreported the results at the Tour of Colorado, and he had a fit in front of the media in the parking lot. It was easy to call Talansky a prima donna, but when we'd meet for training rides in Girona, he'd send a text message if he was running five minutes late, and prima donnas don't care if they keep you waiting. Talansky was probably making seven figures that year, so he had a nice apartment, but he always wore a T-shirt and jeans—no flashy car or designer shoes—but when we stopped at a café, I'd put a few euros on the counter and he always pushed it back. Andrew was exactly the right mix of "normal, good guy" and generous.

I bet fewer athletes would seem like prima donnas if we understood the context: like Tyler Farrar in the sprints, Talansky was in over his head—team leader at races he wasn't capable of winning yet. He was young, on a small team, expected to beat twenty guys who were probably clean now, but maybe pushing the envelope, or enjoying a residual EPO effect from another era. So yeah, Andrew needed a Zbar if he thought it was easier on his stomach. As an athlete at the bottom of the totem pole, you look at guys above you and think, *With a little more effort, a little more focus, I could be him,* but seeing how the pressure could unravel you, my $50,000 salary didn't seem so bad, and the truth is, if I wasn't good enough to go back to the car a few times every day for X-, Y-, or Zbars, I might as well quit. So I sucked it up, pushed my way through the pack, brought Andrew everything he needed, and I descended like a madman if that's what it took. I was in the WorldTour now.

The second stage finished in Girona. We'd been looking forward to a hometown crowd, but with dumping cold rain, the only cheering I heard was from Alex Howes, who was on the roster for Critérium International instead of Catalunya.

"Phil! You suck!" he yelled. Alex and I had become fast friends. It was Joanna's birthday that night, and I'd done my best to be a good fiancé from a distance: I told her where to find the gift I'd hidden in the apartment, sent flowers to her office, put a bottle of champagne on my credit card at the restaurant where she was meeting her friends, and arranged for our roommate to deliver a cake from Sweetsalt. It was a good effort, but you're supposed to be there, and I spent most of the evening texting her, feeling guilty.

CHAPTER 14

WHEN THE RACE entered the Pyrenees, the form I had in San Luis was gone, but I'd gotten into a rhythm with this WorldTour thing.

Every night, we'd get a schedule for the next stage:

09h25 Bags out
09h30 Breakfast
11h30 Leaving for race by bus (30 min.)
12h30 Meeting on the bus
12h50 Neutral start
Total of the race: 169,700km
Weather: 2 degrees C, rain, possible snow, wind SW and
     8 km/h

When my alarm went off at 9:22, I put on the same team-logo T-shirt, underwear, and track pants I'd been wearing all week, I didn't brush my teeth, fix my hair, or look in a mirror, and I was out the door by 9:25. As a marginal gain, riders are supposed to leave suitcases in the hallway for soigneurs to bring down, but I took mine to the truck on the way to breakfast.* By 9:35, I was eating oatmeal and eggs.

The transfer to the start of the stage was luxurious on the Garmin-Sharp bus, custom-built for the 2013 Tour de France. We sat in swiveling leather seats, where bins in the overhead compartments were labeled by name, containing our helmets, shoes, and rain bags filled with everything Pat and Jason told me I'd need. With snow in the forecast, talk among riders was nothing but informal surveys of clothing options.

"Are you going with the thick base layer?"

"I think I'll do a wind vest so I can take it off on the climbs."

"Which shoe covers?"

"Definitely the latex ones. Hey, do these gloves stay dry?"

Every day, like we'd never gotten dressed before.

The middle of the bus had drawers filled with energy bars and a countertop with all the odds and ends laid out: sunscreen, chamois cream, radios, even argyle tape to hold the radio earpiece in place. Every detail was sorted, except we still had to pin our own numbers. With GPS timing chips on our bikes, the idea that we still used safety pins and paper numbers in pro races in 2014 was mind-boggling,† and I'd sort of hoped that in the WorldTour, someone would at least do the pinning for us, but no luck.

I filled my pockets with Zbars for Andrew while Johnny Weltz pulled up the course profile on the flat-screen TV. Well, he tried to, but it froze, so we all squinted at the course map on his laptop instead.

"We never had problems with the flat-screen on my old team," I whined. (BISSELL's vehicle was a Ford Econoline.) When the

---

* I'm a man of the people, so I carry my own bags. Plus, they have wheels, so it's not exactly strenuous.

† Somewhere, the owner of a safety pin factory had a gun to Pat McQuaid's head, yelling, "You will not fix this!"

meeting was over, with twenty minutes to kill before the start, we played air guitar to AC/DC, pounding shots from the bus's twin espresso machines.

Catalunya had brief rider presentations at sign-in, where I was introduced as winner of the first stage ("primeraaaa etapaaaa") of the Tour de San Luis. I was real nonchalant about it: head nod, quick wave to the crowd, closed-mouth smile.

Race organizers had promised that the stage would be canceled or shortened if conditions were unsafe, but fast-forward three hours, it's snowing, and we're still racing. Chris Froome and Alberto Contador finally called for a protest, and everyone obeyed for about two minutes, until one asshole saw it as his big chance, called the rest of us "soft," and went on the attack. Someone chased him down to yell at him, someone else chased *him* down, and then we were racing again. Pro cycling had a union, but they never did much, so this was typical for protests.

I did my job and finished with the groupetto, fifteen minutes behind the leaders, feet numb from the cold, with just enough feeling in my hands to nail Weltz in the chest with a snowball on the way to the bus. Waiting my turn for a shower, I ate a bowl of rice and eggs cooked up by Biso, the driver (his Twitter name is @BisoBus), and looked out the window at a castle built into the mountain, with a balcony over the gate where knights once stood to pour boiling oil on invaders. That put my suffering in perspective as I watched the sea of bundled crowds who'd trekked up the mountain to cheer for us, now hiking back down, with the TV helicopter in the distance. I was cold and wet, in a sport that sometimes seemed broken and amateur, but I was on one of the top teams, competing against the best in the world. This was what I'd dreamed of. I was in the Show.

View from the bus after the stage in Catalunya.

When we arrived at the hotel, soigneurs were waiting outside with room keys and a massage schedule, herding us to the elevator. They'd already brought my suitcase to my room (along with a bottle of sparkling water and a sandwich), but I wouldn't open it. I'd wear the same track suit tomorrow, and I'd left my dirty laundry in the mesh bag with my name misspelled on the bus, which would be cleaned and delivered to me in a couple hours. Riders all bring a big suitcase to every stage race, but we live out of a laundry bag and a backpack by the end.

The hotel was typical for Europe: Wi-Fi was worthless—overloaded by a hundred pro cyclists trying to Skype their wives or girlfriends—and the room was tiny, with two twin beds pushed together into a sort-of-king. Tom and I slid the beds four inches apart so as to not get too intimate, but my hand still found his when I reached for the edge of the mattress to roll over during the night.*

I went straight from massage to dinner, which was the usual bland pasta buffet, but the team provided an assortment of sauces, real Parmigiano Reggiano cheese, and expensive balsamic vinegar, which were all new to me, but I quickly came to appreciate (growing up, we had Kraft Parmesan in a plastic tennis ball can, and vinegar came from a jug in the laundry closet).

After dinner, we headed to the soigneurs' room for more food. They were at the bar with the rest of the staff in the evenings, but they'd taped a room list to the door with a key hidden behind it so we could let ourselves in (every team does it that way, if you ever want to steal some cereal). Crowded around like we hadn't just finished dinner, we poured bowls of chocolate granola and handfuls of nuts. I'd lost track of which stage we were up to or what city we were in, but I felt fine—a plateau of tired and sore. Our phones beeped with the schedule for the next day, and we headed to bed to do it all over again.

---

* Can you imagine pro soccer players sharing a hotel room when they're on the road? I know guys who've slept in bunk beds during the Tour de France.

CHAPTER 15

I WAS TOLD TO try for the early breakaway on stage five, which looked like it would go on the first climb, but I attacked over and over and every time I looked back, Luca Paolini of Team Katusha was dragging me back for their race leader, Joaquim Rodríguez.* If I accelerated on a mountain in a Continental race the year before, the field would be decimated and desperately trying to catch me, but in a WorldTour race, after ten jumps from yours truly, the group was strung out but not shattered, and I was still in the pack at the top.† It turns out there was some feud between Garmin-Sharp and Katusha going back years. Dan Martin beat Joaquim Rodríguez a couple times, Vaughters gave Joaquim a lowball offer or something, and everyone held a grudge. They'd never have let our team into the breakaway, but nobody bothered to tell me.

---

* Paolini twice tested positive for cocaine, which he blamed on a vicious cycle with prescription sleeping pills he used at races. I've heard that cocaine is often used in training as a weight loss aid. I also heard he was using EPO.
† When someone attacks on a climb, we often refer to it as "swinging your dick around." When I swung my dick in the WorldTour, it hit my upper thigh.

I was cramped and gasping in the valley, so Dan rode up to me to give me a little push and some bad news:

"Good effort, Phil, but make sure you eat something now. Remember we have 180k to go."

"Fuck, Dan!" I said, looking down at my computer. "Fuck!"

Thanks to a chocolate pastry from breakfast that I'd wrapped in a napkin, I made it to the finish, but Tom didn't. When you overtrain, it's easy to get hurt or sick, so when he got tangled up in what looked like a minor crash, he dropped out of the race complaining of knee pain.* Tom had grabbed his stuff and found a ride back to Sant Gregori before we finished the stage. I missed his guidance, but I got the whole "king" bed to myself that night.†

I tried for the break again on stage six—a windy, 220k day that started on another long climb—but I hit a rock and went back to the car with a flat tire. By the time I had a new wheel, the pack had exploded, and I caught up to a group of forty stragglers, all in danger of missing "time cut" and having nothing to show for the week except the letters "DNF" (for Did Not Finish) by their name in the results.

With only one stage to go, I'd been looking forward to completing my first WorldTour race, with laps around Las Ramblas—the touristy walking district in Barcelona—but we were minutes behind with 160k still to go.

"What the hell do I do?" I asked Johnny over the radio.

"Eh, is not your fault. You try your best now, eh? And if you don't make it, tomorrow you have some wine on the Ramblas while the boys have to race. Is not so bad, eh?"

Actually, that sounded great. I was almost disappointed when

---

* I'll get some hate mail for this, but I don't think the vegan thing helped, either. I respect the sustainability and animal rights arguments, and I'll probably try it someday, but it's hard to imagine that you can crack the very top of a competitive endurance sport without years of education and fine-tuning and personalization.

† When you get a hotel room to yourself, they call it the "spank tank." No idea why.

the leaders took a nature break and my group rejoined the pack. In Continental races, I'd had to master the "rolling piss," where you pee while coasting on a downhill, but in the WorldTour, everyone stopped together about an hour into each stage. This civil practice saved my bladder many times, but now, it saved my ass.*

Catching up after the flat tire was a hard effort, but I still had the legs to attack on the last climb, trying to help Ryder sneak away for a stage win. It wasn't much, but it was nice to contribute more than just bottles and Zbars.

It was raining and windy again on the final stage, so my ears perked up when we entered Barcelona, waiting for that beautiful sound of "Groupetto!" so I could cruise easy the last few laps, sealing the deal on a solid WorldTour debut. Then the radio crackled.

"Talansky. Rear flat."

On previous teams, I knew where I placed at every race, but I'd stopped looking for my name in the results this year. I was here for a job, and as long as I did it, it didn't matter if I was nineteenth or ninetieth. My result was the team's result; Andrew was in fourth overall, and the front pack was going all-out, so I waited to help him catch up. Digging deep, squinting in the rain, my finish line wasn't the actual finish line anymore. It was the sight of Talansky at the back of the pack. When we got there, I didn't have another pedal stroke in me, so I hopped onto the sidewalk, headed for the bus. All that work, all those bowls of pasta I forced down and everything I learned, all for a DNF. But I'm not a middle-aged soccer mom, and this isn't a 5k. Nobody cares if I finish.

It seemed like we'd been gone ten years when they dropped us off at the service course that night. I drove myself home, slept for a few hours, and woke up with an angry metabolism, so I got back in the car to buy some groceries. The Renault worked fine when I needed it to get home a few hours before, but now it just made a

---

* This is not a poop joke.

clicking noise, so I rode my bike to the market and filled a back-pack with groceries, thinking of Argos, the dog in *The Odyssey*: a strong, healthy animal when his master leaves, but old and flea-ridden when Odysseus returns from his epic journey. Argos finally sees the man he's been waiting for all those years, and then dies. (I forget if Argos licked him first. If he didn't, he should have. I'm not looking it up.) Argos was a great metaphor for the car, but it just needed a jump-start.

CHAPTER 16

I T WAS STILL early in the season, but injuries and illness caused a shuffle in the race schedule after Catalunya. If I didn't keep an eye on the Google Calendar that was shared with all the riders, I'd only find out about my next race when a plane ticket showed up in my in-box, and at a midride coffee stop, Nate Brown got an e-mail about Paris–Roubaix. His face turned red, fearing for his 140-pound body that was soon to be pounded by cobblestones, but the e-mail was meant for Nathan Haas.

I was "reserve" for a handful of smaller races, meaning I could be added to a roster at any minute. I did shorter rides to keep my legs fresh, but the team never needed me, so it turned into a long month of losing fitness at Tom's house. Bored and lonely, I'd want to talk to Joanna every day, which annoyed the hell out of her and was hard to schedule with a nine-hour time difference, so when she was busy, I'd call my mom instead. Mom always answered the phone.

I killed time working on my business and watching Netflix on an old Hewlett-Packard laptop that my dad wanted to throw away. I'm embarrassed to admit how fast I got through the entire

Breaking Bad series, moving on to classic movies like *Magnolia*, which took place a few blocks from where I lived in L.A. I enjoyed the characters' quests for happiness, until the Aimee Mann song came on:

> *It's not what you thought, when you first began it.*
> *You got what you want. Now you can hardly stand it, though.*

I guess those vitamins hadn't helped my testosterone levels, because there I was, alone in Girona, crying at a movie. For years, my goal was to join the WorldTour. I thought it was everything I wanted and I hadn't looked past it, but I'd done it all wrong, and I was miserable.

An hour later, biting into a Big Mac, I understood why Americans found it comforting when they were cracked. When you've been away from the people and things that make you happy, and you feel like a five-year-old because you can't read menus or street signs, everything is just a little more stressful, so McDonald's is an embassy—an oasis. It's a shitty cheeseburger, but it's familiar and you know how it'll make you feel.

I finished *Magnolia* that night. In the last scene, frogs rain from the sky, and the words "But it happened" appear at the bottom of the screen, referring to a rare phenomenon where tornadoes over water can pick up frogs and dump them on land. I guess the message is that you can search for meaning all you want, but sometimes you just have to deal with frog guts.

CHAPTER 17

WITH ANOTHER MONTH in Europe, I made an effort to be social, heading to "Old Town" Girona, the small corner of the city where most of my teammates were clustered. It was only a few kilometers from Tom's house, but it might as well have been another century, with cobblestoned streets built in AD 800 and a cathedral that towers over the city, serenading tourists with its bell every hour.* I should have lived in Old Town all along, where you don't need a car, and you go to the same shops and restaurants as the other pros so it's easy to make friends and enjoy impromptu gelato in the evenings. In the States, pros flocked to Boulder. I'd never wanted to tackle a Colorado winter, but I understood the appeal of living close to other racers, and Girona was Boulder on steroids. Wait. Boulder on EPO? Never mind.

My taste had always been simple (cheap), but it didn't take me long to appreciate Girona's world-class food scene. The guys showed me all the nice restaurants and tasty tapas, but no one I

---

* As a writer, this is cheating, but if that description isn't good enough, Girona is where they film *Game of Thrones*.

Mid-ride coffee stop in Girona.

knew had been to Can Roca, which had three Michelin stars and had just been ranked the number one restaurant in the world. Lunch was twelve courses for 300 euros and the place was booked a year in advance, but I had to take Joanna there.

It wasn't fancy parties with celebrities like other pro sports, but the WorldTour lifestyle would be charming for a few years. With my results in San Luis, the guys said I could expect a two-year contract for something like $150,000. We'd find Joanna a team to race for in Europe, live the dream, spend the off-seasons in L.A., and find new jobs around thirty-five.

Pretty sure I had it all figured out, I asked my teammates what happened to Jacob Rathe, who'd lived in Girona the year before and whose time trial bike I was still riding. He'd raced well, so where was his six-figure contract? They said that Jacob's agent asked Vaughters for too much money so he landed on Jelly Belly, but the guys agreed that they loved him, and the ones who hadn't stayed in touch felt bad about it. It wasn't personal. They just got busy, and there were new guys to get to know. When I'm gone, however it happened, I could only hope that someone would sit at a coffee shop in Girona the next year, telling the new guy they miss me.

CHAPTER 18

A s much as possible, we avoided talk about bikes, focusing on real sports and women. You know— guy stuff. When Dan Martin mentioned that he'd stayed out late to watch a rugby game, they teased him.

"You know you had half a beer and went home at nine thirty, Dan. You're as 'all-in' as anybody."

In the WorldTour, "all-in" means devoting your life to performance: every calorie is nutritious, sleep is maximized, and stress is minimized. When I joined the WorldTour, I thought that the next step was to find balance, but maybe I had it wrong. At the top level of anything, you have to weigh what you value, so what if I could win the Tour de France, but I wasn't a good friend, and I never ate a cookie, called my grandma, or experienced love? I'd have the achievement, but what was it for? Or what if you make all those selfish sacrifices and then you only finish fourth? Fourth sucks. You can wrap your life around one goal, and then failure would be devastating, but if you chase multiple goals, failure is more likely. What if balance means teetering on the edge of a cliff?

The team certainly expected us to be all-in. Just like the bus with everything organized for efficiency, so was life on Garmin-Sharp. If

I was leaving for a race, I'd get an e-mail saying what time to stumble out of the house, and a taxi would be waiting. I didn't ask how I'd get from the airport to the hotel, trusting that when I wandered out from baggage claim, a soigneur would be there in a team car.

If my bike needed a new chain, somebody would take care of it. Want to try a different saddle or a longer stem? I don't think I ever heard the word "no" from a mechanic, and if I stopped at the service course to drop off receipts for reimbursement, they'd grab my bike, wash off the dirt, and change my handlebar tape.*

The service course was a fun window into the workings of the team. One day, they were unloading a truckload of Thule-brand luggage: each rider and staff would get a big rolling suitcase, a trolley bag, a duffel bag, two rain bags, and a backpack. I was taking a photo to post some sponsor love on social media when one of the managers stopped me.

"Thule isn't a sponsor anymore," she said.

"Huh? What's all this, then?" I asked.

"They were a sponsor last year," she explained. "But this year they didn't want to give cash, and we don't take sponsors for just equipment. The team paid for all this."

"So Thule was providing bags *and* cash last year, this year they offered just the luggage but *no* cash, so the team turned it down, but then *bought* the *same* luggage from Thule and took the sponsor logo off of the website?"

"Yep. That's how it works."

I heard it was 60,000 euros, but Thule probably gave them a discount.

---

* Handlebar tape looks easy to wrap, but there's an art to it and it comes out like shit if I do it myself. Top three bar tapers in the world:
  1. Team mechanic Sam Elenes
  2. Sam Elenes
  3. Sam Elenes
  Honorable mention: head mechanic Geoff Brown, but he was usually busy wrapping handlebars for someone more important.

Then the manager directed me to a table covered in stacks of jerseys and handed me a Sharpie.

"Now sign these for our real sponsors."

Tom had showed me how to stretch the fabric to keep it from bunching, but it's nearly impossible to sign a jersey, and I'd still never recognize my own autograph. Sorry, sponsors.

CHAPTER 19

THE NEXT EVENT on my schedule was a one-day race called Brabantse Pijl, where a good performance might mean a shot at the Ardennes classics in Belgium: Amstel Gold, La Flèche Wallonne, and Liège–Bastogne–Liège. Excited at the possibility of racing these "monuments," I did long rides in Girona with short, steep climbs, and then I got an e-mail that I was leaving in two days for an altitude camp in Sierra Nevada. It was short notice, but I didn't have anything else to do, and Alex Howes and Dan Martin were the other guests so it sounded like fun.

Our lodging was an Olympic athletic facility, featuring a running track, soccer field, weight rooms, swimming pools, even trampolines for some reason (that area was locked or I'd have broken my leg, and Howes would be dead). Our rooms were dorm-style, as was the food, and the lobby had Wi-Fi but no chairs, so we spent our evenings on the floor. Perched on a hill above Sierra Nevada's village and ski area,* with a gray cement exterior, it even looked like a medium-security prison.

---

* I could imagine Vaughters's logic: "Team Sky is staying at the hotel 2,500 meters high? We're going to sleep up *there* at 2,570."

It snowed on the mountain, so we spent the first morning in the gym, taking turns on the leg press and writing REDRUM in the steam on the window. In the afternoon, we drove down the mountain for an easy spin, trying to learn how to do wheelies. Ever since Sagan started doing them in the groupetto at Grand Tours, you could finish eightieth or grope a podium girl, but if you cross the line with your front wheel in the air, fans love you and all is forgiven. That part of Spain is filled with citrus and olive groves, and the smell was so powerful, I thought I might skid on olive oil. That's my excuse for not mastering the wheelie.

That trip was my first time rooming with Alex Howes. We'd first met in a crash at the Tour de Toona in Pennsylvania back in 2007, where he slid under a car and smashed his frame to pieces, and I lost most of the skin on my right side. I found his prescription Oakleys in the dirt and we tried not to bleed all over a kind stranger's minivan as they drove us back to the start. He was nineteen and I was twenty-one. Later that year, a fan at the Tour of Utah held out a hot dog as a joke. Alex grabbed it, took a bite, and then attacked, winning the stage, and also my heart.

Howes had been with Vaughters's development team since its inception, so while I was getting dropped at Redlands as an amateur, he was getting dropped in Europe at some of the biggest races in the world. He was a fast sprinter who could make it over tough climbs, but he was in over his head at that age, so results were slim. When he came back to the States for Under-23 nationals every summer, no one knew who Alex was because he hadn't cracked the top twenty all year, but he'd win everything, like a boxer who'd been competing above his weight class, finally getting a fair fight. Now he was twenty-five, starting to be in the mix at bigger events.

Alex was a weirdo, but in a charming and entertaining way. Most of our teammates would come to a bike race and read a cycling magazine on the bus, but he had a *New Yorker*, and when we left the hotel, he'd hide the room key instead of carrying it with him—under a plant in the hallway, behind the fire extinguisher, somewhere different every day. Part Native American, he traveled with a collection of feathers and rocks and set them up on display above his bed.

Dan Martin was a different kind of a weirdo, but also endearing. He'd been a great bike racer since puberty, which came at the expense of other things, like childhood.

"I hate video games," Dan said. "Like, if you just start one, you have to keep going, don't you? And beating it isn't good enough. You have to go again until you get a perfect score on every level. It's maddening."

"Actually, most people don't have to keep doing something until they're perfect at it, Dan." *Is this why Dan is a winner?*

Something else I think Dan missed out on was dating. We were the same age and no one could remember seeing him with a girl, so when a women's running team arrived at the hotel, pointing at our table at dinner, we pressured Dan to talk to them. It took him two days to work up the nerve, but it was good to see him find some balance.

Following the team's protocol for altitude training, I learned what I'd done wrong in Big Bear the year before: you don't stay more than three weeks, because although it does improve your blood levels, power suffers if you're there for too long. The team's coach also explained that a trip of less than two weeks was pointless, since it would make you tired without leading to any adaptation, so naturally I left after less than a week. I'd been taken off the roster for the Ardennes races I was training for, and on for the Circuit de la Sarthe, a five-day stage race in France.

I rode for a couple hours in the morning before my flight, and then sat in the car with director Robbie Hunter as he motorpaced Alex. Robbie was a star sprinter when he raced—one of the guys who got dropped on the climb and caught up by being crazy on the descent—and he drove accordingly, drifting around icy corners with confidence. If my mom was in the car, she'd never have stopped screaming, but we had casual conversation, and I don't think my heart rate broke 45. Robbie was a professional.

He dropped me off early at the Granada airport, where I noticed a family with expensive luggage at the ticket counter, trying to get on the next flight to Rome. *What kind of wasteful lunatic would show up at the airport and buy tickets to fly the same day?* I wondered, browsing at the gift shop, which was filled with postcards of a palace nearby that I'd seen on the Travel Channel. Only a bike racer would spend a week just minutes from Alhambra without going in, but I guess tourists don't get to smell the olive groves. Or experience the dorm food at the training prison.

CHAPTER 20

M Y FLIGHT LANDED late in Paris, and the airport felt like a ghost town. Shops were closed, and the first restroom I saw had orange traffic cones blocking the entrance for cleaning. I headed to an open one on the opposite side of the atrium, and noticed a janitor going the same way with another cone. When I gestured to him that I wanted to use the bathroom before he closed it, he shook his head, speeding up so he'd beat me to the door with the cone. I walked faster, and soon we were both in full sprint, him dragging a cone, and me carrying my suitcase like a football, racing to the bathroom. I took the yellow jersey at Charles de Gaulle International, and confirmed the stereotype that French people are rude.

Director Charly Wegelius followed me in the car for the time trial at the Circuit de la Sarthe, complimenting my effort, position, and pacing afterward, which put me in a good mood until I saw the results. If a director is happy with your performance, and you finished sixty-fourth, he doesn't think much of you. Australian Rohan Dennis was our team leader, finishing a close second to Movistar's Alex Dowsett, while our all-rounder Ramunas Navardauskas was third, putting us in great shape to attack Dowsett for the overall win.

On the way to a hotel, one of the soigneurs forgot that he had bikes on the roof of the car, crushing five Cervélos into the side of a parking garage. Broken bikes are nothing new on a pro team,* but they didn't keep that many spares in the truck. If Rohan and Ramunas weren't sitting second and third overall, the team might have sent us home early, but Wegelius drove north that night while a mechanic went south from a race in Belgium, meeting somewhere in the middle to hand off more frames.

They tried to keep the incident a secret, but at dinner, word got out why our director was absent. Staring at another plate of un-seasoned chicken and overcooked pasta at a French hotel, we did what any athlete would upon finding out they were unsupervised: we marched across the street to a fast-food burger joint. Thomas Dekker put down his credit card, and we enjoyed cheeseburgers, fries, Coke, and something called "Krusty Cheese." I'd been to some of the nicer restaurants in Girona by then, but nothing compared to the joy of that greasy meal.

We'd barely finished eating when Dekker slid a strip of chewing tobacco into his mouth. I was shocked at how many of my teammates were addicted to "snus," as they call it, lining their lip as soon as they got off the bike. It was probably a remnant of the doping era, enjoyed for stimulant qualities, but I only say that because the biggest abusers I saw were Dekker and Hesjedal. Ryder said he had snus in his lip *during the race* when he was leading the Giro.

I worried that Thomas would be fined for wearing non–New Balance shoes, but I had to compliment his shiny high-top sneakers with big silver stars around the top.

"Oh, these? They're Givenchy. Thousand euros. I have three pairs. I was making more money then," he sighed, laughing at

---

* It's normal for a mechanic to spot a crack in a frame, toss the $4,000 hunk of carbon fiber into a Dumpster, and build up a new one for the next stage.

himself. *And as long as he's on the clean team, he'll never make money like that again.*

Dekker was open about his history. He'd won all the World Cups as a junior, becoming a household name in the Netherlands when he joined the now-infamous Team Rabobank at nineteen years old. Thomas's trademark was his long, beautiful hair, so when they told him to cut it for aerodynamics, his father, who'd spent years following him in a car on training rides to help him reach the WorldTour, said that he could quit and come straight home if he wanted.*

So he stuck to his principles when it came to hair, but Dekker said it didn't feel wrong to take his team's advice about EPO.† Soon he was winning big races and making seven figures, and what did he do with that dirty cash? He went to his parents' landlord and bought their house. His dad went to pay rent, and the manager had to tell him that he owned the place now. Years later, when authorities found a test for EPO, they had countless vials of doper blood sitting around. If they'd tested them all it might have sunk the whole sport, so they chose one to make an example of: Thomas Dekker.

Talent often comes with excess and self-destruction. During his suspension, Dekker was known for partying and womanizing, and his DUI was all over the news.‡ He begged Vaughters for a second chance, returning to the pros humbled, and a shell of the racer he'd been as an enhanced twenty-four-year-old.

I'd heard rumors of drugs that brought marginal gains, like xenon gas to improve endurance, or AICAR to help you burn fat more efficiently, but I thought that EPO was a thing of the past

---

* Most of the Rabobank team had pale skin and their heads buzzed. They looked like a pack of emaciated aliens.
† He brought vitamins to his first training camp, and they teased him mercilessly for wasting money.
‡ Like a Dutch Justin Bieber.

until Thomas said that some types were still undetectable, out of your system in twelve hours.

"What about the bio-passport?" I asked, referring to the new protocol in which the UCI took regular blood tests, recording an imprint of each rider's physiology to prevent manipulation.

"Yes, but they look for changes, so it only means you have to keep your blood the same level all the time. If you were doping before bio-passport started, now you *have* to cheat to make sure your numbers don't change."

Pat McCarty got his butt kicked by dirty Dekker when he was coming up, so he'd be annoyed to see us laughing together, but I also enjoyed spending time with Thomas. Unlike some of my teammates who treated me as an outsider, Dekker was warm and inviting, and he always said the right thing. He'd been a bad boy, but he seemed like a good man.

So much of my life on Garmin-Sharp was interacting with people I'd once idolized, but I now knew had stolen from my sport—trying to figure out if I cared enough to try to win them over, if it was okay to like them, and if they'd paid the price by whatever standard I invented. My job was to race my bike, but I also had to be a philosopher, judge, and jury, and there was no right answer. And by the way, if I can't get along, it's going to be a long season on a bus with these guys, and I can go ahead and hang up my dream, because I won't be coming back next year.

CHAPTER 21

WEGELIUS MADE A pep talk out of the broken bikes the next morning.

"It looked for a minute like we might not be able to start today, but the staff and mechanics worked all night to make it happen, so we'd appreciate it if you could reciprocate today with a special performance in the bike race." Charly always spoke like a Dickens novel, but we did perform. Well, I didn't, but Ramunas attacked on the last hill to win solo, and Dowsett was dropped, so Ramunas and Rohan moved up to first and second overall.

It's bittersweet to get to the bus after a stage and find out that your teammate won when you had little to do with it, but Ramunas gave me a hug and thanked me anyway. Sarthe wasn't a WorldTour race so there wasn't much pressure, but I liked how Ramunas handled leadership: always holding doors and giving someone else the front seat. He was so nice, he didn't have to ask for bottles or clothes. I was eager to help him.

Now that we were leading the race, my job was to control the breakaway each day. The first hour is never on TV, but that's where a race is won and lost. It's high speed, complex, and messy to get the right combination of riders up the road, but after a couple days of practice, I knew who to follow, and controlling the race was remarkably easy. Race announcers always try to build suspense, pretending that the breakaway has a chance, but it doesn't. The break only sticks if nobody cares, or if the big teams screw up royally.

WorldTour secrets for leading a race:

1. It's all about numbers in the breakaway—not how hard you ride. If there are four guys up the road, no matter how strong they are, five of us chasing on the front will catch them.
2. For every ten kilometers of racing, the pack can take back one minute. We'd regularly let them out to ten-minute leads on 200k stages.
3. When the gap starts to come down, teams with good sprinters get excited and help you chase. Sometimes they do the work for you entirely.

When we were happy with the breakaway, it was Ramunas's job as GC leader to pull over for a pee stop (I don't think it's a coincidence that leaders' jerseys are always yellow), letting them out to a healthy lead. Then we'd have four hours to reel them in, and I'd go back to the car periodically for bottles, or to hand off extra clothes as the weather warmed up. It's a crazy scene in the caravan, so I accidentally dropped an arm warmer one morning, trying to pass a wad of clothes through the window at fifty kilometers an hour.

"Oops." I looked at the warmer on the ground as we zoomed away. "I think that was Nathan's. You won't tell him it was my fault, right?" I asked Charly.

"I didn't see anything," he said. "I raced in Italy when I was a professional, so I'm good at that."

I don't know if the Italians or Spaniards were worse, but there's nothing like an old doping joke. It turned out to be my own arm warmer.

By the final stage, the caravan was a cinch, and I was master of controlling the early break—the Michael Jordan of a job that nobody knows exists—until someone hooked me into a ditch at sixty kilometers an hour. Now, I'm no Ramunas, but I'm generally a nice guy. I wait my turn at four-way stops, and I'll hold the door for an old lady, even if she's so far away I could pretend I didn't see her.* So I didn't deserve to crash, but gravity doesn't care how hard I trained, how I never doped, and maybe the guy who's not crashing cheats on his wife. Gravity is a jerk.

I find it disrespectful when people use war metaphors for sports. It's not that dangerous and it's not that important, but I'm not using a metaphor here: I was literally in a trench after that crash. I climbed out and dusted myself off while the team car skidded to a stop, and the mechanic rushed over with two spare wheels as I realigned my chain.

"It's fine," I told him.

"You're good?" said Charly from the car.

"Yup." And off I went, back into the pack with a little help from the draft of a Skoda hatchback (but no sticky bottle).

When one of my friends back home crashes on a training ride, his day is done. He's calling his wife for a ride home and complaining for days about his injuries, but in the WorldTour, a crash is nothing. It happens. You keep riding. You do your job. If someone was missing on the bus, it was because he crossed the finish line and went straight to an ambulance to get stitches at the hospital, and if he complained at dinner, it was only about the wait at the emergency room or the nurse who didn't give him her phone number. Pain wasn't a problem. When I rejoined my teammates

---

* Ramunas would carry her through the door, up to her apartment, and then do her laundry.

at the front of the pack, Nathan Haas had already cussed out the guy who hooked me—a touching act of solidarity from a young up-and-comer.

I helped catch the breakaway and dropped out when we hit the final town. It would have been nice to finish, but we'd have to hurry to the airport to make the flight to Barcelona, and I didn't want everyone to miss it because they were waiting on me in the groupetto. I got ready on time, but with Ramunas and Rohan stuck at the award ceremony, the flight took off before we even left the parking lot. Nathan's girlfriend, Laura, had flown in to visit and was already waiting in Barcelona, so he called the logistics manager in a panic to have us booked on the next flight. By the time we got through traffic to the airport, we'd missed that, too, and the manager told us to book tickets at the counter and have it reimbursed. I'd wondered who would show up at the airport to buy a full-price ticket and fly the same day, and I had my answer: me.

The team purchased a total of three flights for each rider that day, flushing money down the toilet to get home from a C-priority race. I'd heard of other examples of waste, like the $800-a-night hotels where Vaughters stayed when he traveled, and one of the managers said that he took her to Can Roca so often, she was bored of the best restaurant in the world. The team could really throw money around, but when it came to signing the clean guy who'd worked his ass off, they couldn't offer more than the minimum salary. Are we rich, or are we poor?

Craving nutrition after weeks of dorm food, hotel buffets, and Krusty Cheese, I stopped at a smoothie stand at the airport, but Nathan put his hand on my shoulder.

"Bro, you don't know what kind of protein they put in those. You shouldn't have that stuff when you get tested like we do."

I killed time by buying a disposable razor instead, because I'd lost my Mach 3 and could only narrow it down to four countries and fifty hotel rooms. You know how there's always one creep shaving in the airport restroom? It was me.

Ramunas playing it safe on a Ryanair flight.

Dan and Alex had just left Sierra Nevada, so I sent a message asking how their training went, mostly hoping to hear about Dan's love life, because it was great to see a hero so vulnerable and human. He went up that mountain single and came down with a girlfriend, and when they got engaged a year later, I called "minister," but you can't really call that sort of thing.

CHAPTER 22

THE TAXI DROPPED me off at Tom's house at three a.m. In that sleepy corner of Catalunya, cats had stopped purring by one, and even the criminals were done criming by two thirty, but the light was on in Tom's kitchen. He was awake, attending a child support hearing via Skype. Note to self: divorce would suck.

I snuck upstairs and slept until noon on the advice of a new coach I'd hired named Frank Overton. He'd worked with World-Tour riders before, so he had the experience I wanted, and he offered to coach me for free if I helped promote his business and let him use my face on his website—a deal this Toyota driver couldn't pass up. We'd decided that after a long spring campaign, with a sore knee from the crash and a flight to L.A. in thirty-six hours, this was a good time to rest, so I told my teammates that I'd be at the coffee shop in Sant Gregori all day, and coffee on me if they wanted to say good-bye. I didn't think anybody would show up, but the day was a slow parade of friends I'd made in just a few months.

I stayed at the coffee shop until midafternoon, when everyone rushed to McKiernan's Irish Pub in Old Town. Climbers gather there to cheer on their teammates at Paris–Roubaix every year, but with lots of packing to do, I watched at home instead. Classics specialists spent weeks studying the course and dialing in custom bikes for this race, all teaming up against heavy favorite Fabian Cancellara, who still finished third. Riding for Trek, the Swiss champion could climb, and time-trial, and he wasn't a bad sprinter. The guy had all the tools, almost like an army knife from—who makes those army knives?

In the Operación Puerto scandal, I'm pretty sure that the blood bags code-named "Luigi" belonged to Cancellara, but it gets better: he'd dominated time trials and one-day races with such ease that conspiracy theorists suggested a hidden motor in his bike. I dismissed it until I heard his former teammates talk about certain events where Cancellara had his own mechanic, his bike was kept separate from everyone else's, and he rode away from a "who's who" of dopers. When you watch the footage, his accelerations don't look natural at all, like he's having trouble staying on the top of the pedals. That fucker probably did have a motor.

I organized my closet at Danielson's house, leaving most of my clothes, along with the old H-P laptop/doorstop (I'd just ordered a MacBook Air with my book advance), my vitamins, a framed picture of Joanna, and all sorts of odds and ends, so I'd only need to bring a small suitcase when I came back for the second half of the season. I parked the Renault out front with the key hidden in a Ziploc bag under a potted plant, and begged my teammates to borrow it while I was gone—for airport runs, trips to the beach, whatever. It was running great after the 1,500 euros I'd spent on repairs, and I didn't want it sitting still for weeks at a time.

I flew from the Barcelona airport, which was familiar by then, as it is for many pros. When Zabriskie retired, he told Lachlan, "If there's one thing I can share with you—with the next generation of professional cyclists—it's that the black marble in the atrium at

BCN is reflective, so you can look up a woman's skirt when you're walking behind her."

The travel day felt easy since I was headed home, and because I was taking a minibreak, my coach said I should eat whatever I wanted and not feel bad about it.

"What if I eat a baby seal or a bald eagle?" I asked. "Should I feel bad about that?"

I settled for the Burger King at the terminal. Since I joined the WorldTour, I'd get recognized pretty often on the bike, but it was rare when I wasn't in uniform, so naturally two teenagers asked for my autograph when I had a mouth full of onion rings and ketchup on my shirt.

A thirty-minute delay led to a seven-hour layover at Heathrow, whose international terminal is full of Gucci and Prada and other overpriced designer stores. Ashamed of the ketchup stain, I thought about Dekker's three pairs of Givenchy high-tops and all the fancy watches on my team, and I decided to buy a new shirt. *You've worked hard, you've earned it, and you're in the WorldTour! Look, there's a sale rack at Burberry. How bad could it be?* The cheapest shirt there was a plain white V-neck for $129, marked down from $178—the bargain of a lifetime.*

---

* No, I didn't buy it! I covered the stained shirt with my hoodie.

CHAPTER 23

I WAS SO EXCITED to see Joanna again, I didn't realize there'd be an adjustment when I got back. We're gone for months like we're off slaying dragons while the loved ones stay behind, and it was hard to explain how cracked I was. I wanted everything to be like I'd left it, but life went on, and I had to work my way back into her routine.

Girls are supposed to like pro athletes. I had a personal momentum—going after what I wanted and getting it, trying to be the best. Women are often attracted to that, and Joanna did get a kick out of it when someone asked for an autograph, but it couldn't make up for all the sheets stained from road rash or the parties she went to alone. She didn't have a car, so she'd been driving my Matrix to work and to visit friends in the evenings. Now she had to commute on her bike, and there was a tired dude on the sofa who just wanted to cook dinner and go to bed early. At the apartment, the closet was full and her stuff had overflowed into my only dresser, but there wasn't much point unpacking for just a few weeks, so I continued to live out of my suitcase, which almost fit under the bed. Home didn't feel much like home.

I ran into one of her coworkers that week at the grocery store.

"Oh! You're here for once!" she said. She didn't mean it as an insult, but as much as I'd tried to convince myself that I'd made a good effort to be part of Joanna's life—that I wasn't a jerk for proposing and leaving—little moments like that tell you how it really is.

At Liège–Bastogne–Liège the following week, Dan Martin caught the remnants of the breakaway in the final five hundred meters, in perfect position to repeat his victory at one of the most prestigious races in the world until his rear wheel slid out in the last corner. It was torture to watch him crash, knowing the months that Dan put into that race, how important it was to him. I'm sure he wanted to hide in a cave for a year, but Dan stepped off of the bus to talk to the media.

"I just took the turn too fast," he admitted. No bike throwing. No whining. No excuses. There are winners, and then there are champions.

Thinking I'd be well rested after a few days at home, I went to Mt. Wilson for intervals, but three days in a row, I started up the hot, chip-seal pavement of Highway 2, couldn't get my heart rate over 90 beats per minute, and went home for a nap. As a hopeless optimist, I always brought enough Clif Bars for a five-hour ride, so I'd give them to homeless people on my way back. One was so happy, he offered me the rest of his cigarette.

I eventually put in some good workouts before the Tour of California, focusing on my time trial bike. I'd be in the worker role for the long stages, so the TT would be my only shot at a result, and I was looking forward to it.

CHAPTER 24

EXPECTING GOOD MEDIA coverage at my home race, my publisher had scheduled the book release for the week before the Tour of California. I was happy to get nice reviews right away, but the people who didn't like it were more interesting. You could go through those pages a hundred times and you'd never guess the sentence that pushed someone's button, like a comment about broccoli that led to hate mail from a nutritionist. And please understand that he wasn't just touting the health benefits of broccoli. That e-mail was hateful. To all nutritionists out there: I like kale and spinach, I love beets, and this is just my opinion, but fuck broccoli. Or at least cover it in cheese.

Recently retired George Hincapie was another hater. My introduction took a jab at dopers and their tell-alls, which George thought was directed at his ghostwritten piece-of-shit book, which came out around the same time. He called Tom to ask what my problem was, and I told him that my intro was referring to Tyler Hamilton's ghostwritten piece of shit, and I didn't know that Hincapie even had one coming out. I was tickled that he was insulted, though. Who the hell cares what I say?

I was friends with one doper, but I'd never spoken to George, so I could still resent Lance Armstrong's former sidekick, who'd made a career out of being in the right place at the right time— like Forrest Gump but with less of a moral compass (and maybe not that bright). I heard that George was worth $40 million, but a book titled *The Loyal Lieutenant* with a foreword written by Armstrong was a few years too late to fool anyone, so his reviews were brutal, and my book (with a fraction of the marketing budget) outsold his. You could beat me on the bike, Georgie, but leave the books to the English majors.

I was good friends with several guys on a Continental team sponsored by Hincapie's clothing company, and it was fun to watch his confusion over whether to like me or not. For months, I kept getting notifications that George was following me on Twitter, which of course meant that at some point he'd been annoyed and unfollowed. The fourth time I got the "George Hincapie is now following you" notification, I immediately posted a picture of a racer with his new CLEAN tattoo, just to piss him off.*

The team sent us to Palo Alto a few days before the Tour of California, on a secret mission to court potential sponsors† and do PR for current ones. When they talk about lead-up to a big race, media often use the "calm before the storm" cliché, but in the WorldTour, those days are the hard part. The pedaling is what we train for, so the storm was the media schedule in Palo Alto that ran from eight a.m. until dinner every day. I was assigned to make YouTube videos for Cervélo one afternoon.

"You're funny and we have two camera guys. What do you want to do?" asked their marketing person.

I'd been in L.A. long enough to know that I wrote, directed,

---

* A handful of pros and amateurs had gotten the tattoo by then—even some that I'd never met. It made me feel like Brad Pitt in *Fight Club*—minus the abs and the multiple personality disorder.

† Vaughters kept tweeting about Nest thermostats, for example, but they never made it onto the jersey.

and starred in three short films that afternoon on an hour's notice. They came out okay (funny, but no Emmy buzz).

The eye of the storm was a trip to an Italian restaurant, whose
owner was a cycling fan. We looked forward to a great lunch until we
found out that someone from the team had called ahead. This was
an important race, so while pro cycling was our bread and butter,
there'd be no gluten and no dairy. If you're familiar with the concept
of "edging" in sex, an Italian meal with no pasta or cheese is the food
equivalent (if you're under eighteen, don't look up "edging").

We finally arrived at the race hotel, and I hadn't even made it
to my room before USADA grabbed me for a blood test. I was on
a first-name basis with the phlebotomist, whose home territory
included L.A. (his name was Ruben, and I always told him I hate
sauerkraut). Since I'd left my vitamins in Girona, on the form
where it asks you to declare your supplements, I put "no pills, but
lots of cookies from strangers if this goes positive."*

We rushed to the Tour of California's "team presentation" after dinner, speeding through Sacramento to get dropped off on a
red carpet at the capitol building. I remembered the presentation
at the same venue the year before, staring in awe as Alex Howes
emerged from Team Garmin's bus, which I imagined was full of
staff and chefs, with rugs and upholstery made from albino tiger
cubs and unicorns. Now I knew that the bus they kept in the
United States was built in the '80s, falling apart, and dressed up
outside with a $12,000 sticker, but being on the cool team at my
home race still gave me goose bumps. I had over an hour to savor
it, sitting on the floor in tights with my teammates—all so we
could stand on a stage for thirty seconds and wave to a room of
rich guys who'd probably paid $1,000 per table.

Back in Europe, the Giro d'Italia had just started. I'd heard that

---

* It didn't, and I'm proud to report that of the hundreds of folks who had the opportunity, no one ever tried to poison me or ruin my life.

our team tried to schedule a special training camp to prepare for the team time trial (TTT) on the first stage, but riders refused, citing too many altitude trips and days on the road already. I respected their stand for balance until a pileup in the TTT sent Dan Martin home and crippled our GC hopes before the race even started.

That put even more pressure on the Tour of California squad, but our start wasn't much better, as Lachlan had visa issues and couldn't make it into the country. Howes was on vacation when he got the call to take Lachlan's spot, but he brought a stomach bug, spending most of his night at the luxurious Doubletree on their luxurious toilet. Oh, and guess who got to share a hotel room with him?

The first stage was hot and almost two hundred kilometers so the pack started slow, and I heard a few of the Continental riders joking that they thought these WorldTour teams were supposed to make the race *harder*. I remembered being one of those guys, but UCI races aren't harder all the time. Some days, it goes easy, easy, easy, and skips right over hard, directly to impossible.

Crosswinds split the field near the end and our entire team missed the front group, but with a little help from a tailwind, I got Rohan Dennis back to the leaders, so we were still looking good at the end—except Howes, who looked so pale, I told him he should go home. "I'll come good," he kept saying.

Vaughters patted me on the pack after the stage, saying I was the only one who did my job that day, and the Continental riders who'd joked that the race was too easy? They finished in the groupetto, probably wondering what the hell happened. I remembered being one of those guys, too.

At the hotel, one of the mechanics handed me a road bike with triathlon-style, clip-on aerobars and asked how it felt. When I did a lap around the parking lot, the seat was low and my knees hit the bars at the top of pedal stroke, but that mechanic was always a jerk to me, so I tried to keep the interaction short.

"I mean, it's alright. What's it for? A spare to go on the roof in the time trial tomorrow?"

"I'm glad you said it was alright. Your TT bike was broken on the flight and we don't have any spares, so you'll be racing on this," he said, lighting a cigarette as he walked away.*

I'd put thirty hours on that bike in the last two weeks to prepare for this race—foiled by Southwest Airlines.

Bradley Wiggins must have flown United, because his bike worked fine when he won the TT. I'd noticed Wiggins in the pack, with legs like pistons and a motionless upper body, and you could tell he was serious about the Tour of Cali, because Team Sky—known for a bottomless wallet when they needed a win—had a ton of staff that week. When I walked past their bus, two men were loading laundry into the same washer, while another stood behind them, just watching. I'm sure he was maximizing detergent efficiency and calculating the rolling resistance of the laundry bags. Marginal gains.

With all of their attention to detail, one thing that Sky hadn't addressed was the damn bib number. I checked with Ian Boswell, their token American, who confirmed that just like everyone else, Team Sky takes their wind-tunnel-tested speed suits, and has riders—who shave their legs for aerodynamics—use safety pins to attach wax paper numbers, which then flap around in the wind all day.

"So Wiggins and Froome do their own numbers?"

"Yeah. That is funny, huh?"

Imagine handing Shaquille O'Neal a blank jersey and a bag of pins.†

---

* This guy butted heads with everybody, and I heard that he was eventually left on the side of the road during the 2015 Tour de France, after mouthing off to Charly one too many times.

† Ian did say that he'd gone months without ever doing his own laundry, which almost makes up for it.

I placed somewhere in the forties or fifties in the time trial (you don't look too closely when you're in the forties or fifties, nor do you Google it when you write a book), which was pretty good for a road bike. If I'd had my time trial bike, I would have finished around sixteenth, and then I'd find an excuse to convince myself I deserved a top ten.

Rohan came in second—his fifth podium that year without a win, so his foul mouth was almost as world-class as his legs when he got to the bus. I thought the rice was a little overcooked, for example, but to my angry Australian teammate, it was "dryer than a nun's cunt."

That night, Rohan bet Caleb Fairly $1,000 that he could go twenty-four hours without cussing. We thought that Caleb would be an easy winner, but he got nervous when Rohan made it through breakfast, because pro cycling is no place for four-digit bets. Finally, in the car on the way to the stage, Rohan said what we all say when we're stuck in fucking California traffic, and when he realized that he'd lost, it was a stream of pent-up vulgarity as his mouth demons were liberated. I cried laughing.

I looked after Rohan in the race, replacing his bottles, ice socks, and food every few minutes. It was crosswindy on the Mt. Diablo stage, so I rode next to him, where I'd get no draft but he'd stay fresh for the final climb. With a powerful build and a little fat on his belly, Rohan was known for his time trial ability more than his climbing, but while others attacked each other on Diablo, he saved energy until two hundred meters to go, where he took off, won the stage, and actually gained a few seconds on Wiggins, putting himself within striking distance of the overall win.

"Maybe my legs were better because I'm allowed to cuss again," Rohan suggested.

"Everyone thought Wiggins would walk away with it, but now we've got a bike race, thanks to your foul mouth," I said.

"Well, you're all fucking welcome."

We had grits at dinner that night, which made this Georgia boy very happy, as well as Ben King, who told a story about a friend who asked a waitress what grits were.

"Well, lemme put it to ya real simple, honey," said the waitress. "It's like oatmeal, but it's grits." If that's not hilarious, you have to hear Ben say it in a southern accent.

Howes told the doctor that his bowel movements were improving, but it sounded like the Fourth of July when he went to the bathroom that night. He didn't even want to eat a cookie to feel better, which was a shame because the cookie thing had snowballed since I joined the WorldTour,* with more treats from fans awaiting me every day (Ted King had the same thing with maple syrup). Some folks baked from scratch or spent hard-earned money at their favorite café to fill a gift box, and then others would show up with a measly bag of Chips Ahoy. I'd thank Chips Ahoy guy, take a picture with his kids, and then joke about it later.

"How dare someone offer me a packaged cookie!" I scoffed, like a spoiled princess.

"Don't they know who you are?" laughed one of the soigneurs. "Hey! Can you tweet and see if someone will make us some gingersnaps?"

And like magic, gingersnaps appeared the next day. For keeping the staff well fed, I got the first massage some nights, and I noticed that a mechanic had put my spare bike on the far outside on the roof of the car (a spot that's usually reserved for the team leader, since it's more accessible in an emergency).

Howes finally got over his stomach bug, right after I caught it from him. I woke up every hour one night with a headache and my heart racing, and in the morning, I couldn't poop after breakfast.

---

* Once, I was recognized at a coffee shop eating a brownie, and the guy got angry, like I was Bob Dylan playing an electric guitar.

This might not sound like a big deal, but the prerace poop is serious for a pro cyclist. We start eating exactly three and a half hours from the race start, knowing that it takes three hours to process a bowl of oatmeal. On the bus, guys would get halfway dressed, and you could tell who's pooped by whether they've zipped their jersey.

I got into racing after I left for college, and since my dad had tried to steer me away from it, I never really wanted my parents to come to races. Now that I was in the WorldTour, they understood how important it was to me so they'd booked some plane tickets to watch.

By the time my parents arrived, I hadn't moved my bowels for days, and everything I ate came back up. I suffered through a few stages, but when I developed a fever, the doctor told me to quit. Mom and Dad had taken time off of work and flown across the country to see what their son could achieve at his physical peak, and they found me pale and constipated, asking for a ride to my crappy apartment.

The doctor had said that taking a laxative between stages would lead to dehydration, but now that I was out, I had my parents drop me off at my car and headed straight to the Vons pharmacy aisle. A nurse friend recommended magnesium citrate, which comes in a tiny glass bottle like you might find filled with whiskey on an airplane. On the back, it said, "Serving size: 1 bottle," so I washed it down with a few swigs of prune juice in the parking lot.

Vons was only a mile from my apartment, but as soon as the liquids hit my stomach, I knew it would be a photo finish. I ran two stop signs, parallel parked on Cahuenga Boulevard, and left my suitcase in the car as I bolted toward the building.

Maybe if I let out some hostages in the hallway, I can renegotiate before the explosion.

Does Phil shit himself? Find out when you turn the page!

I MADE IT to the bathroom with my pants good as new, and you know it's true because I was honest about pissing myself in Argentina. It was great to be five pounds lighter and sleep in my own bed that night, but with another DNF, the one-year contract was starting to worry me, so for the last day of the Tour of California, I contributed to the team the only way that I could: I delivered a cookie cake to the race hotel. They'd never fire the guy who brings a cookie cake. Right?

A friend made an oversized foam cutout of my face, which Nate Brown brought onto the podium when they won the "team overall" prize. I'm told that my face also attended the after party before it found its way back to me, eventually coming to rest in my parents' basement (symbolism: I end up in my parents' basement). They'd planned to stay a few extra days in Los Angeles, but they left early because Dad wasn't feeling well. It turned out that his cancer had returned, but after a quick surgery, doctors said they got it all.

I called my nutritionist to see if he had any ideas to keep my stomach from acting up again. Since veggies are hard to find on the road, he recommended chlorophyll pills, which turned my poop green, but my bowel movements were like a German train (enormous and loud, but also regular).

CHAPTER 25

ONCE AGAIN, NATIONAL championships took place a week later in Chattanooga. I wanted a crack at the individual time trial, but the team saw that Taylor Phinney was signed up, and he was so good, it wasn't even worth the cost of a hotel room to try to beat him. The son of two world-class cyclists, Taylor had just won a stage at the Tour of California for Team BMC and was considered the best up-and-coming American male—our only hope for a Paris–Roubaix win or an Olympic medal anytime soon.

After my near miss the year before with BISSELL, I could have argued that I deserved to be one of the team leaders in the road race, but I kept quiet when they said we were working for Tom and Alex. Ben King jumped into the early break, so the pack slowed down and guys started chatting. It was my first time in a pack with all of the Continental teams that year, so I was surprised when a few of them patted me on the back, congratulating me for making it to Europe, some of the younger guys saying they enjoyed my book. It never occurred to me that just as I'd looked up to Ted King, they'd now see me as proof that their dream was worthy and attainable, not knowing that it had been some of the toughest months of my career.

I appreciated the encouragement, but while these guys looked up to me, I couldn't help but look down on them. Many of them simply had no shot—they'd never be good enough to win a big race. I remembered one older guy who'd posted a selfie from a hospital, with a forced smile and his arm in a sling. This was his glorious comeback, and now he was bumping elbows and fighting for position again, taking risks, making sacrifices. *For what?*

Chasing a dream is a one-way relationship: you have to love it and give it everything or it won't work out, but you can't expect loyalty in return. Some guys are realistic about the results and just enjoy the process, but for others, the dream had thrown them away long before and they were still going after it—or maybe they were running away from something else. I had friends who were in it so long, trying to stay above water in their own little world was all they knew, and they'd gotten good at it, with side jobs and host families, living out of their cars, just as I would have been if I hadn't won Redlands by two seconds—if I hadn't met Tom Danielson against my will. If you're lost in the forest, you might get hungry, so you'll teach yourself to hunt. And then maybe you'll make a shelter when you get cold. It all seems reasonable, but one step at a time, the forest becomes home, and you forget you were trying to get out.

My team only had Ben King in the breakaway against eleven other riders, so smaller teams looked to Garmin-Sharp to chase it down. With eighty guys racing against us, our director had us ride slow on the flat parts, only pushing the pace on the climb, where drafting was less of a factor and we could punish the pack. My friend Mike Creed was directing a Continental team called SmartStop, and he came up with a name for this tactic: he said we were "big-dicking" everyone.

My dick did a great fifteen-minute effort the first time up Lookout Mountain, so I was surprised to see that Taylor Phinney was still there at the top. Taylor had been feeling so good, I heard he'd offered cash to a couple guys to work for him in the finale. Bribes are against the rules, but they're pretty common, and it would be a win-win since Taylor probably had a bonus in his contract for a national championship. I was hurt that he didn't offer me any money, but then again, I might have talked about it in some book.

Taylor attacked on the descent, which is full of sweeping corners, but if you've done it once or twice, you know they're all full speed except one bend that you need to brake for (which had claimed a collarbone in the women's race that morning). A few guys behind Phinney, I could tell that he didn't know which bend, and instead of a soft, protective hay bale in the corner, there was a motorcycle. The lead police officer had misjudged the turn and stopped short, so Phinney went into the guardrail. One other rider crashed, and he stayed with Taylor while the rest of us rode past, trying not to look at his cringing face or shattered knee. The show must go on.

I rode just as fast the second and third times up Lookout, so the breakaway was still within reach, and I knew I had one more effort in me as we approached it the last time. I was next to Jesse Anthony in the pack, with defending champ Freddie Rodriguez in front of us.

"See that guy, Jesse?" I said, loud enough for Freddie to hear me. "I'm about to send his ass home, as long as he doesn't hold on to a fucking car again. Isn't it cool that I get to decide when he goes home?"

Jesse laughed, and I big-dicked the climb until only five guys were left. Howes attacked, and I waited for Freddie so I could keep an eye on him. He shoved me into a curb when we got back to the city, and I kept it upright while the rest of the groupetto yelled at him. I take it all back about looking down on those guys.

Howes heroically made it across to the breakaway, where three guys from team SmartStop were ganging up on Ben. SmartStop hadn't been invited to the Tour of California, which didn't bode well for sponsorship, but their riders were well rested and desperate for results, so our director should have told Ben to stop pulling on the first lap. He could have handled the three teammates racing against him if he'd saved his energy, but if you tell Ben King it's a bad move to pull as hard as you can in the break, he'll show you a closet full of stars-and-stripes jerseys he got by doing exactly that, starting as a junior, all the way up to USA Pro nationals, which he won in a stunning upset as a twenty-one-year-old on a Continental team, earning his first WorldTour contract.

But Ben's breakaway streak finally came to an end in Chattanooga. When Alex got across, he found a salt-encrusted, cramping teammate, and had to settle for third behind two guys from SmartStop. We'd barely crossed the line before an angry e-mail came from Vaughters, mostly blaming the director. They go in and out like riders, and his contract wasn't renewed at the end of the year.

CHAPTER 26

MY COACH HAD me take a week off the bike after Chattanooga, to reset for the second half of the season. Joanna had come out to try her first national championship, so we went from Tennessee to Jekyll Island, where I'd rented a house near the beach. Driving through the marshes of South Georgia, I called the Jekyll Island Club Hotel and ordered a dozen Fudge Brownie Chip cookies to make sure they'd be fresh. I hadn't been there in almost a decade, so I feared that the cookie had been built up in my head, that maybe it wouldn't hold up to memory, but the damn things tasted exactly like they were supposed to. You can trust a cookie.

We were at the café for the fifth time in four days when I got a call from a reporter at the *Wall Street Journal* who wanted to write about my book. I hope my creative writing professor at UF saw the complimentary half-page article that came out a few weeks later. A–, my ass.

Our next trip was to New York for Joanna's friend's wedding—a bad idea because other guests, parents, and strangers kept asking why we hadn't pulled the trigger yet on ours, leading to an argument on the way back to the hotel. We seemed to get along,

I'm successful enough, and I often caught girls smiling at me in public so I can't be too bad-looking, but she wasn't ready to set a date, and God bless her for not caving to pressure and wanting a divorce later.

Since I wasn't riding, I'd been going to the gym every morning, where I always love the rapid, measurable improvement. I struggled with ninety pounds on the leg press the first day, but twenty-four hours later I was throwing around 180.* When I went back for the next workout, the morning after bickering with my fiancée and just a couple hours of sleep, I could barely budge 135. I knew that stress could affect strength, but I'd never seen it quantified like that.

While I was lifting weights in Brooklyn, Nairo Quintana was winning the Giro d'Italia. I'd finished one spot behind him at the Tour de San Luis, so by the transitive property of pro cycling, I reasoned that I could be top ten at the Giro.

The other news story was that Rohan Dennis was making a rare midseason transfer to BMC. The rumor was that Phinney's knee was so bad, he might never race again, so BMC was looking to replace their time trial specialist, and while I always got along with Rohan, I heard that he'd been rude to some of our teammates and staff, so Vaughters was happy to sell him.

By June, my hectic schedule came to an abrupt halt. After a spring of endless travel and logistics with multiple events going on at once, there's only one thing that sponsors care about in the summer: the Tour de France. If you're a cycling fan, it's easy to see the Tour as just another big race, but to the general public, it's like gymnastics or swimming at the Olympics: the athletes compete constantly, but the world only pays attention once every four years, and sponsors know it.

The "long list" for the Tour began with sixteen riders, all told

---

* Sparing us both the metric system here.

to prepare for that race exclusively, knowing that only nine would make the final squad. Then all year, they fought for it. You get a big win and you're probably safe, but one by one, guys were cut, like a reality TV show: you have a bad race, you put on a couple pounds, you tell a soigneur that your knee hurts, and somewhere, they're putting a line through your name. The shared Google Calendar with the race rosters was taken down, so guys peeked at the mechanics' room in the back of the service course. If they were building a new bike with your name on it, that meant you were in. Maybe.

The final selection took place at two races in June, where the long list tried to prove themselves while the rest of us sat on the sofa. *You'd better win the Tour, Talansky,* I'd thought, when I was struggling to deliver his Zbars in Catalunya. Then he won the Dauphiné, a huge stage race in France, which is good enough. You get all the Zbars you want from me if you win a race like that (and if that's not reward enough, you're also the designated leader when they finally announce the Tour roster).

Ramunas got the final spot over David Millar. Millar was retiring at the end of the year, so this would have been his farewell Tour, but he hadn't been riding well, perhaps too focused on a movie about Lance Armstrong he was involved in and renovations on his house in Girona. Millar showed a common mistake among successful athletes (not that I would know): you've worked hard, so it's important to pause, appreciate what you've done, and spend your money, but while he was finding balance and patting himself on the back, there was a long line of guys hungry to take his place. Besides, Millar was getting over a cold, and you can't bring germs to a Grand Tour. With weakened immune systems, one cell of a bacterium could take down the whole team in the first week.

Millar lashed out at Vaughters and Wegelius on Twitter for days, probably drunk. It was fun to watch, but he was overshadowed by a bigger snub when Team Sky opted to work for Chris Froome, leaving former champion Brad Wiggins at home. That would be like if the Beatles had a reunion but they didn't invite Paul McCartney.

The next race on my schedule was the Tour of Austria, which takes place during the Tour de France, so nobody cares about it unless you're me and it's your only bike race of the whole summer. I did a long training block, enjoying the benefits of my tough spring with some of the best power numbers I'd ever seen. On the last ride of a thirty-two-hour week, I set a new record on Decker Canyon and staggered to my car, just as I had when I finished the Tour de Phil, but I didn't eat a box of Dunkers this time. Motivated for Austria, I had a balanced meal at the Natural Café in Westlake Village with Jesse, Stefano, and Katie.

When they make the final selection for the Tour, the guys who get cut usually take it as a chance to enjoy a vacation, but this year, with rumors of a bad job market, some of them asked the team to use their hard-earned form in Austria instead of France, so an e-mail from Wegelius informed me that they'd given someone else my spot. I begged and argued and sent power files to show how prepared I was, but the decision had been made: I was "flicked," and wouldn't race until the Tour of Utah in August.* That's when I got a box of Dunkers.

I told myself it didn't matter. Like my dad said, nobody cares about a bike race. I could just train at home and sleep in my own bed with my fiancée, earning the same paycheck whether they raced me or not. But I wasn't convinced. I'd been so glad to get home from Europe in April, and then I was only there for a few weeks, and all I wanted was to fight for wheels in the rain and eat dry chicken at a shitty European hotel. My laundry hamper overflowed with filthy, salt-crusted argyle from weeks of flogging myself and nights going to bed early and sore, but it was all for nothing.

---

* "Flicked" is a term cyclists use for getting taken off a race or kicked off a team. We also use it for breakups.

Not to mention: getting squeezed out of a race roster isn't a great sign if you're looking for a raise at the end of the year—or a contract at all. I'd been hearing rumors about a merger between Garmin-Sharp and Team Cannondale, which meant jobs would be cut, but McQuaid assured me that they just didn't feel like spending $1,000 on a plane ticket for one race and I shouldn't read anything into it.

I felt like a caged animal, sitting at home all summer without racing. Angry at my team, I was surprised to find myself still interested, watching the Tour on my computer as much as I could. I was gutted when Talansky crashed and dropped out on the eighth day, but Ramunas salvaged the race for us with a gutsy stage win, followed by a podium finish in Paris on the last day. Fans were surprised at his sprint result, but I wasn't. I remembered a moment at training camp, where Ramunas had gone a few seconds ahead of the group on a long, flat stretch of highway. When he finished his interval, the director decided to play a prank: the rest of the team drafted behind the car, so we'd shoot by Ramunas and he'd have to catch up. He must have been tired from his effort, but the big Lithuanian shifted gears when he saw us coming, stood up, and in two pedal strokes, he'd gone from fifteen kilometers per hour to fifty, and was safely with us in the pack.

"You almost got me!" he'd laughed.

He wasn't even really trying, but it was the most impressive sprint I'd ever seen.

Teammates who'd shared a hotel room with Ramunas will tell you that he could sleep twelve hours a night if you let him, and when you check out, you know how you get on your knees and look under the bed to make sure you didn't forget anything? Ramunas just lifts the whole frame and mattress to eye level with one hand and looks underneath. That guy can also do some impressive things on a bike.

CHAPTER 27

M Y LEGS WANTED to race, but my next trip was to Vermont for Cervélo's bike launch and dealer summit. I was the only rider in attendance, but management still sent a strict uniform and daily schedule:

Team casual apparel
- Team T-shirt
- Warm-up pants
- Team baseball cap—wear facing the front, not backward*
- New Balance team version sneakers
- Castelli socks
- Garmin watch

Breakfast: 8:00 a.m.

Ride with dealers: 9:30 a.m.

Take a shit: 10:45 a.m.

Take notes for a book, in which you complain about the schedule and uniform: also 10:45 a.m.

---

* This was known as the "Danielson rule." Backward caps were his thing.

Lunch and meet and greet: 1:00 p.m.
Etc.

It was embarrassing to be the "token pro" in a room full of bike shop owners, like I was back at the wedding in New York, except instead of asking about my wedding date, they wanted to know what I was doing in Vermont instead of a bike race. *I don't know. I guess I'm not good enough.*

My job was to lead the group on "bike demo" rides through the New England countryside. The whole idea is silly, because high-end bikes are all great. People always ask me what the best brand is, which is like asking who's prettier between Scarlett Johansson and Angelina Jolie: they're both tens, so it comes down to personality and preference.* Pros take weeks to get to know a frame, where it's stiff, where it gives, exactly how it wants to take a corner, so I tried not to laugh as each dealer would excuse himself from the pack to "test" Cervélo's new offering. He'd sprint up a hill, huffing and puffing, and then coast back and say, "Yeah, that's a pretty good bike!" Ramunas just won a Tour stage on it, but this chubby, forty-five-year-old shop manager had to see for himself.

I made friends and did my job well, so from a sponsorship perspective, the Cervélo trip was probably more valuable than if I'd finished fifth overall at the Volta a Catalunya, and I left with renewed hope that I'd keep my spot on the team, until I heard that the Garmin-Sharp/Cannondale merger rumor was true. Cervélo would be moving to MTN-Qhubeka, a new team based in South Africa. I asked Cervélo to put a word in.

The UCI has a rule that teams have to wait until August 1 to talk to new riders about contracts, but it's so widely ignored, some teams are full before the "transfer window" even opens. I e-mailed

---

* Scarlett, if you're reading this, it's you, 100 percent.

Vaughters and McQuaid a nice letter that I'd like to stay with Garmin-Cannondale, and then all of July, I stared at my phone for a reply. If I woke up to pee at two a.m., I'd refresh my in-box, as if JV had come to his senses in the middle of the night, unable to sleep until my contract was ironed out, or McQuaid was having desperate meetings with MTN-Qhubeka to get his 10 percent. After weeks without a response, I had to accept that the high-altitude races in Utah and Colorado would be my only chance to prove myself, so I said good-bye to Joanna and packed my car. If you're racing high up, you have to acclimate, and there are no shortcuts. Okay, some guys know a shortcut, but I go to Big Bear.

Instead of bumming at my friend's place again, I got a hotel this time, but for three weeks, I climbed the same roads and had dinner alone at the same restaurants as I had the year before. One afternoon, the bottom of the mountain was 114 degrees, but it hailed at the top and flooded the streets in Big Bear City, so I took shelter at a liquor store a mile from home. I bought a coffee to establish myself as a paying customer, but the owner still kicked me out, complaining that I was dripping water on the floor. I've already left a scathing Yelp review, but if you ever find yourself needing liquor in Big Bear City, go to the Safeway.

I didn't have much fun, but it was a successful trip. I lived like a monk, did my work, ate salads, and, following the altitude protocol I'd learned in Sierra Nevada, I watched my power go up as my weight went down.

CHAPTER 28

AFTER MONTHS APART, I was relieved that my team-mates remembered my name when I saw them in Utah. Howes and Ben King were full of stories from their first Tour de France (Alex went to the after party and woke up on a golf course the next morning). I could tell that the Tour of Utah felt completely insignificant after our sport's biggest event, but they were all muscles and veins, enjoying the fitness that shows up after the hardest race in the world, and ready to help Tom Daniel-son repeat his 2013 win. Tom had done his part, eating meat again and putting on some weight, healthy and recovered from a tough spring.

Our director in Utah was a Spaniard named Bingen Fernan-dez. All year, directors had given me the easy tasks—get bottles, ride the front, and help the leaders—important stuff, but anyone can do it, so I told Bingen that I was climbing well and I needed more responsibility to keep my job. On the fourth stage, he gave it to me.

The course started up Ogden Pass, then down a fast descent where I paid close attention, counting the bends, noting which were full speed and which might need a tap on the brakes, because we'd go back over the same road near the end of the stage, and Bingen said it would be my job to launch Danielson to the stage win. I helped control the breakaways as we looped through the valley, but mostly I hid in the pack, saving energy for the finish. *Will I be able to do this?*

I'd never touched the front on a climb at a big race, but two hours later, Tom was coaching me from behind, managing my speed, telling me where to recover and where to hit it as I dragged the pack up a mountain.

Right away, I was in the zone. My ears popped from the effort, so my whole existence was my heartbeat and my breath, echoing through my head. When I looked back halfway up, the pack was already split into small groups.

"Nice, Phil!" said a voice that I knew was just behind me, but sounded a million miles away. "You're killing it! This is some WorldTour shit!" *I'm doing it.*

One kilometer from the top, a Colombian rider attacked and Tom said to let him go, that my pace was perfect and we had plenty of time to catch him. When I looked back again at the KOM line, only a few of the best climbers had hung on to my pace. *I did it.*

My job was done, so the rest was just showing off. I sat low on my bike on the descent, flying into corners I'd memorized hours before, scaring the hell out of everyone behind me. At the bottom, our team was down to me, Howes, and Danielson when Andy Schleck rode up to yell at me.

"Hey! Easy on the descents, huh?"

The Schleck brothers managed to slide under the radar when the dopers confessed. They were barely capable of results in the post-EPO era, but they still acted like stars.

"Go home, Andy," said Howes. Alex had a thing where every time a Schleck bothered him, he'd politely tell him to go home, like if a friend had too much to drink at a party and was embarrassing himself.

My power meter said I should have died fifteen minutes before, but I ripped through the valley, keeping Tom and Alex in good position and ensuring that anyone I'd just dropped wouldn't see the front group again. I caught the Colombian when we made the left turn onto the final climb.

"Don't look at him, Phil. Just go right by him," said Tom.

Intimidation tactic from scrawny bike racers: You never make eye contact with the guy you catch. You cruise past him like he's nothing.

I led a few minutes up Powder Mountain, and there were seven guys left in the group when I finally blew up. Riding in easy to the finish, I looked down the switchbacks and smiled at the destruction I'd caused, while shrapnel riders passed me, still racing for fifteenth. That's when you make eye contact, maybe give him a smile. Especially if his last name is Schleck.

Tom had barely cracked a top ten that year, but he came through, taking the stage and the overall lead. He jumped off the podium to give me a big hug, with a tear in his eye. We were even.

Second on the stage was Chris Horner, who I'd seen parading through the lobby the night before with a bag from McDonald's. That was his thing: puffing a TUE prescription inhaler and probably getting cortisone treatments, and then eating garbage where everyone would see him and talk about it. Horner thought he was playing a mind game, telling us he wasn't trying, but the truth is, we all ate like shit that week, because the Tour of Utah was sponsored by Subway. As an American, I've had many Subway sandwiches, so I know they're bad, but I hadn't thought about it until I witnessed Thomas Dekker's first bite. He made a face, and then posed a sincere question that we all should have asked long ago:

"Phil. Do people pay money for this?"

Thomas was also refreshing his e-mail every few minutes hoping to hear from Vaughters, but it seemed like he'd lost motivation when he plugged his iPhone into the bus's speakers, singing along to a Dr. Dre/Snoop Dogg song called "Still D.R.E." It started with a conversation.

Snoop: Still doing this shit, huh, Dre?

Dre: Oh, for sho'!

"Still doing this shit, huh?" Thomas would ask when I passed him in the hallway.

"Oh, for sho', Thomas!" was the correct answer.

Young American Lawson Craddock had joined Giant-Shimano—a Dutch team known for antidoping, and cheap meals and accommodations for their riders. He said that they had Michael Jackson's "They Don't Care about Us" repeating on their bus.

Since I'd proved my climbing prowess, Bingen gave other guys the grunt work of pulling on the flat roads, so at the end of the week, Alex and I were still fresh, ready to help on Guardsman Pass. The toughest mountain of the week, Guardsman always finished in a small group, but with a long descent and a valley before the final climb to Snowbird, Tom would need teammates to keep his lead.

BMC put three riders in the early breakaway that day. It was strange for them to be so aggressive, but they were all far behind overall, so we didn't worry about it until the middle of the stage, when everyone was joking around and trading energy bars as Cadel Evans shot out of sight at three times our speed. We reacted quickly to bring back the former Tour de France winner, but soon we were on a tricky descent, which Cadel must have studied—or he's suicidal—because we took some risks and still lost time. Before we knew it, he'd joined his teammates in the breakaway, they were pulling their asses off, and we were in trouble. With a budget of $40 million a year from their billionaire benefactor, BMC didn't mess around.

My team had four guys on the front chasing as hard as they could, but we still lost time in the valley. I tried to be encouraging when I brought Dekker a water bottle.

"Still doing this shit, huh, Thomas?"

"Oh, for sho'!" He coughed, because you can't laugh at high altitude.

Our plan was to see how far I could make it up Guardsman, and then Alex would take over for the descent and the valley. This was the stage that he'd won in heroic hot-dog-grabbing fashion at nineteen, but now he was having a bad day, drifting back when Guardsman had barely started.

"I'm really sorry, Phil. All you," he said.

I wasn't mad at all, because I saw an opportunity to prove myself for the team. All I had to do was take two minutes out of one of the best climbers in the world on this mountain. *Gulp.*

Tom asked how I was feeling, like a concerned mother.

"Well, not awesome," I admitted. "But nobody's awesome. How are you? Don't say awes—"

"—I'm awesome!" He cut me off.

I laugh/coughed and pushed to the front, and for the next two hours, I dominated the TV screen as the group shrank behind me, once again with Tom cheering me on from behind. Grandma, I know that you always wanted to see me on television, and I'm sorry it wasn't *Jeopardy.*

We lost some time when Tom's shifters stopped working on the descent, but the gap went from four minutes to one and a half by the base of Snowbird, where I called it a day as Tom raced away. The shifters probably cost us another stage win, but we kept the GC lead, and I'd saved the day.

Friends were cheering when they watched, sure that this performance would change my life, solidifying my spot in the WorldTour. Opponents patted me on the back at the finish, impressed at my improvement since the year before. I was expecting a contract when I opened an e-mail from Vaughters, but it was two measly lines of encouragement and gratitude. Those are great, but they don't pay the bills.

With one stage left, Dekker dropped out. It was tough to watch him realize he'd be leaving the sport, because it was clear that at least part of him (legs and lungs) still wanted it. Another part of Dekker (you guessed it) took a taxi to the bars in Park City that night, where he met a woman and fell in love at first sight, and somewhere on her mile-long driveway, he found out that she was a billionaire. That's like a millionaire, but with a "b."

Tom had no trouble keeping his jersey on the final stage, and my groupetto hit 120 kilometers per hour on the last descent into Park City. It would have really hurt to crash at that speed, but it was also fun as hell, and I was happy to get to the bus faster, knowing there'd be beer and pizza waiting. We were careful not to party too much, with less than a week until the start of Colorado and early flights to Aspen in the morning.

CHAPTER 29

BINGEN WENT HOME from Utah, so we were unsupervised for a few days in Snowmass Village, an affluent ski town above Aspen, putting meals at fancy restaurants on the team's credit card. Garmin-Sharp had a policy that they wouldn't pay for alcohol, but food was covered, so someone asked the waiter to bring two bottles of wine and call them pizzas on the receipt. It was the perfect crime.

Over in Spain, Chris Horner's scheme hadn't gone so well. He'd finished second overall in Utah, but pre-Vuelta blood tests revealed low cortisol levels, so they didn't let him start the race. It looked like he'd tried to use his TUE prerace steroid preparation again, but he overdid it and fell outside of the legal range.

The suite in Snowmass Village had one bedroom with two twin beds and another with one queen. I was the low man on the team totem pole, but Ben King insisted that I take the better room, because I'm older and he's a gentleman. Also, I had a cough that nobody wanted to catch.

We all enjoyed deep talks with Ben. A devout Christian, he'd had plenty of girlfriends but was saving his virginity for marriage.

Dekker thought he was insane, but as an athlete, I had to admire it. When Ben broke his ankle, he did seven-hour rides on a stationary trainer, which is exactly the same as saving yourself for marriage if you think about it: discipline and self-control. Okay, also insanity, but Ben didn't mind the teasing, accustomed to being a little different. When he went home to Virginia, he'd go hunting and fishing, wearing camo, and I bet his redneck buddies laughed at the weirdo kid with shaved legs, United Gold status, and an apartment in Lucca.

It was a relaxing week of bonding and coffee rides, with daily massage and my first time working with two of the team's chiropractors. During treatment, both would identify problem spots via stretching and short muscle balance tests. One treated it by holding a laser over the affected region, and the other would softly touch somewhere random (for example, he would tap my armpit or my forehead to treat a hamstring). Then they'd pronounce me cured, which was confusing, but the body works in mysterious ways and it did make me feel better. I was tired and everything hurt, but here's this expert who went to college and studied things I can't pronounce, promising that everything is fixed. Maybe it was a placebo, but sore from Utah, with another race coming up in a few days, I'll take it.*

Under pressure after a disappointing Tour de France and with a merger looming, head directors Charly Wegelius and Robbie Hunter were also worried about their jobs, so the fun stopped when they showed up. I was walking around the hotel with a

---

* The chiropractors had been with the team for years, so they also had good stories, like the time the bus passed a statue of a cyclist on the way to a Tour stage, defaced with a three-foot syringe made of PVC pipe. They stopped and took down the needle as a good deed, so when the team's PR manager climbed onto the bus that night, she saw riders passing around a novelty-sized syringe and had a fit. In the old days, guys would put needles in a Coke can and throw them out with the trash. I should have asked how they disposed of this one.

photographer from Castelli, who'd lined up a picture of me reading my book with a bag of cookies, when Charly stepped into the shot.

"Phil, you should be resting," he said, and then walked away, without even addressing the guy with the camera he'd interrupted.

"Hi, Charly," I said.

"That guy sucks," observed the photographer.

"I *was* resting," I said. "Now I'm stressed out."

Directors are supposed to walk in and start playing us like a musician picks up an instrument, and keeping us motivated is part of their job, but directors have different styles and riders all have their own needs. Charly probably rode well under pressure when he was racing, so every time I passed him in a hallway, he'd find a way to mention that I was out of contract, but in my generation, everyone gets a trophy and we're all winners. If I needed threats to perform, I'd never have made it this far, and I hate pressure. I want to be coddled.

We met the Cannondale team at a coffee shop one afternoon, where Ivan Basso bought a round of espresso. I'd watched Basso battle Armstrong at the Tour de France when I was a teenager, but now he was overweight and well past his prime, because in cycling, they don't let you retire at the top. You're underpaid until you get the big results, but then you're overpaid for your past, even though you'll never repeat it.

We all knew that Ivan was signed to Saxo Bank for 2015, but I tweeted a picture of him in his Cannondale jersey, with the caption "No merger is complete until Basso buys my coffee." Vaughters quickly texted and told me to delete it, since the news wasn't public yet. He hadn't returned my calls about a contract all summer, so it was good to know I had the right phone number.

I was next to Basso before the first stage, when announcers introduced the top riders.

"Former winner of the Giro d'Italia, riding for Team Cannondale—"

"—Birillo!" Ivan yelled, referring to his Operación Puerto code name. He was admitting that those blood bags were his, that he'd doped at the peak of his career, that the best thing he ever did was a lie, but in a pack of bike racers, it got a big laugh. Ivan held on to my jersey on one of the climbs later, I suppose as a fee for the coffee. I let him hang for a few minutes, for nineteen-year-old me, who would have been honored.

Tejay van Garderen was the favorite in Colorado, so his BMC team controlled the race while we protected Tom, our best chance for the GC, and Alex, who wanted to go for a stage win. At the end of the first day, the pack exploded on the run-in to Aspen, and Howes escaped with his training partner and best friend Kiel Reijnen, riding for UnitedHealthcare. It's touching to see friends in a breakaway together, until you realize that only one gets to win. Alex had bragged that very morning that he could dust Kiel in a sprint, but he jumped too early and Kiel got it.

I'd been teammates with Kiel on Jelly Belly, so I'd known him for years, and I can't think of anyone who'd waited longer or worked harder for his first big win (okay, me, but Kiel's second). It's rare to be happy with a result if the winner is on another team, but everyone loves Kiel.

"We're all smiling when you win," I told him, with a quick hug at the finish.

"Thanks. That matters." He smiled.

Really, it's all that matters. A lot of guys win a bike race and think they're setting the world on fire because they were the fastest for a day. I think the real winner is the guy who crosses the line first and the losers are happy for him (unfortunately, sarcastic guys with CLEAN tattoos get a mixed reaction when we win).

We had dinner at a mansion in Aspen that night. You know the Simon shopping malls all over America? That guy's house. He was a fan of the team, and his place had enough bathrooms for eight of us to shower at the same time (Dekker used the outdoor one by the pool). Seeing all the beautiful paintings and antiques, I can't believe they didn't frisk us when we left.*

After the near miss in Aspen, the second day was perfect for a small sprinter like Howes, with a long dirt section and a short climb near the end to drop the big sprinters. The directors said that our mission was to make sure the break was caught, and to lead Alex over the flat section in the final climb so he'd be in good position with five hundred meters to go.

"It's going to be difficult, but we need everyone there on that part," said Robbie, pointing at the map like a general. "If Tom and Alex have to cover attacks in the last kilometer, we won't win the stage."

At the halfway point, Ben was on the front and the race was under control, but I noticed that he kept looking off into the woods.

"What's up, Ben? What are you looking at?"

"I want to see a moose," he said. Damn redneck, always thinking about hunting. It's one thing to be comfortable at 300 watts, but quite another to be bored.

Ben had to settle for a fan wearing a football helmet with moose antlers attached. "Moose Guy" had been at every major race in the United States for years, alternating jerseys that said "Voigt" or "Horner" on the back. He'd drive out to the middle of nowhere and chase us up a hill on foot, cheering on his dumb heroes. These are our fans.

Ben paid more attention when the weather changed, which happens fast at high altitude. A sudden storm had us shivering at the beginning of the downhill dirt section, which would have been fun in dry conditions, but in the rain, tires slip, brakes barely work, and mud covered my sunglasses so I could barely see. I took

---

* I didn't steal anything. I just mean I could have.

Bottle duty in Colorado.

them off and tried to clean the lenses at seventy kilometers an hour, but I had to drop them when I rounded a bend to find a group of riders crashing or possibly mud wrestling. That meant that mud sprayed into my face instead, so for the rest of the descent, I mostly rode with my eyes closed, opening them just long enough to memorize the road ahead. I made it, but don't try that at home.

My eyes opened when officials finally decided to neutralize us for safety, but since race radios were banned at smaller races that year, they weren't able to communicate their decision until we'd reached the pavement at the bottom of the descent.* Everyone stopped, and our mechanic ran out from the car to see if we needed anything. Half-frozen, blind, covered in mud, with throbbing legs, I asked if he had any spare glasses to replace the ones I'd lost.

---

* Radios are useful to tell riders when there's an ambulance coming, or a dangerous turn, for example, but they also enabled regular time checks to the breakaway, so a basic safety measure was banned at most events that year, to "make the races more interesting." Instead, we got the same time checks from a motorcycle. One guy would drive the big, heavy machine next to the pack, and another would sit behind him, writing numbers on a whiteboard and showing it to us. This made sense to someone.

"Nah, dude, I don't. But if it makes you feel better, you look really badass."

I sighed. *I've never felt worse in my life. Why the hell would I care how I look?* And then I glanced around, hoping there was a photographer nearby.

As officials tried to figure out what to do, riders planned a strike. We'd ride slowly to the finish—a protest against—well, I don't know—but somebody had screwed up big time to let us race that ridiculous dirt descent and then stop the race 5k from the finish. Robbie Hunter heard the rumor and emerged from the team car, yelling that we will not fucking protest if we want to keep our jobs. Robbie had only retired from racing a year before, so you'd think he'd agree that our safety would outweigh results and sponsor interests, but it was a good finish for Howes and we needed a win.

There was one guy from the breakaway still ahead before officials stopped us, so they gave him a two-and-a-half-minute lead when the race restarted. We could see him in the distance as we started the last climb, losing time, but awfully far away. Tom started to unzip his vest, so I rode up to him.

"Here, I'll take that back to the car for you," I said.

"No! We need you at the front!" he barked, tossing a $140 vest into the grass on the side of the road.

For eight years, I'd raced for teams that gave me one vest if I was lucky. On Garmin-Sharp, we each got a whole box of vests in January, along with five types of gloves, ten sets each of arm, leg, and knee warmers, and something like thirty jerseys. And if that wasn't enough, they had a box of spare everything in the bus. I was disgusted that Tom could be so wasteful, but I threw mine, too, just for the novelty.* It was 3k to go, but Jesse Anthony told

---

* When Stefano rode for Toyota-United, they had forty pairs of sunglasses each, so they'd toss them on the mountaintop finishes as a joke.

me later that he still almost stopped and picked them up to sell on eBay (Optum was a one-vest team).

Our directors had wanted all of us at the front on the plateau with 2k to go, but after the race went to hell, guess which twenty-eight-year-old WorldTour rookie was the only one who pulled it off? I put Alex in perfect position, but the breakaway stayed clear and we had to settle with another painful second place. I'd given everything, so my legs were locked up in the last five hundred meters when the team car slowed down beside me. We were leading the "team overall" competition, which is calculated by the third-best finisher on each stage, so Robbie yelled that although I'd just given everything I fucking had less than a minute ago, I needed to give it all I fucking had, again. I claim that I need to be coddled, but I sure do go harder when a director screams at me from a car. I sprinted to the finish and came in eighteenth on the stage—better than I'd ever placed at a big race for BISSELL— and I wasn't even trying.

The hotel was around the corner from the finish, and someone handed me a key with my room number on it (it was probably a soigneur, but it might have been an angel). You're supposed to drop off your bike with the mechanics after a stage, but I left my $10,000 Cervélo on the ground by the hotel entrance and staggered inside. I sat on the floor of the shower, still fully clothed with my race shoes and helmet, watching a trail of dirt flow toward the drain. I heard that some guys showered together, too cold to wait for their turn.

Our chefs made dinner on the bus that night, and Charly and Robbie called a meeting.

"Boys, we have some news. We don't know what it means to any of us exactly, but it's going to be public tomorrow and we wanted you to hear it from us first."

"Let me guess," someone said. "There's a merger, right? Worst-kept secret in cycling."

"One of you has tested positive," said Robbie Hunter.

Forks dropped, and eight sets of Bambi eyes looked up at Robbie, then each other. You could feel the blood pressure skyrocket in the room, until he started laughing.

"Ha! No, it's just the merger, fellas! I got you good!"

On the hilly stage into Breckenridge, we had Ben King and Janier Acevedo in the breakaway.

"You guys must be happy," said Matt Busche, pointing out that we had a good shot at a stage win.

"I've never been happy," I said, just because I didn't want to talk to him.

Janier finished second, while I set a pace on the last climb that dropped BMC's Ben Hermans, earning more pats on the back and moving Tom up to second overall.

After working hard in the mountains all week, I expected the time trial to be a recovery day, but we were still chasing the team overall prize so Charly said I'd have to give 110 percent. Hoping to get on his good side, I didn't point out the minor detail that my legs were fried from four days on the front, or that the mechanics had just built my new time trial bike, so I hadn't touched one since Southwest killed mine three months before. And I definitely didn't mention the mathematical fallacy of asking for 110 percent.

I gave it 100 percent and finished twelfth. Nobody cares about twelfth, but it was arguably my best time trial result ever. Now think how well I would have done if I'd had a bike to train on or my legs were fresh. Actually, looking at the results, I think I'd have been around seventh, and nobody cares about seventh, either. Never mind.

The team cares about the podium, where Danielson stood next to Tejay. That locked up second place overall with one stage remaining, but BMC passed us for the team prize. Their director must have asked for 114 percent.

I took a nap that afternoon, setting an alarm for a meeting with Andrew McQuaid. He flew in to get contracts sorted for his clients, but I didn't get much face time. In fact, our meeting took place in the doorway after his fourth knock, and I'd only been awake for forty-five seconds when he said that UnitedHealthcare wasn't interested in me. A second-tier team, they'd be a step down from the WorldTour and I was better than any of their climbers, but I'd been reaching out to their manager for five years without even a response to an e-mail. Somebody told me that they don't hire anyone who's outspoken against doping. I wish I was making that up. Another possible factor: their director was always a jerk in the caravan, and I might have thrown one too many water bottles at his car over the years, calling him a dickhead. I stand by it.

McQuaid knew all the details about the merger: Vaughters would retain ownership of the team and control of the roster, but guys with multiyear contracts from Team Cannondale would have the option to stay. Andrew said one of those was his client Elia Viviani, who was moving to Team Sky. When that was finalized, a spot would open up for me, but Andrew would pitch me to other teams just in case. Quick-Step and Trek had seen me ride well and I'd heard that they were on the lookout for more Americans.

I followed up with a note to Vaughters, saying it was nice to hear that they still had room for me on the team. He actually responded for once, saying he never would have told McQuaid that I would get Viviani's spot, and I "should definitely be talking to other teams."

McQuaid didn't respond when I forwarded him JV's message calling him a liar, so I was glad to be assigned to a meet and greet that night. Sponsor events are usually a chore during a stage race, but it did mean there'd be an open bar. While my teammates had a real dinner, Dekker and I snacked on cheese, crackers, and wine—perfect race fuel.

I was buzzed from a glass and a half of Cabernet, but I'll never forget the conversation between Thomas and a man who sat beside us while we were signing posters. He said that Dekker seemed like a nice guy, so he'd like him to date his niece.

"She's six feet tall, a model, and you don't need to worry that she wants your money," he explained, pulling up a picture on his phone. "She has a $30 million trust fund." Thomas politely turned him down.

"You seem like a nice guy?" I whispered, after he left. "Thomas, you know I love you, but you're one of the worst guys I know!"

"It's true," laughed Thomas.

"Besides, I'm right here!" I continued. "He didn't offer me a niece with a trust fund, or a second cousin with a Winnebago! I don't seem like a nice guy?"

"Also why is he a pimp for his family?" wondered Thomas. This stuff never happens on Continental teams.

I thought the wine would help but I still had trouble sleeping that night, stressed about my job. I told myself over and over that it's only bike racing. We're just a bunch of dudes flying around, wasting resources,* riding in circles for crowds of weirdos. I could easily get a job that pays better, and all the jerseys and trophies we're chasing are pointless.

The last stage was a big goal for Garmin-Sharp, starting in Boulder, where the team was founded, and finishing in Denver, where Vaughters lived. More importantly, with Alex Howes's friends and family in the crowd, a course that passed his high school, and two second-place finishes that week, he wanted it bad.

Voigt made the early breakaway, hoping for a win in his last race before retirement, and we went to work, on a Hail Mary strategy that Wegelius cooked up: we let Jens out to a huge lead,

---

* One morning at the Tour of Colorado, I saw a soigneur filling team-logo water bottles from a case of plastic twenty-ounce water bottles, throwing the empties in the trash.

and I set a hard pace on the first climb, dropping sprinters one by one until we thought Alex was the fastest guy left, then I pulled my heart out on the flat roads into Denver to keep them from catching up. On the front for hours, I dug deep, blew up, and rallied several times, burying myself for Alex—and for my job. Maybe I wasn't good enough to get my own results, but I could make up for that in loyalty. It must have been a slow news day, because apparently the commentators went on and on about my effort and dedication.

With 40k to go, Tom brought me caffeine gels and the sprinters faded behind us. With 20k to go, I started to close in on the breakaway, and Voigt's teammate Andy Schleck appeared next to me.

"What are you doing?" he asked.

"What's it look like?"

"This is the last race of Jens's career. You guys are going to let him win, aren't you?"

"No!" I laughed.

"Go *home*, Andy!" said Alex.

Whether he doped or not, Jens didn't strike me as a guy who wanted to be gifted a race, anyway. I patted him on the back when we caught him, and with 8k to go I blew up for good, watching the group ride away in the distance.

It was probably the best effort of my life, and now I wondered if it would all be for nothing. I'd sweated all day with the faith that Alex could do something he'd never done before. What if after all that, Kiel beat him in the sprint again? I'd done my job perfectly, but so had most of the folks on the *Hindenburg*, and now it was out of my control.

On the finish stretch, fans stuck their hands over the fence for high fives and congratulations.

"Way to go, Garmin!"

"Alex owes you a cookie, Phil!"

Holy shit, he did it. I was supposed to go to the bus and take a shower, but I shoved my way into the restricted podium tent instead. Alex saw me coming and bolted from his seat, lifting me in the air with a hug and planting a firm kiss on my lips. He was crying and kept saying "thank you." I cried, too. I'm crying writing this again. Low testosterone, remember? Hang on, I need a break.

Okay, I took some deep breaths. What was my point here? Oh yeah: I'd been telling myself that bike racing doesn't matter, that it wouldn't be a big deal if I lost my job and had to give up. But if that was true, why was I crying and hugging some dude at a finish line again?

Charly put his hand on my shoulder as I staggered onto the bus. "Nice work, Phil. Thank you," he said in his calm tone.

Vaughters was there, too. "That was a very special ride, Phil. You left it all out there for us."

Contract. Contract. Contract. Contract.

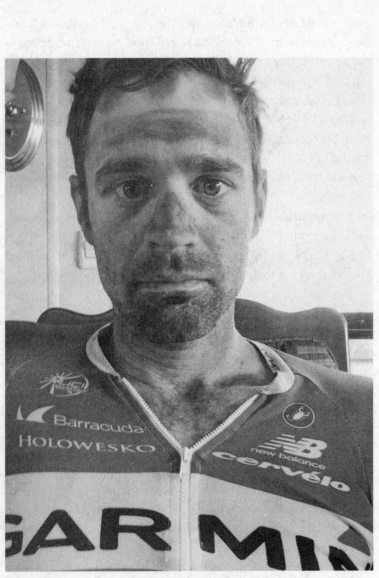

Denver all over my face.

CHAPTER 30

MY OLD BOSS Omer Kem had made it clear that I should always travel with a team-logo polo shirt, but the season was almost over and no one had ever asked me to wear it. If he knew anything at all about the WorldTour, he would have said to bring decent clothes for the after party instead. To avoid sponsor fines, I'd packed only team-issue gear, but for Euro pros, although every square centimeter of the suitcase is prime real estate, one corner is always reserved for jeans, a nice shirt, expensive shoes, cologne, and hair gel so you can look sharp while you hit on the podium girls. My teammates were ashamed to admit they knew me, wearing a tracksuit like an amateur.

I borrowed a shirt and boarded the shuttle to Vaughters's house for dinner and drinks, where Alex and Tom wasted no time, cornering our boss and demanding he give me a contract. JV finally sat beside me in a folding chair on his lawn, and said that the merger complicated things, but I earned it and he'd have an offer by Wednesday. A weight lifted, and Alex started bringing me drinks, still thanking me for my work on the road. It was nice to think I played a role in a day that made him so happy, but I told him I'd have to tell his girlfriend if he kissed me again.

Someone was heavy with the tequila, so I don't remember how I got from Vaughters's house to the after party or back to the hotel, but I do remember Howes and Phinney entering the room around three a.m., waking me up by flipping my mattress and spilling me onto the floor.

Alex kissed me one last time and passed out, but the alarm went off two hours later, because we had an eight a.m. flight to catch. Not to go home and rest after three weeks of hard work on the road—we were off to Kansas, for a meet and greet at Garmin's headquarters.

I've noticed two humbling phenomena in my years as a pro, both of which factored into this Kansas trip:

- No matter how deep you go, you can always race again the next day if you have to, but as soon as a stage race is over, your brain flips a switch and your legs turn to cement.
- As good as I get, I'd always marvel at how small the discrepancy is between a pro and an amateur. It takes years of dedication to improve that last 10 percent, but on flat roads, a weekend warrior could hang out all day in my draft.

So what happens after a stage race, a night with three hours of sleep, too much to drink, an early flight from cool, dry, high altitude to 100 degrees, humid, and sea level, fueled on airport breakfast burritos? Basically, my teammates and I were in no condition to ride bikes at all. We glared at our Cervélos lined up against the bus, like a prisoner would at a firing squad.

Locals were so excited to ride with pros, they whacked each hill as hard as they could, so I found myself suffering at the back with Tom and Alex. A mere twenty-four hours before, we were heroes—my name was spray-painted on the ground and fans held posters for the "cookie monster," as we laughed at Andy Schleck and tore up an international field on the way to victory and the

cheers of thousands. Today, we were sunburned between corn-
fields somewhere in Kansas, suffering to hold the wheels of
middle-aged men in T-shirts and sandals.

"I threw up in my mouth, but I swallowed it," I confided to
Dekker.

"They work us like a cheap hooker," he said. Not that he would
know—Dekker only patronized the finest hookers in Amsterdam.

After the ride, we did not have a nap. We had an autograph
signing, where you have to be perky and friendly, smiling for photos that I was pretty sure would never be looked at again. And in
the evening, the tired, overworked athletes did not get an early
night at the hotel. We went bowling with company executives.

Yes, I said bowling.

Moneybags Dekker suggested we make it interesting and each
put in $20, which was fine with me, because one summer in high
school, Chamblee Lanes gave us coupons for a free game each day.
They probably expected to make money on shoe rentals, and who
would go all the way there to play just one round? The answer: me
and my friend JC. We bought $6 bowling shoes at Kmart, played
one game per day, didn't even use their vending machines, and by
the end of that summer, I could do that spin thing, and my average score was in the 180s. I only rolled a 133 in Kansas, but it was
still good enough to take everyone's money. Europeans suck at
bowling.

Garmin tried to make us feel better, catering in real Kansas
City BBQ for lunch the next day. It was delicious, but I laughed
when Caleb scooped his third helping of pulled pork.

"Next race is Alberta! No mountains there, right?" He smiled.
"I can put on a few."

Caleb wasn't a bad rider, but he never did much in the World-
Tour, so I wondered how he kept his job. The answer was another
loophole in the rules: the UCI has the minimum salary require-
ment, but there's nothing that prevents a rider from bringing a

sponsor to a team. Sometimes that's Mark Cavendish, whose personal deal with Oakley turned into a full sponsorship when he joined MTN-Qhubeka. Other times, it's someone in Caleb's family who writes a check to the team on the condition that they'll hire him. How much does it cost to buy your way into the World-Tour? No number from $50,000 to $500,000 would surprise me.

Caleb wasn't the only one, but he never talked about it, because some guys say that "personal sponsors" lower everyone's value, but the way I see it, my parents paid my college tuition, and someone bought Caleb an opportunity to excel in cycling. Few teams had full rosters, so it's not like he was taking up a spot that would have gone to someone more deserving—in fact, his money might have made it possible for JV to hire someone like me. On the other hand, a WorldTour jersey is supposed to be sacred. Either you buy it full price at a bike shop like a smart person, or you earn it, with hard work, sweat, and hopefully not too much blood. Given that Caleb was probably paying to be on Garmin-Sharp, it must have hurt that he was also losing his "job" in the merger, but he wasn't worried about finding another team.*

I had a later flight home from Kansas, so my teammates were gone by the time I got to the breakfast buffet, where I took one look at the powdered eggs and headed to the lobby to order a taxi. A hundred twenty-nine dollars was too much for a shirt at Burberry, but I hadn't opened my wallet for three weeks, so $30 for a cab, a chicken biscuit, and a sweet tea at Chick-fil-A was well worth it.†

I furiously checked my in-box *and* my spam box, but there was no contract from Vaughters by Wednesday like he'd promised, so

---

* Caleb "retired" in 2016 to become a rider's agent, and many of his friends actually hired him. So the guy who paid for his contract is now negotiating on behalf of his clients.

† I know they're a shitty company, and I'm sorry, but if you grew up in Atlanta, you'd understand. Boston has Dunkin' Donuts, L.A. has In-N-Out Burger, and Atlanta has Chick-fil-A. It feels like home to me.

I left a voice mail on Friday. Saturday morning, I got a response in a text message.

"Let's see how you do in Alberta," it said.

That's when I did something I'm not proud of, but I was desperate. I ordered EPO off the Internet, and injected—nah, I hope you didn't believe that. I'd have no clue where to get EPO or what to do with it, but I'll say this: to all the low-level cheaters out there—the guys who think they need it just to get by—I understand. Of course, your dream is dead if you've gotten to that point, so go get a job at Starbucks. Sell insurance. Sweep floors. But I do feel your pain. Anyway, all the EPO in the world wouldn't have made much difference for my skinny legs on the flat roads in Canada.

CHAPTER 31

THE TOUR OF Alberta was only a week after Colorado, making it a six-week trip with nineteen days of racing. We had another change of directors, but the riders were almost the same. Ben King thought his season was done when he left Kansas, so he was probably fishing when he got the call for Alberta.

"When you finish your last race," he advised, "as long as your contract is set, turn off your phone for at least two months. It's the only way you're safe."

The first stage was a short time trial, which started off flat, with a few turns and speed bumps leading into a steep climb. I'm sure I didn't look graceful jumping the speed bumps, but I only botched it and hit my private parts once, so I was insulted when the German director who followed me in the car gave me a lecture, calling me unprofessional for "looking shit" and obviously not putting in the training on the time trial bike. He didn't apologize when I told him that the team never sent me a new one after my frame broke in May, or when results were posted and I finished a whopping sixth place, but the best part was that he kept forgetting my name. Some directors look at riders the way a farmer sees cattle: don't get close emotionally, because you're just going to slaughter them.

Tom was third, which put me 1.6 seconds off the podium. Could I have made that up if I'd had a bike to train on during the summer? Would I have been more aerodynamic or faster in the corners or smoother jumping the speed bumps? What if a caterpillar farted ten thousand years ago?

It was a good result, but WorldTour teams don't care about Alberta, so it was time to look for a backup in the minor leagues. When I started racing in 2006, there were thirteen well-funded Continental teams to beg for jobs every year. Now that I'd be in demand, it was down to two.

First, I spoke with Jonas Carney, director of Optum Pro Cycling, which was home to good friends Jesse Anthony and Brad Huff. Jonas couldn't imagine that Vaughters would leave me out after the year I'd just had, but he humored me, asking what I'd want for a salary. A couple months before, I was expecting six figures to stay in the WorldTour, but Optum's budget was a tenth of Garmin-Sharp's, so I told Jonas $50,000. He said that was fair but there was a long line behind me for that roster spot, so he'd need an answer fast.

Next, I spoke to SmartStop. They had a smaller budget than Optum's but great results thanks to the leadership of Mike Creed. A former WorldTour rider, Creed was the face of the team in the media, but they wanted to be defined by their riders instead of the guy in the car, so I'd be a good name to solve their image problem. Creed thought it would be a fun project to get me back to Europe, proposing a race schedule that focused solely on a result at the Tour of California, with training camps where he'd motorpace and cook for me, and no obligations that might conflict with my best performance at our target race. His bosses kept saying how excited they were to have me, and then they offered a salary of $25,000. Joanna didn't want to move to Georgia, so I told them that if that was the best they could do, I'd have to go some-where else.

"Well, there's empty space on our jersey that we're trying to sell," they said. "If you can find some sponsors, we'll let you keep the money, and you can wait as long as you want for an answer in case it works out with Vaughters later."

So during the Tour of Alberta, I became a salesman by night, e-mailing everyone I knew in the industry to see if they'd sponsor me to ride for SmartStop, and by day, I battled through heavy crosswinds with Tom. We were placed well overall thanks to the time trial, but Tom and I kept finding ourselves in the second or third groups, suffering to catch up. On the fourth stage, the sixth time we missed a split, Ramunas looked comfortable at the front, so when I started to pull us back to the leaders, Tom put his hand on my shoulder.

"No, Phil. Now is when we give up. This isn't our race anymore."

"Phew," I sighed.

I'd been taught to never give up, but if you can't accept your limitations, you might as well beat yourself with a baseball bat. Ramunas moved up to second overall, and nobody noticed that the climbers lost five minutes.

Helping Ramunas was too easy, so I found a challenge in the next stage, in the form of a pile of riders on the ground when I came out of a turn. I didn't crash exactly, but my chest pounded my handlebars when I stopped short. I'd only broken one bone before: the fracture in my wrist in the San Dimas crash, which I barely noticed because the rest of my body was in worse shape (also, I was unconscious). This time, I knew right away that I'd broken some ribs. Remember the coach who'd said that working on bone density in the off-season would be a waste of time? He's lucky I'd already fired him.

I told the team doctor that night, who said there was nothing we could do about it.

"Do I keep racing?"

"Oh sure! It's just going to hurt like hell."

Most teams have a doctor on staff. It was comforting to know that we had a professional to treat road rash or medicine if we got sick, but the doctor isn't there to make us feel better, necessarily. His job is to make sure we can perform. In Alberta, he prescribed me a "walk it off."

I took one look at the buffet that night and convinced the guys to join me at the hotel restaurant for burgers instead. Caleb ordered a milk shake and fries (Alberta is flat, after all), and being away from "race meal" restored everyone's mood, like a mini vacation. It was nice to joke around, but laughing is torture with busted ribs.

Someone turned on the Vuelta a España, and we watched replays of Ryder Hesjedal's controversial crash. He was ejected from his bike, but the wheels kept spinning while he slid on the ground, so the media exploded with accusations of a hidden motor in his frame.

I didn't even really like Ryder, but I think it's safe to chalk that up to physics.* He didn't have his own mechanic, so he would have had to install the motor himself in a bike that he didn't have access to because it lives in a truck at the service course. I think Nate Brown was his roommate at the Vuelta, so where would he have committed this crime? The hotel hallway in the middle of the night? More importantly, in a world of marginal gains where we're all fighting tooth and nail for 10 watts, if Ryder had a motor, it's fair to say he would have won at least one race that year.

At the start line the next day, I waited for the cameraman to look at me, and then I pulled an imaginary cord from my handlebars like I was starting a lawn mower. Ben nudged me to knock it off, but with my aching ribs, I could have used a motor. The pain

---

* Yes, even though I got a C.

caused me to ride crooked, favoring one leg (soigneurs said my left hamstring was in knots and the right side was good as new).

My chest stung with every breath those days—it hurt just to pull on a pair of socks, the weather was cold and rainy, and the courses didn't suit me—but I did my job every day. I went ballistic on a hill near the end of the last stage, tore the group to shreds for Ramunas, and swung out of the way, job done. I expected to ride the last wet lap around Edmonton alone, but I found crashed riders in every turn, untangling their bikes from each other or waiting for a spare from their team car. I passed so many dudes, I thought I might win the stage. Almost half of the pack DNFed.

With the contract hanging over my head, there was so much pressure, it felt like my value as a person was whatever I did each day, and every stage was trying out for a job I already had. With another strong week under my belt, I messaged Vaughters from the bus to point out that I'd proved myself for the hundredth time.

"Sorry, I just need to see how you can do in a WorldTour race," he said. "Let's talk after Beijing."

This may sound crazy, but I started to get the feeling that JV wasn't being completely honest with me. The Tour of Beijing was a month away and Optum was already pushing me for an answer, but I'd had a decent response from my sponsor search, negotiating a total of $20,000 if I rode for SmartStop, bringing my potential salary there up to a doable $45,000.

CHAPTER 32

From Alberta, we headed to Montreal and Quebec for two one-day WorldTour races. All the cycling news sites had reported that I was still looking for a contract, which I hoped would pressure Vaughters or help McQuaid as he shopped me around, but the market was a bloodbath. My job would come down to one of the last few spots on Cannondale-Garmin, so my heart sank to hear that Joe Dombrowski had transferred over from Team Sky. The talented American climber must have taken a hefty pay cut since he'd just had risky artery surgery, but I had to admit it was a smart move by JV.

I'd only talked to Joe a couple times, so I was surprised to get a message from him: "Hey, Phil, I know that space is tight on Cannondale-Garmin. Just wanted to say good luck and I hope my move doesn't push you out."

It says a lot about Joe that he reached out, but I had no problem with him. The apology should have come from Andrew McQuaid, who was also Joe's agent. While he was telling me that there was no news from Vaughters, McQuaid was negotiating a contract for another American climber to take one of the final spots—and that, ladies and gentlemen, is a conflict of interest. If an agent has more than a few clients, he's deciding which teams to sell them to, so Andrew wasn't really working for anyone but himself.

That left one spot on Cannondale-Garmin, which would come down to me and Ted King: the maple-syrup-chugging master of marketability versus the cookie-monster apprentice who'd followed him into the WorldTour. This is real life.

Ted was a solid domestique, but I thought I'd be the obvious choice. I was younger, with a stage win, a GC podium, and a handful of top tens and twenties in my first European season, while his résumé was blank after five years,* but Ted's agent was pulling strings, hoping that sponsors would pressure JV to take him over me. The guy who showed me the way was trying to kick me out, but I couldn't be mad because I'd have done the same in his shoes. Ted simply navigated the business better than I had, but I put butter on my pancakes instead of maple syrup the next morning. Fuck maple syrup.

Doping news trumped contract rumors in Quebec City when we learned that two riders from Team Astana had tested positive for EPO at another race, raising suspicions of a teamwide doping program. Astana's table was next to ours at breakfast, and half the room was glaring at them. They kept their heads down. This is also real life.

I had a feeling that a bad showing at either of the one-day races would have been justification to finally fire me, while a top ten could have saved my job, so of course my best effort was right in the middle. I pulled on the front and helped Ramunas hit the podium, but nothing special.

We went out to a nice dinner in Quebec—not paid for by the team for some reason. I didn't mind buying myself a steak, but with no job on the horizon, I said "no, thanks" to rounds of appetizers, and yelled "no, thanks!" when someone ordered a $100

---

* The joke was that if you clicked "Race Results" on his website, you got a "404 Error."

*Alex Howes with champagne and
coffee, the two essential liquids.*

bottle of wine and offered me a glass. Then the bill came, split
evenly, except four orders of nachos ended up on my tab. All year,
teammates had paid for my coffee and I thought it was a gift, but
we were even after $86 in tortilla chips and cheese.

After a little too much to drink, some guys played a game
where they held their hand over the glass candleholder at the
table, to see who could bear the heat until the flame starved of
oxygen and burned out. I wasn't surprised that only Ramunas
succeeded.

"Is just physical pain," he explained, laughing at the blister on his palm. I don't know if he was joking.

Before we went home, the Americans attended a meeting about a new branch of the CPA—the historically ineffective pro cycling riders' union. So far, they only represented Spain, Italy, and France, but Christian Vande Velde (who'd retired after he confessed to doping along with Zabriskie and Danielson) was hoping to add a new chapter that would allow input from Americans and other nationalities. With the help of a sympathetic lawyer, we could bring the CPA from not helping riders of three countries to being worthless worldwide. But it was a start.

I suspect that Vande Velde was looking to give back to my generation. He knew he'd played a role in the absence of new sponsors and hoped that a union could improve our working conditions, establishing guidelines about racing in bad weather, for example. He'd already put a lot of his own money into it, so they asked for fund-raising ideas to pay fees and expenses.

I raised my hand.

"Someone tell Lance that if he pays for all of it, we'll all sign a press release that we're not mad anymore and the public should forgive him."

Lance does a "poor me, I keep getting sued" routine, but I'm sure he made good investments. He could probably lose every lawsuit and still find $100,000 in his seat cushions.

The room went silent. Everyone knew it was a good idea and some guys were still friendly with Lance, but they were scared to ask him. We agreed to pay modest annual dues instead, like they do in other sports.

Vande Velde sent a summary of the meeting to all of the Americans in the WorldTour, explaining the dues and the overall strategy for those who couldn't attend, and I enjoyed some of the "reply all" responses as I worked my way through the airport.

Dear CPA,

I don't pay people to do nothing. I have enough joke emails a day already. Please take me off this list.

Good luck not doing what your teams want,

Danny Pate
Team Sky

It was an interesting point. As I'd learned in Colorado when Robbie Hunter said we couldn't protest the dirt stage, it would be tough if our employers wanted us to keep racing when the union said we shouldn't. *Except that's the whole point of a union, you dumbass, and the one who won't join is the one who's ruining it for everyone.*

The next response was from Tom Peterson, who'd just finished his last race for Team Giant-Shimano, and wouldn't be continuing as a professional cyclist.

Tejay et al.,

Take me off this list of fags. You guys can all play with your money without me.

4ever yours,
Tom Peterson

I'd been advised to avoid Peterson and I was starting to learn why, but his point was more valid than Pate's, since the dues probably should have been a percentage of salary rather than a flat fee of 500 euros each.

Another e-mail followed from Peterson a few minutes later:

aww I pushed send too early. . . .

FUCK all y'all!

Wherever you are, Tom Peterson, fuck you, too.

CHAPTER 33

FORMER TEAMMATE JIM Stemper called when I was back in L.A. He'd played a big role as a domestique when I won Redlands, but two years later he was working as an engineer. Jim had read the articles about my job search and wanted to tell me that it wouldn't be so bad if I had to stop, and he still loved riding his bike.

"It doesn't remind you of what you're missing?" I asked.

"It's like passing your father's grave every day," he said. "But I don't want to do anything else."

I also talked to Isaac Howe, who was still begging for contracts from Continental teams.

"I know I'm good enough," he said. "I'm just tired of dragging my dick through glass waiting for someone to notice."

Another friend who has a way with words.

Still hopeful to stay with Cannondale-Garmin (but constantly asking Optum to "give me a few more days"), I trained hard for Beijing, with the usual climbs in the Santa Monica Mountains and group rides for intensity. It was on the race-paced "Nichols Ride" (named for Nichols Canyon in Hollywood) that I ran into a guy named Matt Wikstrom, a vice president at a sports marketing company called Wasserman Media Group and agent to some of my friends and teammates. Wikstrom had followed my season and read my book, so I told him how McQuaid had betrayed me, but I didn't know what to do.

"I'm just so tired of dragging my dick through glass, begging for contracts," I said, plagiarizing Isaac. "Maybe the dream is dead and nobody has the heart to tell me."

"You deserve to be in the WorldTour," said Wikstrom. "You were second overall in San Luis and I watched you tear up three stage races last month. Just stop leaving it up to someone else."

Wikstrom was self-made, successful, and overqualified to represent pro cyclists, so I suspected that this part of his job was mostly for fun. Helping cyclists was a puzzle for him—a break from his real work. We barely knew each other and McQuaid was still my agent, but Wikstrom helped me compose e-mails to every WorldTour manager that week, which read like business proposals instead of begging: "Here's what I can bring to your team and why it's in your best interest to hire me." I was probably still screwed, but it felt good to take control, and for someone I respected to believe in me.

Almost all of the top teams responded (which was already better than I'd gotten from Vaughters), but most said they were full, wishing me luck. Quick-Step, Trek, and MTN-Qhubeka were all impressed with my season and said they might have had a spot if they knew I was available a month before. So remember when McQuaid said he'd shop me around to other teams? I guess he hadn't.

If there's any advice I can give an aspiring pro cyclist, it's that if you hire a bad agent, make sure you invest in one of those shockproof cell phone cases, because it was damn satisfying to throw my phone against a cement wall. The only reason I picked it up was because I was so excited to fire him.

I threw it again after an angry call that afternoon from one of the sponsors I'd been in touch with.

"Hey, Phil, so I talked to a guy named Omer today? He said SmartStop had just hired him, and then he asked for way more cash than we'd agreed on."

It turned out that Team SmartStop had picked up my polo-shirted nemesis to bring in sponsors, so he'd contacted the ones that I'd found and demanded more money—a win-win for Omer, since the only risk was pissing me off and he didn't like me anyway. I tipped my cap to him and told Creed that I was out.* This meant I was back to just one offer: $50,000 from Optum, and Vaughters still wasn't returning my calls.

I wasn't the only one who suffered from JV's silent treatment over the years. In fact, from what I could tell, he'd never actually fired anyone—he'd just ignore you until you got the message. I'm sure it's not easy to "break up" with riders every year, because it's not just losing a paycheck—it's heartbreak and failure, and it's very public. JV was a kingmaker: he pointed his finger and said "you," and your life was changed forever. When he signed someone, he'd tweet about it, sharing the joy, accepting praise from fans and media, so it hurt that when it was over, he made us go through it alone—no "I'm sorry we can't take you back," "thanks for your work," or even "good luck." A former team member sent me a picture of T-shirts he'd had made that said "Friends don't let friends ride for Garmin," which he'd been giving to all the guys JV had burned over the years. I didn't get one, though. He'd run out.

Still, I couldn't bring myself to give up the dream without some sort of answer from Vaughters. I went back to fifteen-year-old obese Phil, staring at my phone, leaving voice mails every day, while he was the pretty girl, ignoring me, too much of a coward to say it was over.

Optum extended their deadline until Saturday, so on Friday

---

* SmartStop ran out of funds midseason, so this was a blessing. I'd have brought in more money than they paid me, and I'm sure I would have quit racing entirely. I'd survived that on Kenda, but I didn't have another one in me.

morning I sat at Sweetsalt with an espresso before the group ride and texted Vaughters one last time:

"Optum needs an answer tomorrow. What would you do if you were me?"

I hit "send," put the phone in my pocket, and rode off with my friends.

I'd felt good in my buildup to Beijing, and my power meter said I was going well, but I found myself gritting my teeth, side by side with a local guy as we raced up San Fernando Road in Glendale. Close to the top, I put some distance on him and started coasting, but he had one more kick, beating me to the imaginary KOM line. It was my first defeat on a Sweet Ride, but I didn't worry about it, eager to check my phone again. Standing in the shade while we waited for the pack to catch up, I read the reply from JV.

"I'd take the sure thing," it said.

I'd seen this coming for months, and for weeks I'd been practically begging for it, so I was surprised to be so devastated, setting my bike computer back to miles and feet.* I wasn't a Euro pro anymore. I was out of the Show.

My head spun with broken dreams and injustice, but when I looked up from my phone, I wasn't a victim. I was on top of a canyon in Pasadena with my friends. I told them what had happened, and their responses all sounded like condolences. They could see that part of me had died.

The guys stopped for breakfast but I kept riding, over Mulholland and down Franklin Avenue, hoping that an overpriced coffee on Sunset Boulevard might cheer me up. I was in no mood for argyle (I'd turned my jersey inside out), but to get from Franklin to Sunset, Argyle Avenue is the safest route, so I worked my way to the center lane, made the left turn, and found the shoulder filled with industrial staples, instantly puncturing both of my tires.

---

* Yes, you can set your brain back, too. Isn't that a relief?

If this was a work of fiction, the editor would tell me to delete the part about my flat tires on Argyle Avenue.

"It's not believable," they'd say. "Too much of a coincidence."

But it happened.

I was carrying two tubes, so at least I didn't have to call a taxi. With a crowd of homeless onlookers under the 101 Freeway, I filled my tires with my mini hand pump, wincing from the pain of my broken ribs with each squeeze. *Is just physical pain.*

That night, I called Jonas Carney and told him I'd go with Optum, but he wasn't quite ready. Carney had raced alongside my old coach Matt Koschara—clean in the dirtiest era—and he hated dopers with a passion, so before I signed, he needed to know how the hell I could be friends with Tom Danielson. I did my best to explain it, but I heard that Jonas called Brad Huff next, to confirm that I wasn't an idiot.

I signed the contract, but I was pretty sure I'd tear it up in a few weeks and quit. Sure, there'd be plenty of upside riding for Optum—I'd live at home, I'd spend more time with Joanna, and $50,000 was enough to pay the bills—but if the dream was dead, was there a point? Shouldn't I just focus on my business full-time, since I was already making more money selling bike products than using them? I'd have to answer that later. For now, it was time to pack my bikes for my last trip with Garmin-Sharp: the five-day Tour of Beijing and Japan Cup a week later.

The news reported that Ted King got the last spot on Cannondale-Garmin, but Howes cheered me up, offering to buy the car I'd left in Girona. He found the key I'd hidden at Tom's house, drove it around to make sure it worked, and sent $2,500 the same day, like a prince.

CHAPTER 34

BOARDING THE PLANE from L.A. to Beijing, I made small talk with a BMC rider, who stopped at a plush sleeping pod in business class and pulled out $300 noise-canceling headphones. It was a long walk from there to seat 78D in economy class, where I wore plastic earbuds and watched *Amadeus* on my laptop. As an L.A. resident, I'm actually required to write a movie review and act like an expert, so I'll explain that it's a strong story about Salieri, a great composer who dedicates his life to music, only to be outshined by the genius of young Mozart, who he eventually tries to murder out of jealousy. The only weakness in the film was the fact that I'm six-one, crammed into a tiny seat for thirteen hours.

The flight from Amsterdam to Beijing landed at the same time as mine, so I stumbled into my teammates at baggage claim. Someone herded us onto a bus along with dozens of other riders, and there was a collective groan when we heard that the hotel was two hours away. We accepted our fate and settled into our seats, looking forward to a light dinner and a heavy sleep, but after an hour and a half on the road, we pulled back to the airport parking lot where we'd started. Groans turned to yelling, the driver went outside to smoke a cigarette, and no one could tell us why we were there or when we might leave.

Hesjedal went to the terminal, returning with a bucket of Kentucky Fried Chicken and beer from a vending machine (75¢ each), so a small crowd of pro cyclists sat on the blacktop under a streetlight for hours, taking turns buying more rounds to make the best of a situation we couldn't control or understand.

"For every hour we're stuck here, we all have at least one drink," someone said.

Dan Martin had flown straight to China after winning the Tour of Lombardy. An elite athlete, millionaire, and finely tuned machine—from years of hard work, guided by some of the top experts in endurance sports—was eating a bucket of chicken and washing it down with cheap beer. It was like pouring piss into a Ferrari.

It turned out to be a completely unnecessary customs issue involving all of the $10,000 bikes we'd brought in. Someone paid someone else a deposit, recorded the serial numbers, and the riders/hostages got back on the bus, headed to the hotel for real this time, except grumpier and half-drunk.

We raided the shop when the bus stopped for gas, spending currency that was so foreign, it didn't feel like a waste. Tyler Farrar returned to his seat with what looked like pickled hot dogs, and the smell was powerful when he opened the package, waking the lucky few who'd managed to fall asleep. Then he ripped open a hole in the fabric of the seat in front of him, so the hot dog had sex with the hole, but Tyler accidentally dropped it in, which was hilarious on my fourth beer and thirtieth hour of no sleep. (Actually, let me think about it . . . yep, still funny now.)

I arrived at the hotel with one of the hot dogs out of the fly of my shorts, flopping it around while the guys took pictures, and Dekker responded by holding a hairbrush in his foreskin. Thomas loved showing off his giant foreskin, which really was impressive.* Stretching it over the brush's handle, he said he could fit ten quarters in there. Think about that next time you hold a quarter.

"Still doing this shit, huh, Thomas?"

"Oh, for sho'!"

The hotel was north of Beijing, in a small village that was under construction for the 2022 Winter Olympics. They hadn't been confirmed as the host yet, but they were already building hotels and arenas, and the hills echoed with tractors and bulldozers. What if they didn't win the bid? Would a brand-new city have been abandoned? You bet it would. That's China.

It was sad to walk past the work sites near the hotel, where labor laws and unions haven't caught up to the rest of the world. Construction helmets are rare, and men were welding with no safety masks, turning away to keep the sparks out of their faces (and I did five hundred words whining about dirt in my eyes in Colorado). They build faster and cheaper in China, but you also notice people walking around with glass eyes and missing limbs. Our mechanic fell into a hole in the sidewalk and needed stitches.

Owned by the UCI, with mandatory attendance from World-Tour teams, the Tour of Beijing was a remnant of Pat McQuaid's corrupt leadership. The race would be shut down after 2014, but that didn't make it any easier to read the letter placed on each table at dinner, warning of potential meat contamination that might lead to positive drug tests. The concern was with certain "controlled substances" like DHEA, a steroid hormone that's found in your body naturally but considered doping if they catch you above a certain amount. Easily detectable, it would be an odd choice for performance enhancement, and of the handful of positive tests

---

* If you look down, you may very well be standing on it right now.

over the years, several are from riders who you couldn't imagine cheating.

So KFC turned out to be the last meat that we ate in China. Team soigneurs rationed canned tuna and beef jerky to go with our rice, but replacing five thousand calories every day was a chore. I ate the DHEA eggs at breakfast when nobody was looking, but I knew from previous races that vegetables were out of the question.*

Checking out of the hotel before the first stage, the front desk had a bill for each team for hundreds of dollars, accusing us of stealing coat hangers, TV remotes, light bulbs, and gas masks from our rooms.

"No one wants your coat hangers!" I heard our soigneur arguing. "And what kind of a lunatic would steal a gas mask? We're not paying for that!"

You might wonder why they'd even have gas masks in hotel rooms, but it would make perfect sense if you saw the haze through the windows. While staff argued about the charges, the riders, directors, and race organizers met in the lobby, debating whether it was safe to race in the polluted air. Dan Martin downloaded an air quality app on his phone, and we studied particulate readings, all suddenly experts. The worst it ever gets in Los Angeles is 100 (which is where doctors say it's unsafe to exercise outside), so the race organization compromised: it was 285 now, but they'd cancel the race if it reached 300. It was almost as if our health wasn't their highest priority.

"I mean, what's the difference between 285 and 300?" asked Ryder. "Either way, it's bad for you."

---

* At the 2010 Tour of Qinghai Lake, Kiel Reijnen ended up at the hospital with severe stomach pain. The doctor said that his intestines were in a knot, and they wanted to cut him open to untie them. Fortunately he refused, because it turned out to be a case of basic food poisoning, probably caused by veggies washed in tap water.

"Fifteen is the difference, I think, no?" said Thomas Dekker, leaning back in a chair, shirtless, wearing a stolen gas mask.

Lachlan sat in the corner, lighting a match. "Two eighty-six," he counted. He lit another. "Two eighty-seven."

Twenty minutes before the start, we finished our espressos and filled our pockets with Snickers and bottles of Coca-Cola. It was October, and no one could handle energy bars or sports drinks anymore, so for one more week, we'd fake our way through with sugar and caffeine. Other teams might toss in a tramadol—the inexplicably legal, gray area narcotic painkiller.

Teammate Steele von Hoff was in the same boat as I'd been a few weeks before: Andrew McQuaid as an agent (not returning his phone calls), no results, no word from Vaughters, and a ticking clock as other teams filled up. Farrar was signed to MTN-Qhubeka, so he graciously offered to work for Steele in the sprint instead of the other way around.

"Just stay on my wheel, Steele," he said. "I'll drop you off with two hundred meters to go."

I felt bad for Steele when I saw the video of the finale: he's positioned behind Tyler in the last kilometer, but when Team Sky comes up, Steele pushes over onto their train, just before Tyler opens it up and blows the doors off of them. The guy who took Steele's spot behind Tyler won the stage, while Steele got pinched against the barricades, barely finishing in the top ten. That was the result he needed to keep his dream alive, but one bad decision at forty miles an hour, and it was done.

We piled into the van and drove over a ridge to the next hotel. Looking down on Beijing reminded me of the scene in *The Matrix* where they reveal what the world has really become: clouds were red with pollution but rainbow colored on the edges like an oily puddle, and in the valley, all we could see through the window was a thick gray. Cannon sounds echoed against the mountains and a translator explained that they "seed" the clouds by shooting chemicals into the sky, manufacturing rain to clear the air. I slapped myself for all the time I spent separating my recycling back home, like that matters at all.* AC Milan's exhibition soccer game was canceled that night (they have a union), as was Mariah Carey's concert, but our hotel was a chorus of coughing, with bloodshot eyes, headaches, and sore throats.

I'd crossed ten time zones to get to Beijing and I was hopped up on caffeine, so I needed a sleeping pill the first couple nights. Garmin-Sharp couldn't afford to send a doctor to the race, but we didn't need one. We had Dr. Dre. I knocked on Dekker's door.

"Still doing this shit, huh, Thomas?" I asked, doing my best Snoop impression. "Do you have your stash of sleeping pills?"

"Oh, for sho'! What kind of sleep do you like? On the taxi to the airport, I take one of these." He held up a blue pill, which looked innocent. "I don't remember anything from the trip. I land and go to baggage claim, not sure if I even check my bike. Then it comes out, and I say, 'Good one, Thomas!'"

I took half of that one.

I couldn't believe how well I raced that week. I helped our team leaders with bottles and clothes, made all the front groups in the crosswinds, felt relaxed on descents, and when we compared power output after the stages, mine was about the same as everybody else's, which means I wasn't wasting energy like I had at the beginning of the year. It took until October and I'd already lost my job, but I'd finally gotten the hang of the WorldTour. *Damn it.*

Dan finished second to BMC's Philippe Gilbert on a hilltop finish and Tyler won a stage in a field sprint, so we were raking in prize money, and with contract pressure finally off for everyone but poor Steele, we had a great time, despite the pollution and canned-tuna dinners. Lachlan and I bought cheap remote-control cars at a toy store by the hotel, and we raced them in the hallway.

---

* Yes, I still do it. Don't e-mail me.

Steele had a remote-control helicopter, but he just sat in his room with his feet up.

"Where's Steele? Why isn't he playing with us?" asked Lachlan.

"I dunno, man. It's like he's trying to get a job or something."

We laughed. Lachlan was signed to Jelly Belly after an ugly contract battle with Vaughters. I'll get the details wrong, but I think it went something like this: Lachlan was on the first year of a two-year contract when he won the stage at Utah, so Vaughters offered $200,000 to add another year. Lachlan agreed, and then a contract showed up for $90,000.

"No big deal, JV," said Lachlan, confused. "If you don't have the money, we won't extend the contract just yet, and we'll see what happens next year."

Vaughters's counteroffer: if Lachlan didn't sign, he'd send him to all the worst races the next season, so he'd get no results and wouldn't be worth $90,000 to anyone.

Lachlan's response: "Bring it on."

As I understand it, the Morton family is filthy rich. Have you ever heard of Morton Salt? That's nothing to do with them, but I heard his dad had a patent on some sort of magnet that's used in high-end appliances and cars. The point is, Lachlan didn't buy himself a spot in the WorldTour like Caleb did. He wasn't in it for the money, but he sure as hell wasn't in it to make money for somebody else. He raced like shit that year and ended up on Jelly Belly, so JV won, but to me, Lachlan was a scrawny, 130-pound superhero.

A rumor circulated that more Astana riders had tested positive, and a scandal might get their whole team kicked out of the WorldTour. Nothing came of it, but Lachlan and I did our best to steer the cars under their feet when they walked by. He finally drove his into the street and got it run over (I have video), and I smashed mine in the hallway and left it in a corner with a beer can, implying a DUI situation.

The remnants of Lachlan's remote-control car.

Stage four was the big mountaintop finish, and our only chance for Dan to drop Philippe Gilbert to take the overall lead. Ten kilometers from the last climb, the break was still several minutes ahead, so I pulled hard on the front with Lachlan and Nathan Haas. We ate up the breakaway, and at the bottom of the last climb, I ate a Snickers.*

The group split to pieces on the climb, with BMC setting the pace. My domestique job was finished, but I found myself comfortably in the lead group, so I rode up to Dan. He was as surprised to see me as I was to be there, but I acted nonchalant about it.

_____

* To all the sports scientists out there: I did that entire stage race on Snickers and Coke, and I've never ridden better.

"Dan, do you need bottles or anything?"

"No. I'm good, thanks."

"Yeah? You're feeling good? Want me to make it harder at the front?"

Dan gave me a look.

"Sure. If you can."

I shot past BMC's team and upped the pace. It was just a few minutes, but it was a WorldTour race where everyone thought I'd be eaten alive, and I was in front at the hardest point, with big names getting dropped from my effort. Ryder attacked when I ran out of steam, putting pressure on BMC to catch him, and Dan didn't make up any time on Gilbert like we'd hoped, but he won the stage.

Cyclists are trained to be lazy—don't stand if you can lean, don't lean if you can sit, don't sit if you can lie down, etc.—but I broke all the rules after the finish that day. In second overall, Dan had to focus on recovery, as did Tyler, seeking sprint glory and prize money, and Steele, still full of misplaced contract hope.* They sat in the van while I kept riding up a dirt path at the end of the parking lot. Around a few bends, the wind blew away the sounds of the announcers, and I wasn't at a bike race anymore. I was at a temple on top of a mountain, staring down at the Great Wall, taking pictures so I'd never have to go back.

On the drive, the guys all patted me on the back.

"Didn't know you could do that at a WorldTour race, Phil," Lachlan said with a grin.

"I can't believe that was the same guy I raced with in West Flanders a few months ago," said Nathan Haas. "You've learned more in a season than some guys do in three!" Nathan's a sweetheart.

---

* If you think Steele was in denial, one guy who was riding for Cannondale lost his job in the merger and spent 2015 doing charity rides and unsanctioned races, telling people he was still on the team.

After the final stage, our prize split was $7,500 each, so we went out on the town. Some racers spent their prize money at brothels,* which are hard to avoid in Beijing. We looked for a bar and thought we found one, but then a row of women in lingerie lined up in front of us. We looked at each other, shook our heads, and kept walking, finally ending up at a dark hotel restaurant (their brothel was in the basement).

With a few drinks in him, Ryder complained about the merger. He had another year on his contract, but the rumor is that Cannondale's new boss wanted to get rid of the ex-dopers on the team,† so Vaughters had tried to buy him out (probably Tom, too). I remember the exact moment that I stopped feeling bad for Ryder: "I was so mad," he said, "I had to look at my bank balance to cheer myself up."

From the team's inception, Vaughters offered a million-dollar bonus for a Grand Tour win, thinking it would never happen. They probably had to spread payments over several years when Ryder won the Giro, but he already had millions put away from his years of doping as a mountain biker.

Then we listened to Steele, who was still hoping to stay with Cannondale-Garmin, but Dan and Nathan already had plane tickets to their first training camp, so we tried to tell Steele it was over as he drunkenly scrolled through the international rider rankings on his phone.

"If I'm out of the top five hundred, I don't deserve to stay in the WorldTour, and I'll shut up," he promised. He was ranked 526.

We looked at mine next: 480. Ranked 480th in the world, after all that. It doesn't sound impressive, but where do you rank in the whole world at your job, you judgmental ass? (Sorry. Sensitive topic.)

---

* This won't be surprising, but I noticed that many of the riders who got away with doping were the same ones who cheated on their wives. I heard about one guy who called his two girlfriends before bed every night, ending both conversations with "I love you."
† Hence Basso's departure. Cannondale deserves some credit for this if it's true.

I'm a happy drunk, so I tried to look at the bright side. "Hang on! So if there was a plane crash, and 479 of the best riders in the world were on it, I'd be number one!"

Dan—ranked fifty-first—glared at me.

"I mean, God forbid!"

"You'd be ranked number one, until someone else started riding a bike," Haas pointed out, ranked 202 at only twenty-five years old.

Pizza Hut was closed by the time we left the bar, but we did find a TGI Fridays for milk shakes.

CHAPTER 35

THE NEXT MORNING was a short flight to Japan, where we went straight to McDonald's for double patties of gray, cheap meat, agreeing that it was the best food we'd ever tasted after a week of canned tuna. Uncracked, the color returned to our faces, and I swear my legs felt better by the time I stood up.

Before we left for the train station, Nathan ran to a magazine store.

"Hang on, guys. I need some lip balm."

"Don't say 'bomb' at an airport!" I cautioned.

High on cheeseburgers, everyone laughed like it was the first joke they'd ever heard.

"Jesus, you're fast!" said Dan. *Dan Martin said I was fast!*

Our roster for Japan Cup all came from Beijing, except good old Bingen Fernandez flew in direct, and Dekker swapped out for Caleb Fairly, who'd been at home in Colorado. It came out that Caleb had signed to Giant for 2015 (they picked up two young riders at the same time, who might not have realized that Caleb was paying their salary and they owed him a coffee), but he showed up to his last race of the year carrying a few extra pounds, not shy to admit he hadn't ridden his bike in a month, and refusing to shave his thick leg hair. I understood that Caleb was insulted at being left off of Cannondale-Garmin, but it was still disrespectful to his teammates.

At Japan Cup's opening ceremony, we stood on the stage at an outdoor arena as a high-energy announcer introduced us to fans, with lights, lasers, and loud American pop music (I mentioned we were in Japan, right?). I was trying not to swallow my tongue when Steele got my attention.

"Phil! Phil! Look at Caleb! His shorts have popped!"

I looked past Steele to the far end of the stage. After all the pulled pork in Kansas, milk shakes in Alberta, and a month off the bike, Caleb had gone from a size extra small to more of a medium, and he was paying the price, using his hand to cover a blown seam. (I don't know if I believe in God or karma, but I do believe in high-end Lycra.)

"The sumo match is tomorrow, Caleb!" said Team Sky's Bernie Eisel.

Fans packed the small host town of Utsonomiya, mobbing us for photos and autographs every time we entered the hotel. We'd pose for a picture and they'd print it out at home, returning the next day with a small gift if we signed it. In other words, they were exactly like the Belgian pedalphiles, except pleasant and sober, but I still used the hotel's back entrance to avoid them, because sometimes you just want to run to the Utsonomiya 7-Eleven to buy some cashews and fizzy water and you don't want to deal with adoring Japanese mobs. You know what I mean, right? I'm sure you've said that lots of times.

Race organizers asked us to do a short ride with locals and volunteers one morning, and when we returned, WorldTour riders each got an envelope with $100 cash. "Don't tell the smaller teams," whispered our translator. "We don't pay them." The rich got even richer in the criterium that afternoon, where I helped control the race for Steele, who finished a respectable second place to Sky's Chris Sutton. I bet Steele stared at his phone all night for a contract from JV, but second place at Japan Cup crit doesn't keep you in the WorldTour.*

Crowds lined up for the Japan Cup criterium.

---

* He joined a respectable second-tier team, keeping his apartment in Girona and his dream intact.

The main event at Japan Cup was the hilly road race. Part bike race, part performance, they allowed a handful of local teams to start, including some keirin riders who looked like they'd never ridden up a hill.* It was understood that WorldTour guys would let a breakaway go with the Japanese teams represented, allow them some glory, and the real race would start when we caught them in the last 60k. Haas had won the year before, so we took the responsibility to control the race. Despite his leg hair, Caleb rode well for the first half, and then Dan Martin took over on the front.

Dan pulled for a long time, reeling in the breakaway and hitting the climb fast enough to split the group in half. I was safely in his draft on the flat sections but I suffered on the uphills, worried because it would be my job to take over the pacemaking when Dan was done, and there was no way I'd be able to match his speed. But Dan never asked me to take a turn. He stayed on the front by himself for over an hour, increasing the speed every few minutes as the pack blew apart behind us.

It was a pull that made me rethink my life. It had been a long trip and a long season, and Dan hadn't trained for this race. With a beer the night before, a Snickers in his pocket, and another year on his contract, this might have been one of his worst days, but the effort I was watching was something I couldn't do at my best.

I'd had my butt kicked plenty that year. I was going all-out when Quintana danced away from me in Argentina, but this was more humbling: ability without caring or trying, like Ramunas sprinting into the group at training camp when we tried to prank him, or Dylan van Baarle attacking the car during a motorpace session. I had talent, a world-class power-to-weight ratio, an off-the-chart VO_2 max, and a work ethic to get the most out of it, but so did everyone else here. To be special in the WorldTour took

---

* Keirin is a track cycling event, popular for gambling in Japan. Some of those guys make seven-figure salaries—and I don't mean yen.

something else—let's call it Real Talent. On a narrow road in Japan, with a heart rate of 170, dodging Dan Martin's beads of sweat, I had to admit that I didn't have it. Dan never doped, and the difference between us was only 1 or 2 percent, but it might as well have been the Pacific Ocean.

For ten years, I'd been on an upward curve. I'd start the season supporting teammates, but they were bringing me bottles by July. Here I was in October, I'd learned fast and I was stronger than ever, but I was still taking jackets to the car. My curve had flattened out, and it was only a matter of time before it would start going down. All those coaches and teachers and clichés were wrong: everyone's not a winner. No one wants to talk about natural ability, because Real Talent isn't inspiring or fair, but if you're born a six, hard work and sacrifice can only get you to a nine.*

Dan Martin is Mozart, and I'm Salieri.

But I didn't try to murder Dan. In fact, I was grateful. It was good to know that no matter what, I'd never be the best, and no amount of vitamins or kale shakes would change that. I could put premium in my Toyota, but it would never keep up with Dan's Ferrari filled with piss, so if I decided to quit, at least I'd leave with a sense of satisfaction. A weight was lifted.

Sadly, that weight was only metaphorical, because when Dan finally blew up on the last climb, I was clinging for dear life to the back of the group. I was pretty sure I could hang on and help Nathan, but Mozart scurried past me at the top. It was the first time that it didn't look effortless, but he'd recovered from an hour-long pull in the first thirty seconds of a climb and managed to rally by the top. Dan neutralized every attack for the last twenty kilometers, and Nathan won.

I'd almost finished my first beer at our team's tent when Dan

---

* I know some guys who were born a ten and drank or smoked their way down to a nine. I don't respect that, but a ten looks like a lot of pressure, so I understand.

got there, asking the mechanic for a stationary trainer to do a proper, professional cooldown. Of course the mechanic hadn't brought a trainer to the last race of the year, so he felt bad until Dan started laughing.

"Gotcha! Hand me a beer."

It was off-season, even for all-in, Real Talent.

Now that the race was over, fans were ravenous for souvenirs. I sold the sweaty jersey off my back for $75 (clean jerseys went for $50), rode the twenty minutes back to the hotel in just my shorts, and locals were knocking on my door before I was out of the shower, eager to buy more stuff. This was an annual tradition at Japan Cup, and teams all set up a shopping mall in their section of the hotel. Nathan's win raised the demand for argyle, so the real winner was the racist soigneur, who'd come prepared with extra suitcases of team gear.

WorldTour teams each had a banquet room at the hotel that evening where fans could meet riders. It had traditional seating on the floor, but my hamstrings were so tight, I could barely bend them.

"That's what happens after 25,000 kilometers of riding since January," Nathan offered.

It felt like just 24,980, but maybe I should have stretched more often.

Team Cannondale's party was in the next room, separated by an accordion-style fabric partition.

"Why don't they just pull the wall down, kick me and Steele out, and get this merger over with?" I asked.

We finally escaped the hotel, heading out to spend the cash from the gear we'd sold, joined by Joanna and Nathan's girlfriend, Laura Fletcher. Laura was a journalist and producer for a cycling news site, so they'd bought her a ticket to cover the race. I paid for Joanna's, and Nathan and I had arranged for the team to book our return tickets a week later, in a sly move to get vacations at a discount.

Our season ended with the only nightlife in Utsonomiya: a strip of tiny "glass bars," with eight seats in a U-shape and a bartender in the middle. Nathan bought the first round. He had the glow of a winner, and I could tell that Dan took pride in helping to make it happen for his friend, just as I did with Alex in Denver and Tom had for me in Argentina. We drank, we chatted, and we joked around. It took all year, but I'd almost forgotten what these guys meant to me, and I was talking to a room full of winners as if they really were my peers. I loved this sport, I loved my teammates, and I was going to miss them. More rounds of sake followed, and we stumbled back to our rooms, where soigneurs had left bottled water by our doors, knowing we'd need to rehydrate. They think of everything.*

*Glass bar in Japan with (left to right) Steele,
Dan, Laura, and Nathan.*

---

* Shout-out to Alyssa, who remembered my favorite cereal, and that I prefer salted cashews.

Joanna and I made plans to meet Nathan and Laura in Tokyo, and said good-bye to everyone else. I hadn't told them that I was thinking of quitting, but I hoped for some sort of confirmation— just a hint of permanence in those farewells. *Tell me you don't ever want to see me again. Tell me I'm too old and too slow.*

"We'll miss you, Phil," said Dan. "It's silly that you're not in the WorldTour next year. We need guys like you."

Damn it. Real Talent is born on third base. Some of them act like they hit a triple, but not Dan.

Bingen smiled and put out his hand for a shake. "I know you'll be back in the WorldTour, Phil." I hugged him so he wouldn't see my tears.

Joanna and I spent a great weekend with a triathlete couple I'd met through Instagram named "Iron Sam" and Emi. They took us to hiking trails, temples, and restaurants, and then dropped us off at a train station to fend for ourselves. For a few days, we got lost in small towns, relaxed in traditional hot spring spas, got lost in grocery stores, hiked around Mt. Fuji, got lost in train stations, and ate all sorts of delicious foods that we couldn't identify.

Joanna got her nails done in Shibuya at a place that played Taylor Swift's "Shake It Off" on repeat, while I purchased a pair of bright blue Puma high-tops with a furry texture that I've never had the guts to wear in the United States. At the end of the week, we found Nathan and Laura in Tokyo and sang karaoke.

Japan Cup put me in business class on the return trip and Joanna's ticket was economy, so I took the other half of Dekker's sleeping pill as we boarded, promising to trade seats with her when I woke up. My first time in one of those magical sleeping pods, I put my feet up, pushed in the earplugs, and pulled the mask over my eyes, but the words from Dan, Nathan, and Bingen kept echoing in my head. I thought that part of me would have been excited to move on from racing, to throw myself into my business, but that wasn't appealing at all. Neither was writing for a cycling magazine, or any other job I might have been qualified for. If you'd offered me $500,000 a year to be a cookie taster, I'd have hated the sound of it.* Lots of guys took a step down from the WorldTour over the years, confident that they could work their way back, but as teams and budgets got smaller, I could only think of two who'd been able to do it. I was probably fooling myself to think that I could be third, but I had to try. I gave up on sleep and snuck back to economy class to give Joanna her turn in the pod, but she was already snoring.

The UCI requires teams to reimburse door-to-door transportation for riders, but all year, I'd done my best to save Vaughters's money, arguing with gate agents to avoid $150 bike fees and cramming my bags into small taxis at LAX. Now that I was fired, for the last receipt I'd submit to Garmin-Sharp, I ordered an executive driver service. A man in a suit held a card with my name on it at baggage claim and carried everything to his black SUV.

On the way home, I called my coach and told him to get to work on my training plan for 2015, because I was all-in. I might not be able to win in Europe, but I deserved to be there and I was ready to prove it. I'd be Optum's team leader at the big events, I'd know my schedule in advance, I'd go to races that suited my abilities, and I'd be based in California, so I wouldn't struggle with a distance relationship. I just had to keep doing what I knew I was capable of, and as long as nothing went horribly wrong, I'd be back in the WorldTour for 2016, living the dream.

---

* That's a joke. If you're hiring a cookie taster, please call me.

PART 3

The Year When Everything
Went Horribly Wrong

CHAPTER 36

THE FIRST STEP to going all-in was getting rid of my business. I didn't get into it here because my attempt at entrepreneurship could fill another (very boring) book, but when I'd thought I might be done racing, if I wasn't excited about shifting focus to my company, what kind of a plan B was it? My partner had been doing most of the work, but I still had fires to put out, so it had been a source of stress—a marginal loss for my performance. We came up with a fair price and he bought out my half.

Selling the business meant I could put more time in to cycling, and it also helped me escape the crappy apartment, because now I could afford a down payment in Toluca Lake. You pay a premium for nicer neighborhoods in L.A., but I liked the idea of a prestigious zip code after all those years being broke. Both Miley Cyrus *and* Justin Bieber live in Toluca Lake, and Bob Hope's mansion—complete with a golf course—was for sale for $22 million. So that's what you get if you're one of the biggest comedians or pop stars in the world. If you're an above-average climber in the bike race, you go a couple blocks outside of the celebrity enclave, and you offer $420,000 for a one-thousand-square-foot "luxury town house" near a Mexican restaurant called Ernie's. There was no golf course, but it had everything we needed: a garage, a guest bedroom, a washer/dryer, and enough marble and hardwood to earn the term "luxury," so it would be easy to rent out when we moved to Europe. It was also close to Sweetsalt and Joanna's office so she wouldn't have to take my car anymore, and Ernie makes a very decent enchilada.*

I had the money, but with roller-coaster tax returns and a one-year contract, banks weren't excited about giving me a loan, so a twenty-eight-year-old WorldTour rider, published author, and semisuccessful entrepreneur had to ask his parents to cosign, which wasn't a pleasant conversation. Dad agreed that the town house looked like a good investment, but he pointed out that I was making big decisions and setting down roots based on a job I might not have in a year and a girl who didn't want to set a wedding date.

"What if something doesn't work out?" he asked.

"Well, I could always sell it," I reminded him. *And screw you for not believing in me,* I didn't say.

When the loan went through, I made quick enemies with my Realtor, threatening to walk away from the deal until every minor repair was done. After a decade of begging for contracts, I was finally in a position of power in a negotiation, so the poor seller paid for everything Vaughters and McQuaid did to me.

I'd spent years arranging a life with low expenses and low risk because racing had never felt safe or sustainable, but I entered the 2015 season with no fallback plan and a house to pay off. I was all-in, and it felt good, like I believed for the first time that life was going to work out. Joanna had to help with the monthly payments, but my hustle had put a roof over our heads, which made

---

* For a great enchilada, you go to Cascabel on Riverside. But there's nothing wrong with Ernie's.

me feel successful and grown-up. I was a provider. Maybe I could raise a family someday, after all.

It looked like 2015 would be a tough year on the Continental circuit. Mancebo had moved overseas to a team called Skydive Dubai (probably for a big raise, plus I heard they could go skydiving for free), but I wasn't excited to race against my former teammate Lachlan Morton, and after all the issues with Chris Horner's blood levels, WorldTour teams wouldn't touch him and he found his way onto a tiny American program. Most of his teammates were unpaid,* so Horner wouldn't have much help, but any Grand Tour winner would be tough to beat.

When my Garmin-Sharp contract ended on January 1, I immediately felt less relevant, like less of a man. If I saw a group of cyclists in 2014, someone was always wearing my jersey, and I couldn't go for a ride without being recognized. If I showed up at a bike shop, maybe I only needed to pump my tires, but the mechanic would insist on a full tune-up for Mr. WorldTour, and they'd never let me pay.

"Oh, your money's no good here, Phil! Can you sign this T-shirt for us?"

In 2015, my money was good again at bike shops, hundreds of followers vanished on social media (fuck 'em), and nobody wanted a photo anymore.

---

* I heard that Horner pulled in $125,000. Living the dream!

CHAPTER 37

OPTUM'S TRAINING CAMP was held at a rental house on the ocean, an hour north of L.A. Looking around at my new teammates, it wasn't like the year before, with a "who's who" of world-class champions and questionable characters. Almost everyone went to college, and the closest we had to a doper was Tom Zirbel, who'd served a suspension for DHEA in what must have been a tainted supplement or some sort of mistake.* I went out for coffee with some of my younger teammates the first day, and was hit with a tough realization: *I'm the highest-paid guy here. Now I have to buy the espresso.*

I didn't have to worry about being accepted socially this year, because Brad Huff and Jesse Anthony were already two of my best friends, and I'd spent lots of time with Will Routley and Tom Soladay before. Routley missed the Olympics for mountain bikes twice—to Ryder Hesjedal and another Canadian who was probably on EPO—but he wasn't too bitter. He was racing his bike for a living, happily married, running an organic farm in the off-season.

---

* If you asked him what happened, Zirbel would shrug. He sent every vitamin to a lab and obsessed over it for years, but he never figured it out.

Me and Brad Huff, climber and sprinter.

Then there were some teammates I didn't know, including a Canadian named Mike Woods, who everyone called "Woodsy." He'd sent me an e-mail a few weeks before camp:

Hey dude,
    Just read your book over the weekend. It was great. Couldn't put it down.
    Looking forward to the season.

—Mike

I'd heard that Mike was a promising runner as a teenager. He went under four minutes in the mile at seventeen years old, dreaming of the Olympics, but injuries forced him to switch to bikes after college. Now he was twenty-nine—the same age as me—hoping to make Team Canada 2016 for cycling instead, but with only a couple years of experience on small teams, I didn't think Woodsy had much of a chance.

I had a blast with the guys and I was excited to spend the year with them, but there was one thing I couldn't figure out about my new team: what's Optum and how do we sell it? On Garmin-Sharp, training camp included lectures from sponsors, educating us on their products and what to promote, but nobody sweat that little detail on Continental teams, which was probably why sponsors didn't last. I was the only one who'd ever tried to sell vacuums for BISSELL, and all anyone knew about Optum was that it had something to do with health insurance (but they didn't provide us health insurance).

Compared to WorldTour camps with hard climbs and motor-pacing, Optum's rides were alarmingly easy. In a big group, WorldTour protocol was to take a hard, ten-minute pull and then swing off to the back, but here, I'd take my turn on the front, and someone would yell at me to slow down. "Guys, we have to train!" I wanted to scream.

It was a wasted week for fitness, except for "Camp Champ," a few days where we'd compete against each other with prizes for winners and pride on the line. Camp Champ started with a race up Gibraltar: a tough climb in Santa Barbara with steep sections near the top. We'd barely started the thirty-minute effort when it was already down to me and Mike Woods.

I controlled the pace at first, expecting "Woodsy" to drop anchor any minute, but instead, he came around me and we took turns in the wind, flying up the climb together. It was fun, but I wasn't happy to think that I might be evenly matched with this rookie.

Then we got to the steep sections, and it wasn't even anymore. When Woods stood up on his bike, something strange happened: he was still attached to the pedals and holding his handlebars, but Mike wasn't riding a bike at all—he was running, and a huge varicose vein popped out of his right calf, like an alien growing inside of him. That gave me something to stare at when he took over the pace, until he dropped me in the last five hundred meters. My confidence took a hit. *Who is this guy, and how can I lead the team and get back to Europe if I can't even win training camp?*

That night, Mike uploaded his power file to see where our effort ranked all-time on Gibraltar. I looked over his shoulder and noticed his username: "Rusty Woods." This was the guy who broke Ryder Hesjedal's record in Hawaii, and I was in trouble.

On the next Camp Champ day, we raced up a climb called Fernwood, where I'd trained many times. You might think it's an advantage to be familiar with a climb, but knowing the road didn't improve my power-to-weight ratio. Woods would drop me, wait for me to catch up, ask which way to go at the next fork in the road, and then drop me again. My power meter said 430 watts when he disappeared around a bend for the fourth time, and I finally had to face it: Woodsy had Real Talent. I wasn't the best climber in the world, but I was up there, and he made me look average.

When I got to the top, I could tell he was proud that he'd beaten me, but Mike didn't gloat. He smiled, put out his hand for a fist bump, and said, "Nice one, buddy!" Woodsy called everyone "buddy," and he meant it. A college graduate and fellow English major, he told stories about his coaching business and his job at a shoe store, and I enjoyed his positivity, impressed at how hard he'd worked and the adversity he'd overcome. My new teammate was jeopardizing my career, and I couldn't even hate him.

The third Camp Champ event was a flat time trial. I finished a close second to Zirbel—the best time trialist on the Continental scene—and Woods was way down, because the TT bike puts you in a low, aerodynamic position, where you rarely stand up. *Guess you can't run on that thing, eh, buddy?* I saw that if I wanted to lead the team, time trials would be the only way to do it, so I spent a day with a bike fitter after training camp, working on my position and efficiency.

CHAPTER 38

OPTUM'S FIRST EVENT was Volta ao Algarve, a stage race in Portugal in February—arguably the biggest race we'd do all year. We flew into Lisbon early and settled in to two small apartments in a town called Vilamoura at the southern tip of the country. Planning to peak for California, I was using Algarve as training, with a no-stress attitude of "do my best, help the team, and see what happens." When we checked in to the hotel the night before the first stage, I found a dead blackbird in my room, but it's okay because I don't believe in omens.

Canadian Eric Wohlberg was our director. He had great energy, but after a career on North American Continental teams, he didn't quite know how things worked in Europe, planning early departures for each stage, "just in case," like how my mom wants to be at the airport two hours before the flight takes off. Organizers were still building the stage while we sat beside the van in folding camp chairs for our prerace meeting, bundled up against the morning cold.

Pointing at a map, Wohlberg gave a rundown of the course and how he thought the stage might play out.

"This part's going to be windy. Be at the front there. You're looking at a real shit fight 20k later, so make sure you're at the front for that part. You've gotta fuck them before they fuck you, boys. This descent looks pretty dangerous, so start at the front."

"Ride at the front" is the advice they give junior riders when they don't have anything real to say, so my mind wandered, but then suddenly everyone was looking at me, wanting to know what I thought. On Garmin-Sharp, I was a fly on the wall at meetings and nobody asked my opinion, but now I was the most experienced on the team. Basically, we were screwed, but I had some good ideas of how the big teams would race and what we should watch out for.

"Here's where you might get dropped if it's windy." I pointed. "But don't kill yourself because here's where you catch back on."

WorldTour teams finally arrived in their fancy buses, and the shadow of Cannondale-Garmin's rig loomed over our cargo van. I stared longingly through the steam of my breath, remembering the reclining seats, the stocked refrigerator, and the staff asking if they could get you anything, and then the door opened and Sebastian Langeveld's big smile popped out, inviting me in for espresso. "Later, suckers!" I said to my teammates, climbing up the stairs.

From the riders to the staff, everyone on the bus wanted a hug, and I was relieved that I wasn't dead to them after a few months. I'd been a good teammate, which didn't earn me a contract, but I got some friends out of it, and a shot of espresso in a plastic cup.*

In the race, though, I didn't have enough friends. The year before, I'd grown accustomed to a certain amount of respect in the pack—if I wanted a spot in line, I could usually have it—but now, my Optum jersey looked like a turnstile to WorldTour riders. I got pushed around and had to work hard to stay at the front.

The night before the second stage, I had a dream that I attacked

---

* Half a shot, because I spilled some getting off the bus.

solo and won, so I went for it in the final laps around a small village, to prove once and for all that I should have stayed with Cannondale-Garmin. Fans lined the streets on the steep climb, screaming in my ear as I flew by, and for a minute it felt like San Luis all over again.

If the WorldTour teams hesitated and gave me just a bit of a leash, I'd have won and looked like a genius, but they kept me close and caught me with a few miles to go, so I looked like an idiot. After the hard effort, I couldn't hold on to the front group on the last climb, so I lost two minutes and any hope of finishing the week in the top ten overall. Woodsy made it, and a few stages later he came in fourth on the mountaintop finish. I was fifteenth that day, which is pretty damn good, but nobody noticed.

JV had also figured out the identity of "Rusty Woods," and I failed to hide my jealousy when my old boss praised him on Twitter.

"Have fun at Three Days of West Flanders," I said.

When they took my bike off the roof for the final stage, the rear wheel was full of blood and feathers.

"Jesus! Another dead bird!" I said, in disbelief.

"What's that Hitchcock movie?" asked a mechanic.

"It's just called *The Birds*," Woods answered, a little too fast.

There's no such thing as a bad omen. There's no such thing as a bad omen.

That day was expected to finish in a field sprint. Optum had hired Canadian Guillaume Boivin to be a leadout rider to help our main sprinter, Eric Young, position for fast finishes, but I'd overheard Guillaume complaining about it. "I don't get a World-Tour contract by dropping Eric off at two hundred meters to go and finishing thirtieth," he said, plotting to selfishly save his legs for his own result.

Guillaume might have fit in better in an earlier era of stage races, which were designed to be the ultimate tests of endurance and self-reliance. There were no leadouts or domestiques in the 1913 Tour de France, for example, when race leader Eugène Christophe stopped to repair his own broken forks, and was still penalized for receiving assistance, because a young boy pumped the bellows while the yellow jersey welded the steel.

More than a hundred years later, pro cycling had evolved into a pure team sport, with packs and drafting and mechanics, so winning a modern race demands full effort from nine riders. Reality proves no match for tradition, though, so instead of declaring the team as the winner (like they do in baseball, for example), races still only make room for one on the podium. This explains the salary disparity on WorldTour teams (and probably the doping issues), incentivizing guys like Guillaume to race for their own results instead of working for the team.

I tried to help our sprinter myself, dragging him into decent position with a couple miles to go, but it wasn't much and Eric wasn't at his best. Coming out of a cold winter in Colorado, he finished dead last overall in Algarve, but he handled it well.

"There should be a prize for finishing last," he joked that night at dinner. "A jersey or something."

"How about a rusty, tarnished trophy, filled with dog shit?" someone suggested.

"I was thinking two minutes with a podium girl in a closet," said Eric.*

"What would you do with the other minute and a half?" I asked, collecting high fives.

I was twentieth overall, which also earns no trophy. If I hadn't lost time on the second stage because of a dumb dream, I'd have been eighth. Eighth would have been nice.

---

* He's a dreamer, but Eric had hooked up with a podium girl or two. They always go for the sprinters.

CHAPTER 39

THE TEAM KEPT us in Portugal another three weeks for two amateur races, which wasn't worth all the time away from home, but we wouldn't have been there in the first place if we didn't all love hanging out with a bunch of dudes in a foreign country. Vilamoura had one café with decent Wi-Fi, so we spent the mornings there on our laptops. We were all gathered in the corner booth when Woods showed us an interview with Chris Horner about the upcoming season. "I've won Redlands four times," he'd boasted. "They might as well call it the Chris Horner Cycling Classic."

Redlands had changed its course for 2015, with a stage finish on Oak Glen, a tough climb that hadn't been part of the race since the early 2000s when Horner was winning. I'd bet anything that he called the organizers and asked them to put it back as a personal favor.

"What a cocky bastard!" someone said. "This guy cheated his way to a Vuelta win, and now he's racing in the U.S. against a bunch of clean kids and bragging about how easy it'll be!"

"It's like getting away with murder, and then doing doughnuts in the victim's yard," I agreed.

"We're gonna make him pay for this, buddy!" Woodsy smiled, giving me a fist bump.

In the afternoons, we'd train on climbs along the ocean that reminded me of L.A., except there weren't nearly as many Ferraris and the midride coffee was cheaper. For less than 2 euros each, we sat outside, drinking espresso and eating pasteis de nata, a flaky Portuguese pastry. Local kids would see us and run to get their own bikes, doing jumps off the sidewalk to show off.

"We get paid for this," I reminded everyone, with more high fives and fist bumps.

To spice up the rides, we'd race over hills and sprint for city limits signs. One afternoon, I was first to the top of a climb on a dirt road (Woods took the day off or I'd have been second). It dead-ended at a small farm, where I admired the view and caught my breath while an old man emerged from an olive grove holding a rake. He stared like I was a UFO, and I waved, knowing that five more guys looking exactly like me would blast around the corner any minute, only to make a U-turn and go looking for the next one. Did the farmer tell his wife about their visitors that day? Would she believe him?

If a dirt road got too rough, we'd have to give up and turn around. I'd yell, "Abort!" and then apologize to Jesse, who was raised Christian and pro-life. He always laughed.

The team hired a local soigneur for massage in the afternoons. Jonas was reluctant to sign me because of my friendship with Tom Danielson, but this guy fell through the cracks—a big fan of Alberto Contador.

"Conta-Dor! Best cyclist ever!" he insisted, in a raspy voice.

"Look, if you're including the dopers, Lance Armstrong is obviously the best ever," I argued.

The soigneur was deeply offended and never spoke to me again. When I told the guys about it, Guillaume said that it wasn't

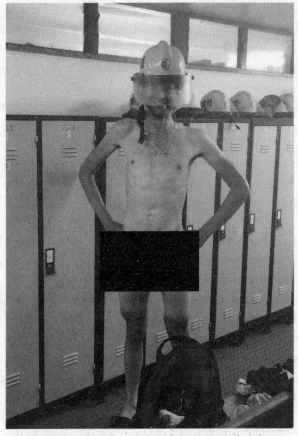

One day, we took the van into the mountains for a longer ride, and when it rained, the soigneur found a fire station where we could change and shower. I forget who took this picture, but I assume they'd rather not be credited.

fair to be friends with one doper and resent others. I argued that it's perfectly fine to consider more than one factor in assessing someone's character, explaining that one was a criminal master-mind who threatened his enemies' livelihoods, while the other was a guy who took some drugs but then earned my friendship and helped make my dreams come true. When I mentioned the tear in Tom's eye on the last mountain in San Luis, I started to cry myself. I went out for a walk so they wouldn't notice.

Guillaume was insisting that there's no such thing as a gray area, but before bed, he pulled a prescription medication that would have been illegal without some doctor claiming that he had asthma. The inhaler sounded like a harmonica, so I bellowed Bob Dylan songs while Zirbel slapped his knees to the beat.

Hummmmmmmm.

"Once upon a time you dressed so fine, you threw the bums a dime in your prime, didn't youuuuuu?"

Hummmmmmmm.

Guillaume had also mentioned that on his previous team, they used *caffeine suppositories* for time trials, but he saw nothing wrong with that.

"So if you order a sandwich, and the waiter sticks it up your ass, there's nothing wrong with that?" asked Woods.

Training took a dent when someone brought a cold to the apartment. Three of us skipped the next race in favor of bed rest, but Woodsy won anyway. Real Talent doesn't need teammates at Portuguese local races.

CHAPTER 40

THE FLIGHT BACK to Los Angeles was turbulent, and the woman next to me kept grabbing my arm, afraid. When we landed, she went straight to the smoking lounge. Quiz: which one is more likely to kill her?

I'd only been gone a month, but it was another adjustment for me and my fiancée when I got home. Joanna had had a busy week, so my car was out of gas, dishes filled the sink, and clothes were all over the floor. I'd just sold my business to buy that house, so I'd only been home five minutes and I was already angry. I thought this year was going to be easier, but we still hadn't gotten it right. I asked Zirbel how he handled it with his family, and he said his son kept asking for Mommy when he picked him up.

I tried to channel the frustration into my training. My next workout was three sets of ten-minute "hill repeats," so I headed to Nichols Canyon in Hollywood, a climb I'd done a hundred times, where my record was 9:50. I felt good when I reached the flat section where the road makes a few sweeping bends, but someone had started building a new house since I'd left, and a small puddle ran into the street from the construction site. In most places, a little water on the road is no big deal, but in the dry hills of Los

Angeles, that's all it took to send me sliding. When you crash at a high heart rate, your blood is pumping hard, so the blood really squirts out, and I found myself trying to calm down the construction workers, begging them not to call an ambulance.*

Normally, I wouldn't finish my workout after a crash, but I was motivated for the San Dimas time trial that weekend. I'd won it twice before so it looked like easy prize money, and I was excited to see how much faster I'd go after a year in the WorldTour. Plus, it would be a good test with the Redlands "Chris Horner" Classic coming up a week later. I brushed myself off, went home to change my torn clothes and clean my wounds, and headed back out for my last two intervals—this time on Benedict Canyon in Beverly Hills, which had no puddles.

---

* I once went to the ER for a few stitches after a crash. There was an old man with a broken leg in the waiting room, but I had so much blood on me, triage took me in first.

CHAPTER 41

OPTUM HAD BOTH a men's team and a women's team with all the same sponsors, but we were segregated when it came to staff, race schedule, and equipment. The men opted not to send a team to San Dimas, so I had to pay the entry fee and handle my own logistics, but the women were sending a full squad with staff and equipment, and kindly offered to lend me a set of climbing wheels for the time trial. I pulled my Toyota into the dirt in the 100-degree sun, across from a shaded area where they were warming up on stationary trainers, grabbed the wheels from their mechanic, and leaned them against my car.

I was starting to get dressed when a friend slammed his brakes to give me a hug, skidding his rear wheel and coming to a stop just short of my chest. It was a tiny impact, but his front brake pierced the scab on my knee and sent a stream of blood down my shin. Afraid of staining my socks, I sat in the car to wipe myself with a napkin, and then noticed the Optum women's van leaving across the street.

I was already looking at a short warm-up, but I might as well take their spot so I could do it in the shade. I turned on the engine, hit the gas to make a quick U-turn, and heard the crunch of the wheels I'd borrowed, which I'd left leaning on the door and were now broken in half under my worn-out tires. I borrowed another set of wheels from strangers and rushed to the start line.

In 2013, my buildup to the San Dimas TT was a month of intervals with Tom Danielson, resulting in a win with a time of 14:03. In 2015, it was a head cold in Portugal and a rough patch in my relationship, which didn't mix well with the ultrasmooth, wet patch of pavement I encountered on Nichols Canyon.* Maybe if I'd slept better and been more focused, I could have avoided that crash, and then I wouldn't have been wiping my bloody leg or run over the wheels. That could have meant a decent warm-up and better pacing in the race, but I went too hard at the start, hemorrhaged time in the last kilometer, and came in fourth with a time of 14:38.

I read a poem that afternoon by Rudyard Kipling, called "If," and I'd like to share some lines here that brought me much-needed inspiration.

> If you can make one heap of all your winnings
> And risk it on one turn of pitch-and-toss,
> And lose, and start again at your beginnings
> And never breathe a word about your loss

Before you call me pretentious for quoting poetry, I only read "If" because it was framed above the urinal at Martha Green's Eating Room in Redlands where I went to meet my dentist friend for lunch. I must have been hydrated, because I read the whole thing, and decided that instead of going back home to L.A. and feeling sorry for myself, I'd go to Big Bear to get back on track.

---

* You know how if you miss a night of sleep or you're in a big rush, you're more likely to spill your coffee? I'm more likely to crash my bike.

The prize money at San Dimas was skewed in favor of the men, so I asked Optum's women's director to pick up my check for fourth place and throw it in with their "heap of winnings." That saved me a drive to San Dimas, made me a hero for gender equality, and helped me feel a little better about the wheels I'd killed.

CHAPTER 42

IN MY FIRST book, I explained why Big Bear was perfect for altitude training, but of all the folks who asked me for advice over the years, only one wanted it bad enough to listen—Mike Woods. He was settled into a rental house with his wife, Elly, and while we trained the next day, she marinated a flank steak that he grilled in the evening. (I brought a kale salad and a bottle of wine. I'm not an animal.)

Elly reminded me of my friend Pat, who'd given up bike racing to team up with his now-wife Gwen, the triathlete. Pat cooked and cleaned so Gwen could focus, and she'd already qualified for the 2016 Olympics. Elly was traveling with Mike, working remotely to pay the bills while he chased a dream. He hadn't won a big race yet, but it was only a matter of time.

Woodsy and I rode together for a week, trading fist bumps at the top of each mountain. Then, determined to outwork him, I'd secretly finish each ride with an extra hour on my time trial bike. I got lots of sleep, and I never even entered Big Bear's fudge shop. Okay, I tried to go once, but they close at eight thirty.*

---

* I'm still angry about this. Who would want fudge before eight thirty?

Mike beat me to the top of Mt. Baldy, which would be the critical GC stage at the Tour of California, and again when we checked out the uphill finish for the Redlands Classic. I hung on as long as I could but finally blew up, watching his alien vein run off into Oak Glen's apple orchards.

I had nightmares about that vein, but I felt ready when I arrived at the host house in Redlands, opening the guidebook that the race hands out. Inside the front cover was a list of previous winners: names like Vaughters. Vande Velde. Mancebo. Former world champion Santiago Botero. Horner. Horner. Horner. Horner. Me.

CHAPTER 43

T HE FIRST STAGE at Redlands was a circuit race, with tight turns and a hill up to the finish line each lap, so Jonas asked me to do the leadout. That typically means throwing elbows at high speed, so I'd always chickened out when I tried on BISSELL, but I wasn't scared after a year in Europe. My timing wasn't perfect and our sprinters got swarmed, but my legs felt great.

The second stage was an out-and-back time trial on the east side of Big Bear Lake—a road that I'd ridden a hundred times but didn't suit my abilities at all. Learning from my disorganization in San Dimas, I loaded my backpack the night before, pinned my numbers, and put my shoes in my rain bag in the team car. In the morning, we had a leisurely breakfast, drove up the mountain, and then, ninety minutes before my race, I realized that my shoes were gone. On Garmin-Sharp, rain bags never left the cars, but on Optum, with fewer staff and vehicles, someone took them out to save space, and there wasn't enough time to drive back to get them.

Shoes are impossible to replace for a pro cyclist. Aside from having a certain size and brand, I used $300 custom insoles, and it usually takes days to get the cleats how I like them. *You want to be a professional? You think you should race in Europe? You can't even remember your shoes! Chris Horner has his shoes. What if Vaughters hears about this? You don't deserve to be in the WorldTour.*

I circled the parking lot in a panic, asking friends on other teams if they had spares, but I couldn't find anything in my size. A spectator overheard and said he had some ten-and-a-halfs at home, so I started my warm-up in sneakers while he went to get them. My teammates were so angry they couldn't look at me, and rivals smirked when word got out, walking by our trailer to see a race favorite setting up new cleats, minutes before I was supposed to go off.

Stefano had just finished when I lined up at the start. I took his advice on pacing and wind conditions and came in fourth, eight seconds behind winner Tom Zirbel. Fourth was disappointing at the uphill TT in San Dimas, but it was a great result on the flat course in Big Bear: five seconds faster than Lachlan, thirty seconds ahead of Horner, and a minute up on Woods. That made me the undisputed team leader, but most importantly, my teammates weren't mad anymore.

"Listen, guys, if there's one thing I learned in the WorldTour, it's the importance of a long cooldown," I lied. "Let's all go ride another thirty minutes, real easy."

They fell for it. I took them straight to the Fudge Shoppe.*

While mechanics packed the van, I changed the cleats back for the spectator who lent me his shoes. For saving my career, I made Jonas give him a team-logo hat.

The third stage was the new course: four long laps of wide-open roads, finishing on top of Oak Glen. Everyone who beat me in the time trial would get dropped, Horner or Lachlan would

---

* Before you call me a hypocrite, I put the fudge in my pocket and didn't eat it until nine p.m.

probably win the stage, and all I had to do was stay close to take the overall lead. My teammates lined up at the front when the climb started, setting the pace as I barked orders from behind, six guys taking turns giving everything they had.

On the rare occasion that someone believes in me, my first thought is, *It's about time. They said I was too old, that I started too late, but I proved them all wrong.* Now, I was back on a Continental team, but at least my new teammates had faith. They trained for months, flew to California and loaded up on breakfast, all building up to this moment so I could get the result. That's when my second thought always kicks in: *They're crazy to think I can do this. I'm gonna buckle and let everyone down. Horner's gonna put two minutes on me.*

Most of the guys pulled for a minute or two, and then it was Woodsy's turn. He was on the front for miles while I sat behind, telling him where to punch it and where to rest, encouraging him like Tom had done for me.

"Nice, Woodsy! You're killing it, buddy!"*

Woods shattered the pack, and with 1,500 meters to go, he was still fresh enough to talk to me.

"Is the yellow jersey dropped?" he asked, looking back for the guy who took the race lead after the time trial.

I laughed. "He's been gone for a while, man. I just can't lose much time to any of these guys."

We sized up the remnants of the lead group. Lachlan was dropped, and Horner drooled, hunched over his handlebars. Everyone else was gasping, clearly on the limit, while Mike and I were having a conversation. *Oh. I don't have to worry about losing time. I'm going to win.* I attacked, hitting the finish with enough of a lead to zip up my jersey and kiss the ring that hung on my neck.

---

* Everyone on Optum was using "buddy" by now. It was contagious.

Finishing the job on Oak Glen.

Woods proved that he was the best climber in the race, still coming in second after selling out for me. He kept riding after he crossed the line, full speed, into my arms with a big smile. I kissed him on the mouth.

A race has so much preparation, buildup, nervousness, and doubt, when you win there's a high of victory, but then the relief is the best part: it's over and nothing went wrong. I tried to ignore the feeling I get when people believe in me and it all works out: *I'm going to pay for this someday.*

Joanna's race finished a few minutes after ours, and it was great to have her there instead of telling her about it on the phone.

She'd asked someone from one of the men's teams for a water bottle, and when he handed it to her, he said, "Tell Phil that the lazy mechanic from his book says hi." I'm not sure who that was, but if you're reading this, lazy mechanic: "Hey."

Chris Horner didn't congratulate me when he finished, but a reporter from Cyclingnews.com did. He'd done the interview where Chris mouthed off about how easy Redlands would be, and he suspected that I was peeved about it. Or I might have texted him and told him I was peeved. Perhaps I didn't say I was peeved, exactly. Maybe I told him that Chris was a cocky sack of shit and we were going to teach him a lesson.

"So, Phil, Chris Horner said that Redlands was his race. How does it feel that you've put over a minute on him after three stages?"

My response was the headline that night:

"It's great to be leading the Chris Horner Cycling Classic."

Woods and I stepped off of the podium and coasted down Oak Glen toward our host house, still laughing. We'd dominated. We were heroes. Gods. Then a red Mini Cooper convertible pulled out in front of us—a quick reminder of our mortality. I had to swerve into Mike as he moved toward the gutter, leaning on each other to take up as little room as possible. Being a pro cyclist is a weird level of fame. You're well-known and respected in this tiny bubble, where you get attention and validation and love in short bursts a few times a year. There's a cheer and roar of the crowd that's a real thrill, but it's crazy how fast it goes quiet. Or it goes "Honk! Get off the road!"

Plenty of fans still supported Horner, but Vaughters didn't, so he sent a message to say that he really enjoyed my quote. Then he said that Ted King was retiring at the end of the season, which would open up a spot for me on Cannondale. I knew what his promises were worth, so until I had a contract in hand, I didn't get my hopes up.

JV's next message was about Woods.

"What's Rusty like? He has the legs, but is he a nice guy? Good bike rider? WorldTour mentality?"

I'm ashamed to admit that I had to think about it before I replied. In the WorldTour, we're all fighting over a few hundred jobs. For North Americans, it's more like fifty. For twenty-nine-year-old climbers with limited experience, it was hard to imagine that there was more than one. I won't pretend that JV would have listened to my recommendation, but it was probably in my best interest to tell him that Woodsy was a prima donna who couldn't handle a corner. That's what I would have done if I didn't like him.

"Woodsy's a champ," I said. "He deserves a shot."

The team did a great job controlling the criterium the next day, but it still got physical and dangerous. With four laps to go, I knew I was taking a bad line through a corner in the fight for position, but I'd ripped faster turns on wet roads all over Europe the year before, so I didn't think I was taking a risk. That made it very confusing when I found myself sliding on my ass.

I'd recently met a guy who was recovering from a bad crash on his rear end. His intestines had spilled out, so he had to carry them to the hospital to get sewn back up.* When Jesse Anthony stopped to help me, that story was the only thing on my mind.

"Phil, are you alright?" he asked.

"Yeah, I think I'm okay, but, dude, did my intestines fall out of my ass?"

Jesse gave me the side eye, with the "you can't be serious" brow, but he had a look at my butt and promised that although I did have blood on my saddle, everything looked fine. Since the crash was within the last five laps, officials gave me the same time as the pack.

---

* Grossed out? He went into way more detail, but I'll leave it at that. You're welcome.

Jesse checking out my butt.

Checking my rear end was above and beyond the call of friendship, so when our massages were finished, I took Jesse on a mandate. At eleven thirty p.m., the night before the final stage of one of the biggest races of the year, while all of our rivals were resting, Jesse and I had burritos and ice cream (carne asada and salted caramel, respectively). And the next morning, I swept the kitchen at the host house and cooked breakfast for the soigneurs. I probably should have gone to bed early and stayed off my feet, focused on my race, but I decided to be a good person instead. If that means I don't win, so be it.

I doubt if Chris Horner swept any floors. He was looking forward to the Sunset circuit race, which he'd won before. When we lined up for introductions, I was chatting with friends when Horner yelled to me from across the street, so everyone could hear.

"Hey, Gaimon, last time I checked, one plus one equals two, so if you win today, that's still only half as many Redlands as I've won."

After a decade in Europe and a Grand Tour win, Chris still had to remind us how good he was. He cared more about Redlands than I did, and I was depriving him of his victory and rubbing his face in it in the media. Now, Horner wanted to talk-trash, but all he could come up with was this bizarre, fraction-based insult. My anger turned to pity, but everyone was staring at me, so I had to say something.

"Dude, you won the Vuelta."

Then the race started, and it was chaos. If you picture the Redlands Classic as a fireworks show, the Sunset stage is the last few minutes where they shoot off whatever's left. Attacks never end on the hills and tight turns, and if you leave the top ten you might as well drop out. My team controlled it well, but when Lachlan joined a breakaway, we had to burn a few guys to catch him, so on the last lap, it was just me and Woodsy left in the front group.

Sensing vulnerability, all the favorites took turns attacking, but I didn't panic. I let them dangle, waited for the climb, and launched up it like I was shot out of a cannon. I caught everyone and went solo over the top, just to show them I could. I controlled the pack on the descent and a few flat laps through town, alternating quick decisions and short efforts, with a list in my head of which riders I had to chase down because they were close to me on GC versus who was a few minutes behind, so catching them was someone else's responsibility.

When I won Redlands in 2012, it came down to two seconds, and when it was over, I sat in the car, shaking with pain and unable to speak. Mentally, I compared it to a chess game, and if the race that year was a lap longer, I'd have fallen to fifth overall. Three years later, it was checkers, and I had all kings. One more lap, and I'd still have won the stage.

Remembering the Rolexes on Garmin-Sharp, I decided to buy gifts for teammates and staff who'd helped me that week. On my budget, it would have been funny to hand out fifteen Casios, but I gave them each a decent bottle of wine instead. I also gave Alex Howes $500, because when Nathan Haas sent congratulations, he mentioned that the Renault had died. Howes blamed himself for leaving it on the street all winter, but I don't think he drove it more than twenty miles, so I wanted to give him something. Is $500 fair? Tell me if it's not fair and I'll send more.*

I partied after that first Redlands win, going out to the bars in Athens, and I paid for it at the next races. This time, my teammates cracked some beers, because Optum had been chasing that win for a decade and never pulled it off, but to me it was hardly worth celebrating. What was once a miracle was now an expectation, and a Continental win didn't feel like much after a year in the WorldTour. Besides, I had bigger fish to fry.

---

* Also: never buy a Renault.

CHAPTER 44

HE TOUR OF CALIFORNIA is a fish.

CHAPTER 45

MY BUTT WAS still swollen and bruised when I got home, but I stopped complaining when I read about a WorldTour race in Spain, where the sprint finish included a series of waist-high metal poles, causing a huge pileup. BMC's Peter Stetina broke his leg, but the new union took action with a protest the next day and a proposal of basic safety requirements for WorldTour events.

It seemed like every year, someone in the WorldTour would end up in a coma or worse—from a crash, or getting hit by a team car or a camera motorcycle. Now, they were going to *talk* about it and make a *proposal*. It's as if you were clinging to driftwood with the *Titanic* sinking in the distance, so you decided it was time to have a discussion about icebergs.

Thomas Dekker also had a roller-coaster spring, attempting cycling's sacred one-hour distance record, riding as many laps as he could around a track to end his career on a high note. He fell short by 270 meters, but don't feel too bad for him, because Thomas went straight to his billionaire girlfriend's mansion in Beverly Hills, starting his retirement with months of relaxing by the pool, socializing with A-list actors, producers, and artists. (His girlfriend is

Jewish, so he also attended a celebrity-filled Passover Seder, and I made him promise not to mention his foreskin.) Our ride through Griffith Park was Dekker's first time on a bike in weeks.

"Still doing this shit, huh, Thomas?"

"Oh"—gasp—"for sho'!"

I'd planned to spend two more weeks in Big Bear to prepare for Gila and California, but Jonas wanted Optum to win a national championship for the team time trial, which was held in Greenville, South Carolina, four days after Redlands finished. I pointed out that a cross-country trip would take away from my altitude training, and we hadn't done much TTT practice, while George Hincapie's young team was in the middle of a TTT-specific training camp.* Our riders were stronger, but I feared that Team Hincapie might beat us on efficiency and experience.

"The last thing we want," I told Jonas, "is to fly out there, compromising our prep for races that matter like Gila and Cali, and then finish second."

Jonas still wanted to go for it, and I didn't need much convincing. I'd been chasing a national championship for ten years, and that stars and stripes jersey was my Moby Dick.

Jesse and I flew together from LAX, with a connection in Dallas, where the weather turned biblical. All flights were canceled, and it was a very long line to get rebooked for the next day. Careful to implement *everything* I'd learned in the WorldTour, I bought us a drink for every extra hour we were trapped at the airport, so I was two margaritas in when I remembered to report my location to USADA for drug testing.

---

* Their budget had been bolstered that year by two giants in finance—Bahamian Mark Holowesko, who seemed like a good guy, and an investment fund called Citadel, which was the villain in a Michael Lewis book about the corrupt high-frequency stock exchange. It seemed that Citadel had robbed America of billions and caused a stock market crash, but my friends had a very nice bus.

Normally, updates to USADA's automated e-mail whereabouts system look like this:

NAME: Phil Gaimon
SPORT: Cycling
<date>
<address>
<1-hour time window I'll be available for testing>

That night in Dallas, this was the best I could do:

Phil Gaimon
Bicycles!

DATE: 4/15 but it's almost 4/16
LOCATION: It's all fucked. I'm at the airport in Dallas right now but I don't know where I'll be tonight. I think I fly to Charlotte tomorrow. I promise I'm not doping.

We slept for a few minutes at a cheap motel, got up early, ate at Waffle House, flew into Raleigh because there wasn't anything to Greenville or Charlotte, and rented a car for the four-hour drive to the race. On the course, inefficiency cost us, and we finished a close second to Hincapie's team, just as I'd feared.

"How'd I end up ahead of you?" I asked Jesse that night, looking at a photo from the race and remembering the order we'd planned at the start.

"And here's one where I'm behind Zirbel, like, a minute later!" he said. It sounded like we were recapping a drunken orgy.

The return trip from North Carolina found me stranded once again, with more bad weather in Dallas. I skipped the margaritas that time, but with my biggest races coming up, I got home with a cough, a fever, a silver medal, and a week of my life I'd never get back.

CHAPTER 46

I ARRIVED IN NEW Mexico with a few of my teammates eight days before the Tour of the Gila, which we
hoped was enough time to catch up on training and acclimate to
the high altitude. The team arranged lodging at a church that
rented out tiny bedrooms, where I kept finding bits of glass in the
carpet, and I didn't feel entirely safe.*

Gila's race organizers asked us to speak at an elementary
school one afternoon. I'd done it before, but I never knew what to
say. Are we supposed to talk about bike racing? Am I supposed to
tell kids how great it is to follow a dream when that barely worked
out for me? Should people who win the lottery tell their friends to
buy a ticket? It's not right to show a pro athlete to a kid in rural
New Mexico. Don't make it seem real. Don't let them think it's
attainable. I just talked about exercise and nutrition.

Mostly, life was boring at the church. One morning, we saw a
quail in the bushes and went to Walmart to buy $8.99 slingshots.
Will Routley actually killed one, spent hours pulling out the guts

---

* I usually make small talk when I meet someone new, but when we meet in a shared
kitchen at $20-a-night accommodations in Silver City, New Mexico, and they're in their
midthirties with teeth like a box of crayons, I just smile and say "hi."

and feathers, and cooked it on the grill.* Later that night, we found a website that listed average penis size by different nationalities, and made a guessing game out of who was biggest.†

The first stage of the Tour of the Gila was a mountaintop finish called Mogollon. Since Woods and I had just finished first and second on Oak Glen, our team should have put two guys on the front to keep the breakaway close, but Jonas didn't like wearing out his domestiques so early in the race, so Guillaume joined a breakaway that went out to twelve minutes, and a Colombian guy who'd tested positive in 2008 easily dropped our sprinter to win the stage. Woods and I were still in good position overall, but Mike was the best climber in the race, so we missed an opportunity to get his first big win. There's rolling the dice, and there's rolling them into a sewer.

We made up for it in a field sprint the next day, lining up at the front like a WorldTour team for the last few miles. I got the timing right in the leadout, and Eric Young took the win. After a decent time trial later in the week, I was in second overall before the final, Gila Monster course. I'd attacked there in 2013 and barely missed the overall win, but I struggled this year, plummeting down the GC while Woodsy won the stage.

Knowing from experience that results in Utah and Colorado would be too late for a WorldTour contract, I'd planned my season around the Tour of California in May. Believing in that target, I thought I could take risks with breakaways in Portugal, or I could squeeze in a win at team time trial nationals in April. I'd put all my eggs in one basket, and now it hit me that my preparation was far from ideal. The big event was coming up, and I wasn't at my best.

---

* There was barely any meat, so I didn't ask for a taste. He said it was gross and slathered it in ketchup.

† This made it awkward when I wanted to borrow Will's tape measure to check my saddle height.

Stefano and Katie had driven to Gila instead of flying, which took nine hours. That would be about the same as packing my bikes, driving to Tucson to catch a plane, and dragging my bags through LAX, but a road trip with my friends would be a hell of a lot more fun. I canceled my plane ticket, jumped in the car with them, and fell asleep in my own bed just after midnight.

CHAPTER 47

A T THE START of the Tour of California, our bike sponsor delivered a custom-painted frame for me, covered in cookies. Pat Lemieux had the idea as a fun PR stunt, and I'd had to overcome resistance from team management, who'd complained about too many bikes to build, low inventory on components, and limited space in the trailer, but finally it was ready. Fans loved it, so it made a great launch platform for our sponsor's new race frame, but there was one little problem: they sent a size 58 and I ride a 56. The "cookie bike" hung around for photos, and then someone shipped it off to the warehouse.

Talansky was Cannondale-Garmin's leader at the Tour of California, riding a plain old green bike with no desserts on it whatsoever. We chatted before the first stage, and he asked if Optum had any Clif Zbars we could give him for the rest of the week. When he dropped out of the race later that day complaining of allergies, some fans accused him of quitting on purpose—that he was being a prima donna and he never planned to finish. I love a conspiracy, but I can tell you that one's not true, or he wouldn't have lined up the snacks.

Our team had been experiencing some technical problems that

spring, with skipping gears, rubbing brakes, and even broken forks, which left the rider holding a set of handlebars suddenly detached from the bike, with nowhere to go but down. I don't want to sound ungrateful, but if we can agree that riders in the WorldTour are stronger, it's fair to say that top teams also get higher-end equipment sponsors, and the cream of the crop when it comes to staff. Factor in the experience they get from big races, and more funding so they're less overworked, and it makes sense that things fall through the cracks on smaller teams. Or they just crack entirely. Continental riders have so many disadvantages, it was a miracle that I'd ever managed to get to Europe, and hard to think I could repeat it.

I thought I'd solved one problem, contacting our wheel sponsor before the Tour of Cali, confirming that we'd been using too much air pressure in our tires.* When we knocked it down to 85 psi, I stayed comfortably in the lead group on the narrow descent from Mt. Hamilton while guys from other teams launched into ditches and trees, and one guy ran into Mike Woods, sending him to the ground. I almost waited for Woodsy, but Jonas was behind us in the team car to help him catch up, so I decided to be selfish.

With one rider from the breakaway dangling just ahead when Woods rejoined the front group, it looked like the WorldTour teams had everything under control, but they never managed to catch the guy. Toms Skujiņš, a twenty-five-year-old Latvian with Team Hincapie, wasn't much of a climber or a sprinter, which only made it more impressive that he'd been winning races all year, culminating with a big one here in California. People like Superman because he was born strong, but that's no achievement, if you think about it. I've always had more respect for Batman, who invented his own superpowers. That was Toms Skujiņš, winning races by cunning and determination—another Continental rider trying to take a WorldTour spot, and I couldn't help but like him.

---

* Harder tires can get you more speed, but less control.

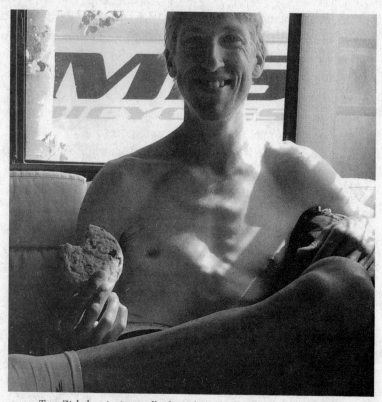

Tom Zirbel, enjoying really the only perk of having me on his team.

When we arrived at the hotel that night, team mechanics were playing hula hoop with a wheel that I'd cracked. Our wheel sponsor's new wide rim design was shown to improve rolling resistance and aerodynamics, but our tire sponsor didn't make a wide tire, so with the lower pressure I wanted, the carbon would crack on bumpy roads. Thus began a months-long battle, where mechanics pumped the tires to high pressure to protect the rims and do their job, and I let air out at the start line to protect my skin and do mine. They got several $1,000 hula hoops out of the deal, so everybody wins.

That night, I had a secret meeting with Doug Ryder, the owner of the MTN-Qhubeka team. I'd contacted him too late to join for 2015, but he'd followed my social media after his sponsors Cervélo and Castelli recommended me. We had such a great conversation, I thought I might leave the room with a contract for 2016, but he said he wouldn't know about money until after the Tour de France, so we should talk again in August.

I had a similar meeting with Drapac, a well-funded middle-tier Australian team that was planning to race more in Europe the next year. No offers, but it looked like I'd have options.

Since they'd first announced the 2015 route for the Tour of California, I'd looked forward to the time trial in Big Bear, where I'd enjoy familiar roads, a home-away-from-hometown cheering section, and hopefully some fudge, but after years of short ski seasons that must have been tough on their economy, the snow showed up in mid-May, and thanks in part to our union, the time trial moved to the Six Flags parking lot in Santa Clarita. The short, flat course wasn't ideal for me, but I came in a respectable thirtieth, with Joanna's dad cheering from the passenger seat in my follow car. Peter Sagan killed us, winning by fifteen seconds.

When Sagan joined Tinkoff-Saxo, I read an interview where his agent patted himself on the back for factoring in different teams' atmospheres and stability when he decided where his star client would go, but he obviously just went with the one that offered the most money, headed by an attention-seeking, chauvinistic Russian oligarch named Oleg Tinkov, who referred to his riders as "toys." Now, after slim results at the spring classics, Tinkov was publicly threatening to cut Sagan's pay and "buy" another rider, like they were slaves or cattle. *This is the dream job we're chasing? You work your way to the top to be berated by this guy?* Sagan was making $4 million a year, but I actually felt bad for him. The only upside was that Oleg also blamed their director,

Bjarne Riis. Bjarne should have been kicked out of the sport long before for doping, so now he was finally fired, as a scapegoat.*

Sagan had already won a sprint stage that week, but he made a statement with the time trial victory, taking the overall lead into the infamous Mt. Baldy stage, where he was expected to lose ten minutes and I hoped to move into the top ten.

Peter was still there after the first climb, just behind Team Sky as they pushed the pace on Glendora Mountain Road. I knew the roads, but the next hour was harder than I'd expected, as the few remaining Continental riders were pushed to the back of the pack, where accelerations were amplified on the rolling terrain. I was too out of breath to show Woods the spot where I once saw a discarded dildo on the ground, and he was dealing with stomach issues, in no mood for my shenanigans.

"I'm afraid I'll shit myself if I go any harder," he confided. (Note to self: look up "confide." I hope it doesn't mean it's a secret and you're not supposed to talk about it in a book.)

When we previewed the course in early April, it was 100 degrees on Baldy, and Woodsy and I stopped for water four times in six hours. Now, in mid-May, there was snow on the ground, but the roads were clear so the cold was refreshing, like a York Peppermint Pattie, except Team Sky was on the front trying to kill us. The pack blew up on the final climb and I finished fifteenth, despite encouragement from Joanna, wearing a cookie monster hat as she chased me in the last kilometer.†

Woods's stomach caught up to him and he finished way down.

"Man, I had nothing today," he admitted, heartbroken.

---

* And who says two wrongs don't make a right?
† Joanna was angry later when she heard that a pretty girl brought me a cookie at the finish line. Still waiting on her to set a wedding date, it was nice to see her jealous, but I only accepted the cookie to be polite. What am I supposed to do, refuse it? I swear I didn't have a bite.

I bent down toward his butt and took a loud sniff. "But you didn't shit yourself!" I put my hand up for a high five.

He forced a smile and gave me a good slap. Woodsy never leaves you hanging.

Joe Dombrowski had only been with Cannondale-Garmin for a few months, but when Talansky got sick, he became their protected rider for California. Years before, he'd come out of nowhere to finish fourth on Mt. Baldy—a ride that landed him a contract with Team Sky and a hefty paycheck. Now, at twenty-four, he had a nice apartment in France, a Porsche, some expensive clothes that looked hilarious on his skinny frame,* and thanks to all of Team Sky's resources and development, he finished fourth on Baldy again, proving that nobody really knows how training works. The real surprise that day was Sagan coming in sixth, still a favorite for the overall win with time bonuses up for grabs on the final stage.

The last day of the Tour of California began in downtown Los Angeles. It was early but my friends came out to cheer, and as the hometown boy, the race organization said they'd introduce me to the crowd along with all the favorites. They knocked on the bus and told me when to be ready, and I continued my prerace rituals: joking around with the guys, drinking coffee, and, of course, the prerace poop, but when it was my turn in the bus's tiny bathroom, it had been a long week, and whoever was in charge of cleaning it had been shirking their (wait for it . . .) duty (!!!!!!), so the toilet was clogged.

Always the good teammate, I searched for something to push it down, and that's when I heard my introduction. Family and friends saw my name on live, national TV and waited for me to cruise up, smiling and waving. Sorry, everyone, I was jamming a chair leg into the shitter on a rented RV.

---

* Next time you're at the mall, see if they have any pants with a twenty-eight-inch waist and thirty-six inseam.

The stage started with pothole-filled laps around the Staples Center (I cracked two rims and Guillaume's fork broke) and finished at the Rose Bowl in Pasadena—a short ride from Toluca Lake, so the crowd was full of friends who couldn't pick me out as the pack whizzed by. The last time I'd done laps at the Rose Bowl, I was staring at the back of a Honda Element, motorpaced by my friend Hrach, who owns a bike shop nearby. The pace was only slightly slower this time, with Teams Quick-Step and Tinkoff beating the crap out of each other, and Sagan eventually taking the overall win.

I showered on the bus and sat by the street after the stage, waiting for Joanna's dad to pick me up as crowds left the venue. With my bike, suitcase, and boxes of cookies from strangers (which I'd eventually pass out to homeless people in the park), it wasn't hard for fans to recognize me. Several stopped for a photo, one asked if I needed a ride, but most just pointed and stared. *Pro cyclists sit on curbs, too!* We went straight to Sweetsalt for lunch, and the guy who played Newman on *Seinfeld* was there, getting pointed at. *Newman eats lunch, too!**

When I got home, I had a look at my training bike in the garage and found a crack in the fork. Our sponsor sent new ones and made changes in their manufacturing, so no one was hurt, but it's weird when part of your job is to be guinea pig.

---

* His name is Wayne Knight, and he lives in Toluca Lake, so I see him often at Trader Joe's. Someone always asks for a photo, he always says yes, and he always drops a $20 bill in the Salvation Army can around the holidays.

CHAPTER 48

CAPPING OFF A nice month for Tinkoff-Saxo, Alberto Contador won the overall at the Giro d'Italia. He crossed the line in Milan holding up three fingers for his three Giro wins, which would include the one that was stripped for a positive drug test. I cheered for Nate Brown, who came in sixty-seventh, close to four hours down after three weeks of racing.

At this point, it was five months into the season and no one had asked about the brand-new Cervélo S3 that was still hanging in my garage. Technically it belonged to Garmin-Sharp, but it's standard practice for pro cyclists to try to keep their bikes at the end of the season. I'm not saying we steal—we just don't send it back unless they ask,* so I saw it as severance pay and sold it on eBay. Instant karma: FedEx crushed it in shipping.

---

* Sometimes we make them ask three or four times, or change our names and flee to another country.

CHAPTER 49

I DIDN'T KNOW HOW to feel about my result at the Tour of Cali. WorldTour teams wouldn't be looking at fourteenth overall and thinking, *I sure need a guy who can do that,* but it wasn't terrible. Instead of analyzing it, I did what we always do: hate myself for a few days, and then move on to the next one! National championships were coming right up in Chattanooga.

With no help from Canadian Mike Woods at U.S. nationals, I was the best climber on the team and I wanted that jersey, so I took Jonas aside before the meeting and told him what I thought our plan should be.

"I'm always good on this course, so let's work for me and not worry about the breakaway. Just put four guys on the front of the pack to keep it under control like BISSELL did when I almost won in 2013. If the whole group is together the last time up the climb, there'll be ten guys left at the top, and I can win this if I'm still fresh there."

Jonas politely said no. He wanted everyone to go for the breakaway.

"I wouldn't want to be the guy in the break with Zirbel attacking me at the end," he said.

"Really?" I asked. "Because I'd give everything I own to be that guy. Zirbel's been in the break here every year! Is he going to win out of it, or will he come back to the group with a lap to go covered in salt like he always does?" (I love Tom Zirbel and he was a great bike racer, but the heat got to him on long days.)

We compromised: I could hide in the pack and save energy, while my teammates would attack instead of working for me. So basically, one of the favorites would race as if he had no team at all.

Optum put three guys in the move, which I had to admit was pretty good, except Talansky was also there, and he dropped them all when he attacked halfway through the race. The next group included me, Matt Busche, Chris Horner, Kiel Reijnen, and Alex Howes. Vaughters's team had managed to lose nationals in upsets every year, but with a solo rider up the road and the best sprinter in the chase group, it looked like they'd finally pull it off.

The way I saw it, there were two ways to get JV's attention so he'd want me back. One was to ride well and ingratiate myself, but I tried that already, so I went the other way this time: I ruined his day, attacking on the climb to bring the front group up to Talansky, and dropping Howes.

Twelve riders were left at the top, so I'd actually put myself in decent position to win, but it started raining on the last lap and I'd forgotten to check my tire pressure at the start. I slid around every turn until I finally crashed.

I found video of the race later and watched myself eat pavement over and over, like you might replay a dunk in a basketball game (if you were into real sports instead of cycling). Eleven guys made it through the turn safely—their wheels didn't skip, and no one even touched their brakes. I hit it last, taking the same line at the same speed, but my tires gripped like I was on ball bearings.

The good news is that wet pavement doesn't tear up your skin like it does when it's dry, so I got up, let some air out, and jumped back on the bike. Jonas was behind me in the car, yelling at me to grab hold of the water bottle he held out the window. After all the bitching I'd done about Freddie Rodriguez two years before on the same course, the guy with a CLEAN tattoo wasn't about to take a "sticky bottle," so Jonas and I were in a fight after that.

The rest of the team cars were behind the leaders, and I caught them at the start of the last lap around the city. When a rider is coming up from behind, standard practice in the caravan is for cars to pull to the outside of a turn so I'd have room to take the fast line, but at nationals, with smaller teams who can't afford staff, one of the cars was probably driven by somebody's dad, who pulled to the inside. If my tires and wheels were getting along, I might have survived the turn, but I was on the ground again before I knew it. I didn't feel like riding around for a third crash, so I headed to the bus, where my teammates were waiting. No one from Optum finished.

Writing about this day, I can't help but remember Dan Martin's interviews after he crashed at Liège, where he internalized and took full responsibility. That's the kind of athlete I'd like to be. I wanted nothing more than to lose a race and feel like it was my fault—that preparation and execution and outside forces all went right, and I just didn't have it—but I'm telling you, those tires had no grip, and our tactics were horrible!

CHAPTER 50

I'M NOT TAKING responsibility for the next race, either. The Tour de Beauce took place at the beginning of June, including a mountaintop finish and a long time trial, so I liked my chances of winning the race overall, but the first stage featured everything I'd come to dread about Continental racing. In the WorldTour, if you ride dangerously in the pack, Chris Froome or Peter Sagan might sit next to you at dinner and give you a lecture.

"These men have families. You're putting us all at risk," I once heard someone tell a guy after he caused a crash, descending like an idiot at a race in Spain. But at smaller races like Beauce, guys were so hungry and desperate, they'd forget that we're all in this together, shoving all day like it was a mile to go, or dive-bombing turns to gain an inch. There were pointless crashes everywhere.

Near the base of the climb on the second stage, I lined up on the left side behind Woods, with our teammate Pierrick Naud blocking the wind until someone swung across the road and slammed into him, sending all three of us to the ground at high speed.* I slid on my back like a turtle, Woods on his belly like a penguin, and Pierrick kind of rolled, generously spreading wounds to all sides.

By the time I untangled myself from the pile of dudes and bikes, there was no hope of a decent result anymore, so I rode easy to the finish, while Woodsy jumped up as fast as he could, chased alone to the base of the climb, and raced his heart out for sixteenth. I teased him for being a rookie and repeated what Tyler told me the year before—how it's better to accept when you're out of it and save your energy for the next stage—but I envied his fire.

Our heroic soigneurs had found a small shack on top of the mountain, where they'd intended to shelter us while we changed clothes after the race, but instead it became an impromptu hospital. Woods had road rash all over the front of his body, including his penis, which he insisted was three feet long before the crash.[†]

Optum was the first team I'd been on that didn't have a doctor. They said it was because doctors were associated with doping, but I suspect it was a cost-saving measure (ill-advised with a health insurance company as title sponsor). Even on Kenda's tiny budget, we had a doctor to clean wounds and test for concussion, but soigneurs helped me scrape myself clean on top of Mt. Mégantic that day,[‡] and Optum's concussion protocol was a mechanic checking to see if your helmet was damaged.

My helmet just had a small dent, but I had a headache on the way back to the hotel, and I kept catching myself staring into the distance, and then sort of waking up. I knew it wouldn't be smart to race the next day, so I squeezed my helmet until it cracked and showed Wohlberg, who was fine letting me sit out the rest of the

---

* On Garmin-Sharp they taught us to always stay with your teammates, but the president and vice president never take the same plane.

[†] Road rash is temporary, but a good dick joke is forever if it makes the book.

[‡] To get the dirt out, you use this rough brush. It probably feels about like taking sandpaper to your skin.

week. Woods also opted not to start the next day (he didn't even waste a helmet), but Pierrick got stitches and hung in there.

Another concussion meant four days alone in a dark hotel room, where I had plenty of time to be moody and second-guess every decision I'd ever made. I knew plenty of guys who enjoyed full careers on the Continental circuit, but after a year in Europe, all I saw were the problems: teams with shoestring budgets, races with no spectators, riders without common sense, and no sign of anything getting fixed. I didn't see much upside to that life, and reading about all the NFL players suffering from long-term effects of concussions, I couldn't deny the risks. Alone in the darkness, I made some phone calls, promising Joanna, my agent, my coach, and my parents that if I couldn't get back to the WorldTour, I'd move on with my life.

My friend Stefano skipped Beauce for a race in Minnesota. He won a stage, which isn't easy as an amateur, but still didn't have any luck finding a job after his team got swallowed up in a merger.

My head felt better when I got back to L.A., so I started to train again, with plenty of time to prepare for Utah and Colorado. On the way to the canyons one morning, I was catching up to another cyclist on Mulholland. He went faster when he saw me coming, and then he crashed in a turn. It served him right for racing me, but I stopped to make sure he was okay. The guy was young, he hadn't hit his head, and I'd seen enough crashes to know this was nothing, but he sat on the guardrail with a tiny patch of road rash on his hip, making that hissing sound.

"Are you alright?" I asked.

"I'm not sure," he kept saying, hunched over and gritting his teeth. "I don't know."

I still had worse under my bibs from the crash at the Tour de Beauce, where I kept riding to the top of a mountain and I didn't make a sound when I cleaned it with pure alcohol. Woods had more road rash *on his penis* and still finished top twenty, but this guy was shaken up from a little scratch. It made me feel tough, telling my friends later about this wimp I met, but that sounds so stupid now. Was I really proud of how much pain I'd put myself through, like that makes me more of a man? Shouldn't I be jealous of the guy on Mulholland with his soft hands, who was so unaccustomed to suffering?

The road rash was much worse at the Tour de France that year. Rohan Dennis won the prologue, but he didn't keep the yellow jersey for long, because organizers borrowed roads from epic one-day events like Paris–Roubaix to maximize carnage and TV ratings—a response to the complaint that riders had become robots in the post-EPO Tour de France, racing according to power meters and science instead of *panache*.*

Still, the guy with the best power-to-weight ratio prevailed, and Froome made it look so easy, accusations of doping far outweighed congratulations. Someone had to cross the line first, but winning and suspicion had become inseparable in our sport. Fans called for physiological and medical data from top riders to prove they were clean, but they'd have been pretty angry about all the gray area asthma medication and cortisone. If top riders embraced "transparency," they'd have to cut out that stuff, and then they wouldn't be at the top for long.

Besides, you can't prove a negative, so even for me, there wasn't much upside to transparency. *Road* magazine did a feature that included my power data from Oak Glen, and the feedback was either accusations that I was doping (because my numbers were so good), or amateurs insisting that they could do better (because my numbers were so bad). Reading Froome's interviews, I tried to imagine what I would do if I won the Tour clean and fans didn't believe me. (First, I'd cry into my pillow of money . . .)

Ivan Basso dropped out of the Tour to get surgery for testicu-

---

* Science in bike racing! Can you imagine?

lar cancer, and Jean-Christophe Péraud (with a name like that, he's gotta be from Cleveland . . . no, wait—France) tore his shorts in a crash, showing viewers at home that both of his testicles were very much intact. Commentators loved him for continuing all the way to Paris with bandages and blood-soaked socks, and then they went on about Froome's training camps at depressing, eight-thousand-foot-high ski resorts, away from his family. Cycling fetishized pain and sacrifice, so even TV promos for the Tour were filled with crashes. It's weird as a rider, understanding that my agony is why folks tune in. Part of me knew I should flee from that, but here's the thing: I like it, too.

Wikstrom and I feverishly contacted teams those weeks, knowing that the Tour de France was when contracts would start to move. Cannondale-Garmin still seemed like my best shot, but we wanted an offer from MTN-Qhubeka or Drapac so Vaughters couldn't lowball me again.

We had some positive responses, so I was optimistic when I left for Big Bear, with Utah and Colorado a few weeks away. The Matrix was up to twelve years old and 240,000 miles, but we made it up the mountain to a cheap motel, where I cooked my meals on an electric burner I still had from my homeless years, reading *Walden* by Henry David Thoreau.

Living alone at a house he built in the woods, Thoreau extolled the virtues of simplicity, so he would have approved of my setup: a small room with a minifridge, one pot, one fork, and one knife. My favorite philosopher/poet was a big proponent of a morning walk and manual labor, but he wouldn't have been happy about all the training. Thoreau would have thought that hundred-mile rides were pointless. *But that's the beauty of it, Henry!*

I was having a great trip until I talked to my parents. They'd been on vacation but they cut it short when my dad wasn't feeling well, and Mom feared the worst. I talked to her on the phone to cheer her up, and then Joanna called during her lunch hour. She had friends who were getting divorced, and she wasn't sure if she even believed in marriage anymore. If I got my WorldTour contract and went off to Girona, she wanted to stay in L.A. and have an open relationship to figure things out.

I'd seen this coming. I'd gone after her the way I had for everything else—doing everything I could, refusing to take no for an answer. That might get you a pro contract and a book deal, but after two years together, I realized it doesn't work on people. I don't consider myself uptight, but I couldn't imagine her going on dates and bringing dudes to my house while I was off racing, so I said that if she meant that, we should split up, and she had six weeks to move out before I got back from Colorado, with no hard feelings.

Unable to focus when I started my intervals that afternoon, I gave up and tossed my bike in the car, hoping to make it to the group ride in Redlands for a decent workout. I squealed my tires down the mountain for forty-five minutes and pulled the bike out of the backseat, only to realize that I'd been so rushed and distracted, I'd left my wheels at the motel.

I should have driven back up to finish my training but I went to a car dealer instead, where I bought a used Lexus hybrid hatchback. I'd just gotten a royalty check from my publisher,* so I got a kick out of the idea that I could get a nice car just from writing about bikes, and between my relationship, my family, and my job, I think I just needed something that would last. My friend JC said he'd buy the Matrix, so the old car stayed in the family.

Since Toyota owns Lexus, the CT 200 wasn't much different from my old car, but it was quieter and nicer inside. Flying up the mountain that night with the moonroof open, I thought of a new motto: "Don't change, just get better." When I talked to Joanna, she'd thought about it and took everything back.

---

* The check hadn't cleared yet, so I spread the car purchase over three credit cards.

Old car on the right. New one on the left. I guess I have a type.

To balance all the climbing with some high-speed training, I signed up for a local criterium that weekend, and the SoCal sprinters laughed when they saw me.

"You know there's no climbs on this course, right, Phil?"

"I hope you've been hitting the gym," Rahsaan Bahati, former national crit champion and king of the local scene, said with a smile.

An hour later, I'd won $200 in lap prizes, bridged to the breakaway, and attacked with three miles to go. Rahsaan hung on and offered to trade prize money checks if I'd let him win. I thought about it, and then dropped him to lap the pack and win solo.

"Please go back to Europe, Phil," he said at the finish, his hand on my shoulder.

Climbers don't win criteriums, but it was easy that day. I sent the file from the race to my coach, who confirmed my power output was better than ever, even though I was six pounds lighter than the year before.*

"You do belong in the WorldTour with these numbers," he said. "And you're going to kill Utah."

I realized later that I forgot to kiss the ring when I crossed the line. Maybe I was mad at Joanna, or the race wasn't that hard and I didn't need her help. Perhaps it had something to do with the guys who were still racing around me because I'd just lapped them, and I wanted both hands on my bars.

I sent Vaughters my power numbers and a photo of my bathroom scale, and just like he had two years before, he gave me an offer, afraid that I'd crack a podium and my price would go up. Was it the six figures I should have had if I hadn't been screwed with the merger? Nope! It was $70,000. But it was an offer. JV was a man of his word.

Seventy thousand dollars was probably more than Drapac could have come up with, and MTN-Qhubeka had just added a new sponsor and lots of big names after a strong Tour de France (they were now called Dimension Data), so it didn't look like they'd have space for me. Wikstrom still wanted to negotiate, but Vaughters was firm with seventy.

Fortunately, I'd heard about a study at Princeton, showing that a household income of $70,000 was enough to meet the needs of the average American, and anything above that didn't improve day-to-day happiness. Life isn't about having nice things—it's about being comfortable and doing what you love.† I don't need to be rich—I just need enough to get a bottle of water at the airport, or not let it ruin my week if I get a parking ticket. Basically, $70,000 is the salary that Thoreau would have wanted, so I told JV that I'd take it and he could send over the contract.

---

* I was emaciated, but I felt great!
† I find this out after I buy a Lexus.

Knowing Vaughters when it comes to answering e-mails or returning calls, I was surprised to see his name pop up when my phone rang. JV explained that with Ted retiring, he wanted someone on the team who could represent sponsors on social media, appear in advertisements, and attend nonrace events, so I'd have as many race days or more than I did on Optum, but not as much as the rest of the team. He wanted to make sure I understood that going in, so I wouldn't get angry if I found myself at a charity ride in Massachusetts instead of a stage race in France.

I sighed. I wanted to race Grand Tours, not fly overseas for photo shoots. If I was going to be a sales rep, I could apply for a *job* at Cannondale and probably make more than $70,000—without having to work on weekends. My effort to be marketable helped get my foot in the door, and now it was coming back to haunt me.

"I understand," I told him. "And thanks for the warning. I'll do a great job if that's my role, but I plan to be so fit, you'll want me at races instead."

"I'll keep my eyes open," JV assured me. "We'll send a contract soon."

It's crazy how riders are expected to do these incredibly demanding races, while simultaneously going through the emotional roller coaster of a cutthroat job market. I feel like I spent half of my twenties worrying about contracts, and I wouldn't be happy until the papers were signed, but I did sleep better that night.

CHAPTER 51

THE TOUR OF Utah provided college dorm suites for each team when we arrived. My teammates and I put down our bags and walked through the courtyard toward the dining hall for dinner, while the Trek team came up the sidewalk from another building.

"What are you doing, walking on the grass?" yelled Fränk Schleck.

"We're just taking a shortcut," Jesse Anthony explained to the washed-up doper. "You know something about shortcuts."

Jesse's usually a nice boy, but Fränk was asking for it. I fell to my knees laughing, which probably was bad for the grass.

We sat outside at the team presentation that night, where Schleck was interviewed on the stage.

"It's nice to see how many great riders there are here in Utah," he said.

One less than you think, Fränk.

That's when I felt a tap on my shoulder. It was Alex Howes.

"Mind if I sit here, you Continental scum?" He smiled, pointing at the chair next to me.

"It's your reputation, WorldTour," I said, giving him a hug.

Tom was next in line for a squeeze, and I lifted him high in the air. He wormed out of it, trying to look serious as the race favorite, but I could still pick him up like a child. They both asked what happened to my face. Apparently I rub my chin when I'm stressed, and there was a big bald spot where my beard hair had stopped growing.

I haven't seen Danielson since that hug, because he got a phone call from USADA that night and made an announcement via Twitter as he fled back to Boulder.

"Tonight has been one of the worst nights of my life. An out of competition test I gave July 9th has tested positive for, from what I understand, synthetic testosterone . . . I have not taken this or any other banned substance. I would never ever take anything like this especially after everything I have gone through the last years. This makes absolutely no sense . . . I spoke with [USADA] and my team and I will have to sit out the Tour of Utah as I wait for the B sample as well as look into all the possible ways that could have produced this result . . . I don't understand how or why this happened and still can't even accept this is true."

To jaded cycling fans, it was the same old story: "I don't know why the test was positive. I don't know what I took. I don't even know where I am. I'm just a dumb athlete who swallows pills at random." But to me, it sounded like one of my best friends was in trouble. I contacted two experts I knew, who both said that synthetic testosterone isn't the kind of thing that gets into a supplement on accident, and the test was accurate as far as they knew.

Jesse Anthony once said that if I went positive and claimed it was a mistake, he'd believe me 99 percent.* It was meant as a compliment, but that 1 percent felt like a knife in my back. He said it was a religious thing—that nobody's perfect—but I think it says a lot about the state of the sport, that you could question the

---

* "Went positive." It's telling that pro cyclists have a slang term for it.

very foundation of people you knew best. Stefano said he'd believe me 100 percent, give me a kidney if I asked for it, and maybe even pick me up at LAX, but among people who don't know me, I'm sure there'd be a lot of "Yes! I knew he only got that tattoo to trick us! Fuck that guy!"

It rained the whole first stage, which I found appropriate. If life was a movie, there would have been rain on the day that my mentor tested positive. After all the times I'd defended him, how could he betray me and make all the haters right? Or if he was telling the truth somehow, would he ever be able to prove it? Either way, if Danielson ever needed a friend, it was me, and now. I must have typed and canceled fifty text messages while I ate my oatmeal that morning, but I never sent one. I couldn't be there for him because I didn't know what to believe, and I was afraid that if I wasn't careful, my verbal contract with Vaughters would vanish in a puff of smoke.

You're supposed to put away the emotional stuff during competition. You can't worry about contracts, your girl, your dad, or if your friend was doping. I'd spent two months training for Utah, and I'd paid out of my own pocket for that motel in Big Bear, where I sprawled on the floor after countless laps of the scorching climb that locals call "Damnation Alley," going to bed hungry to lose weight. Now I was finally at the race, and my head was everywhere else. The weirdo fan in the moose helmet was at the top of the first climb, yelling as usual. With Jens Voigt retired, his football jersey said "Danielson" on the back. Moose must get bad cell service in rural Utah.

With forty miles to go, we descended on the wet highway back toward the city, and Jesse asked how I was doing.

"I'm sad," I told him.

I was just being honest, but then I saw his expression and realized that he was really asking if I needed my rain jacket from the car.

"Oh. I'm fine, dude."

He smiled and helped me work my way to the front of the pack—a gentle reminder that I still had a job to do.

With seven miles to go, Howes and Reijnen attacked, the pack was flying to catch them, and my front tire went flat, which put me in a pickle: if I pulled over to change the wheel, I'd never catch back up and my GC hopes would be over, but if I crashed from riding a flat in pouring rain, GC could be the least of my problems.

I was so bummed by then, I'll admit that I was tempted to stop and wait for the groupetto. I'd be out of the GC, the pressure for a result would be off, and nobody would have blamed me, but I wasn't quite ready to give up. If you have an "incident" within the last three kilometers you get the same time as the pack, so I just needed to hang on for a few wet laps around Logan, Utah. I coasted to the back of the group where I wouldn't put anyone else at risk, waved to the team cars to give me space in case I crashed, and for ten hair-raising turns, I dragged one foot on the ground for balance, barely controlling a front-wheel skid at thirty miles an hour.

White as a ghost, I came to a stop with exactly 3k to go, and a motorcycle official pulled over next to me.

"Here's my flat, and that's the '3k to go' sign. I get the same time as the leaders, right?"

"Yep." He smiled, writing down my number. "I thought you were gonna die on that last lap, but you're a pro, Phil. Loved your book, by the way."

It was a bad day, but I did some things right.

Before Danielson took over the headlines, the big story at the Tour of Utah was Taylor Phinney's return to the peloton. After fourteen months of rehab from his crash in Chattanooga, one leg was still atrophied—visibly smaller than the other—but while I was power-sliding through the circuits, he'd joined Kiel and Alex in the breakaway. Taylor probably could have won, but he led out the sprint for his friends, so Kiel and Alex topped a clean podium that was all we needed to have faith in cycling again.

The news that night barely mentioned Kiel, though, because they got more clicks by interviewing pros who didn't know Danielson and wanted to cheer his downfall.

"Tom and I started around the same age, and we had very different trajectories," said Ben Jacques-Maynes. "I guess now we know why." Ben was one of the top guys in the United States during the doping era, so if you remove the cheaters, he'd have won a lot of big races and should have made it to Europe. Instead, after a long, clean career in the Continental leagues, Ben was retiring at the end of the year.

The guy who stopped to help when I crashed in San Dimas will have to walk around the rest of his life haunted by what could have been, so I don't blame him for his anger, but for many, hating dopers is more of a scapegoat. A lot of guys spent their lives in the back of the pack because they didn't do the work or they just weren't that good, and it's easy to blame cheaters for your own inadequacy. Riders hide behind integrity to feel better about failure, just as I did before I learned the truth: Real Talent is out there, and some of us don't have it. Taylor Phinney didn't even take a multivitamin, and he'd just dusted all of us at his first race back, *with one leg.*

The other topic in the media was whether Vaughters would follow through on his promise to dissolve the team if they ever had a positive test. My phone didn't stop ringing that night, and it wasn't just the cycling news sites—it was ESPN and the *Wall Street Journal.* Nothing I told them could have moved the needle of public opinion (maybe "needle" is a bad word choice) (or the best word choice), and JV had probably already made the phone calls to keep his sponsors intact, but I hoped that somehow, if I said exactly the right thing, I could make a difference. The *Wall Street Journal* article the next day ended with my quote:

"Whatever happened with Tommy D, it would be a shame for the pioneer antidoping program—with a huge number of guys who certainly aren't cheating—to go away. There are some teams and owners that I think cycling would be better off without, but Cannondale-Garmin isn't one of them."

I didn't throw Danielson under the bus, but I still felt bad about it. A good friend would have said that Danielson was innocent, instead of "whatever happened," selfishly protecting my own interests.

The real lesson I learned that night was that the best way to get over bad news is for something worse to happen to put it in perspective. For example, say you lose your wallet, but then you're attacked by wolves. Not too worried about the wallet, are you?

Wi-Fi was unreliable at the dorms, so I tried a different browser, where apparently Joanna had left her Facebook logged in, and a message popped up from a guy she'd met at a race a few weeks before (around the time she'd brought up an open relationship). I did some reading, and I didn't sleep much the rest of the week.

The next few stages, I went for hopeless attacks on the final circuits. I didn't lose time, but I was wasting energy, firing bullets left and right, and Jesse called me out on it.

"It's easy to do the sacrifice move, Phil. It looks cool on TV, but it's a cop-out and it's not fair to the guys working for you."

There's nothing like being cramped and tired and covered in salt and hearing that you're weak, but he was right and I appreciated it.

I'd never mixed it up in a field sprint stage at a big race, but Eric Young said he was feeling good on one of the flat finishes, so I shoved my way up to him with a mile to go, threw some elbows, and shot up to the front to drop him off in perfect position, swinging out of the way just before the sprint would start. I was proud of my leadout, knowing that Vaughters was watching and I'd added another skill to my résumé—until I looked back and saw that Eric had stayed behind BMC's train instead of following me. I was pissed until ten seconds later when he won anyway. If you cross the line first, I can't say you screwed up.

The stage finished in a town called Heber Valley, which I recognized from my first Tour of Utah in 2011. I'd stayed at host housing that year, racing for a team with no mechanic, no massage, and no one to hand us bottles in the feed zone, so I carried extra water in my pocket and barely finished. Now, the streets were lined with eight-foot-tall vinyl posters of me, ripping the group apart on Guardsman Pass the year before, gritting my teeth with Danielson in yellow on my wheel, Horner hanging on for dear life, and the ring from Joanna around my neck. I had mixed emotions about that image, but I'd never get another poster of myself, so Eric Young went from the top of the podium to helping me steal it. We kicked down two heavy wood poles in the dark, and it's still hanging in my garage in Toluca Lake.

The next stage was circuits through Salt Lake City, with a steep kick to the finish every lap that looked perfect for Woodsy. I'd promised Jesse that I wouldn't go for the suicide move again, but I ended up in the early breakaway on accident, cracked both of my rims on a pothole, and wasted energy in the wind for an hour and a half.

We were caught with two laps to go, and I tried to help Mike. I didn't do him much good, but he did his "running on the bike" thing and killed everyone, taking a huge win and the leader's jersey with two stages left. That night, he told the team that he'd also accepted a verbal offer from Vaughters.

"How much?" somebody asked.

"Ninety thousand dollars," he admitted, looking down.

Everyone turned their heads to me, knowing that my offer was for $70,000, but I just smiled and congratulated him. Woodsy was better than me and he deserved it. I was excited to go on the WorldTour journey together, and I'd be honored to bring him bottles. Anyway, neither of us had a contract signed, and I had better reasons to lose sleep: my mom was at the hospital with my dad, and the guy Joanna had been messaging was on his way to L.A. to see her.

"When are you coming over to my house? ☺" she'd asked him.

The guys were nervous at the meeting the next morning. Continental teams usually don't win stages at the Tour of Utah, and they're certainly not supposed to lead the race. Woods pinned his numbers onto a new yellow jersey, but everyone else's eyes were on me. This was the course where I'd had my breakout ride for Danielson, leading up Guardsman Pass, shutting down Cadel Evans, and earning my face on the poster. Now, I learned the hardest part about being good: you're expected to repeat it. I told everyone what to do in the first half of the stage to control the breakaway, knowing that the next thirty miles were on me, and the last three would be up to Woodsy.

Optum's bus didn't have an espresso machine, so before we left the hotel, I crammed two packets into the coffee maker in the room and used half the water, which makes what I call an "almost espresso" (still better than Starbucks). Then I raided the maid's cart and made another one. You don't go to the start line because you're ready. You go because it's time.

My teammates had never played the high-speed chess match of controlling the early breakaway at a big race, so WorldTour teams were aggressive, hoping we'd screw it up and the race would fall apart. Woodsy and I both had to burn matches, but we got to the valley with the full team on the front and the race under control. I had 60k to recover, but when it was my turn to take over on the front, my sleepless week caught up to me and I could barely pedal. I was nowhere near the front group on Guardsman, and I hated myself for leaving Woods there alone.

Joe Dombrowski won the Snowbird stage for Cannondale-Garmin, knocking Woodsy to second overall. Joe had expected to work for Danielson that week, and there was something poetic about the baton being passed from an old doper to a clean kid from Virginia.

I apologized to Woods when he came back from the podium, but he promised that it would've been the same result if I'd been there to help him, and he just got beat by the better guy (internalizing, taking responsibility, like a champion). Then I sat in the gravel behind the bus and called Joanna. Her new friend was coming over that afternoon, and I had to confront her before anything happened that I couldn't forgive. She said I was crazy, jealous, reading into nothing, and they were only friends. That might have been true. Or maybe she just needed attention.

The silver lining that day was that Horner finished way behind. I felt bad for his young teammates—in over their heads, driving Chris's personal camper from his driveway in Oregon because their team couldn't afford to rent one.*

As much as I hated him, I appreciated that Chris was riding so badly this year, because it meant he was clean. For a guy who'd always carried a gun, it would take guts to show up at a knife fight with just a knife, getting your butt kicked every week. I told my teammates that he deserved a little respect for that.

"No, he doesn't! Fuck that guy!" was the unanimous response.

I didn't argue. In an interview that night, Horner insisted that he would have won if the UCI let him use his prescription asthma inhaler, but he still had Woods and Dombrowski right where he wanted them with one stage left. Chris probably thought he was playing mind games or talking trash, but he came off more like the Black Knight in *Monty Python and the Holy Grail*, refusing to accept defeat after his arms and legs were severed. Horner was

---

* Dopers often had RVs or motor homes back in the day, so they could pack up and go somewhere that authorities couldn't find them for a few days, until the drugs would be out of their system.

just a bloody torso, propped up in the dirt, still threatening his opponents.*

Nothing changed for Horner, Dombrowski, or Woods on the final stage into Park City, but nothing changed for me, either, and I finished in the groupetto again. I called Wikstrom from the bus, panicked that JV would take back his offer.

"Do I tell him about everything I have going on? I don't want to make excuses."

"They're not excuses, Phil. You're a mess," said Matt. "I'll talk to him. Just take care of yourself."

---

* "Come back here and take what's coming to you! I'll bite your legs off!" yelled the Black Knight.

CHAPTER 52

THE TOUR OF Colorado started in seven days, so I told the team to cancel my plane ticket home and let me borrow one of the cars instead. I'd head to Colorado early, save a mechanic the nine-hour drive, and a road trip would be good for my head. I put my bikes on the roof, my bags in the back-seat, and all the cookies from kind strangers in the trunk where I couldn't reach them.*

I was just outside of Green River, Wyoming, when my mom called. Dad's cancer was back, it was everywhere, and the doctors gave him a year to live. I told her that miracles can happen and he could beat this, but you know in war movies after an explosion, how they stop the sound and the picture goes dark and blurry, so you're just seeing lights and bodies running around and you don't really know what's happening? That's how I felt for months. I promised that I'd come to Atlanta to see them after the world championship team time trial in Richmond, Virginia, coming up in a few weeks, and then I lost cell service. When I saw the exit to

---

* If I'd kidnapped someone and locked them in the back, they'd have had very mixed feelings about it.

Yellowstone National Park, it was damn tempting to turn left and disappear for a while. I could sleep in the car, ride my bike, and eat cookies. Living the dream?

Howes had given me the key to his house before he headed back to Girona, so I had a free place to stay in Boulder for the week, and Brad Huff had his own relationship issues, so he'd spent the whole summer there on Eric Young's couch. Over coffee, we wondered if our legs would come around.

"How much do we train today?" I asked.

"No more training, Phil! Now we rest," he said. "The hay's in the barn!"*

Danielson was also in town, but I didn't call him. Instead, I reached out to Vaughters. He'd announced that the team would continue, so I was desperate to sign a contract and confused that it was taking so long.

"I'm around this week if you want to grab a coffee," I messaged him. "Or egg Tommy D's house."

I thought it was a good joke, but JV didn't respond until two days later.

"I don't drink coffee. And I don't hate on people."

If you've ever read Vaughters's Twitter feed, he does nothing but hate on people. And I swear I'd seen him drink coffee.

I was greeted with a new cookie bike when I arrived in Steamboat Springs for the Tour of Colorado. They sent the right size this time, but my legs had gotten worse, and I was pack fodder all week.

Phinney won the first stage and showed up at the dinner buffet wearing a black hat with a wide, flat brim like you might see on a bullfighter. People make fun of athletes and celebrities for seeking attention or being extravagant, but Taylor's a good guy and it's not

---

* Brad grew up in Missouri. He can make a good farm metaphor, or he could bale you some hay.

his fault: if you're talented enough, people laugh harder at your jokes and no one tells you no, or "take off that dumb hat." In a way, it's so mentally tough to compete at the highest level, maybe you need yes-men, but self-awareness can atrophy like a muscle, and suddenly Michael Jordan is sporting a Hitler mustache in a Hanes commercial. Or maybe Taylor just liked the hat and I shouldn't read into it.

BMC had given Phinney more than a year to focus on rehab and hat fashion after his crash in Chattanooga, but Peter Stetina was racing in Colorado just four months after he broke his leg. Taylor's injuries were more severe, of course, but it didn't seem like Stetina was quite ready, because he came to dinner leaning on a cane. BMC had already told him that he wouldn't be re-signed at the end of the season.

I saw also Rohan Dennis that week, for the first time since we'd been teammates. BMC had either a great nutritionist or a doctor with some cortisone to help him lose the ten pounds he'd always carried around, because Rohan arrived in Colorado with a climber's build and enough post-Tour fitness to easily win the overall. He was kind of a jerk about it, though, so tensions were high in the pack. There was a lot of yelling, and one crash that looked intentional, and the yellow jersey eventually threw a rice cake at a twenty-four-year-old Continental rider who was probably making $6,000 that year.

Sitting on the bus before stage six, I was about to turn off my phone and head to the start when I saw that my mom was calling. Of course, if you're all-in, you don't answer your phone before the bike race. I should have been thinking about the course and visualizing my role, but I hit the green button instead, and learned that they'd be installing a permanent feeding tube in my dad that afternoon. It wasn't serious surgery, but as I followed attacks an hour later, hoping for another pointless early breakaway, I made a mental note to call after the finish in case something happened in surgery—and to hear his voice once last time, since the feeding tube would make him sound different. Just then, Kiel rode up to me. He said he knew this wasn't the right time, but he'd heard my dad was sick and he was sorry. I thanked him, unwrapping a Clif Organic dark chocolate/almond bar, so if someone saw me crying, I could just say I was emotional because my snack was so damn delicious. Then I wondered something: *what the hell am I doing here?*

A DNF at the Tour of Colorado would probably cost me my WorldTour contract, but I stopped at the feed zone and told the team I had to go to Atlanta. Jonas drove me an hour and a half to the airport, promising to hold my roster spot until JV sent a contract, and that I'd always have a home at Optum if it fell through. I'd disagreed with his race strategy a couple times, but Jonas is a great person where it matters, with a loyalty and humanity you don't see much in cycling.

There were complications with the surgery and Dad was in the hospital most of the week. Mom and I played cards in the waiting room, which was full of cancer patients and tissues. *They know. Just like the hay bales in the corners at a criterium. These fuckers know we're going to cry here.*

I took Dad's wedding ring and eyeglasses when they told him to remove his metal objects for an MRI. He was pretty much blind without the glasses, but when he got back, he asked for the ring first. I excused myself to the bathroom, where I punched the toilet paper dispenser until the plastic shattered. I had to hide my bloody knuckles in my pocket so Mom wouldn't see, but it was very satisfying.

Optum was lucky to be invited to Richmond for the world championships, and it would have been a great milestone to compete at Worlds on U.S. soil, but I gave up my spot and flew to California instead, to take Joanna to Joshua Tree. We'd been fighting from a distance for almost three months, but everything seemed back to normal.

An old friend from Florida went to Richmond to watch the road race. He sent me a photo of Vaughters at a diner with Toms Skujiņš and another old friend: Andrew McQuaid. There's a good chance that McQuaid was trying to convince JV to give Toms my spot, so I should have asked my buddy to eavesdrop, but I had a more pressing concern:

"Is Vaughters drinking coffee?" I asked.

He said he couldn't tell.

Dad was still in and out of the ER, so I flew back to Atlanta again, dividing my time between a crying mom, a terminal relationship, and a terminal father. Sitting on the porch in Tucker, he said he felt bad that I'd dropped out of the Tour of Colorado, and with my last race of the season coming up in Pennsylvania, he frowned when I said I hadn't ridden my bike in four days.

That's when Dad put his hand on my knee and finally gave me the approval I'd been waiting for. "I'm glad you're a pro cyclist. I understand what it means to you, and I'm proud of what you've done. You should follow your dreams as long as you can, son."

Nah, I made that up. Wouldn't it be nice if life worked that way? Dad still called me a biker instead of a cyclist, but the crooked basketball hoop in the driveway told me how he really felt. He did assure me that whatever happened with my contract, he knew I'd figure things out, and he didn't want me to miss another race because of his health. It was nice of him to say, but according to Dad's doctors, I'd probably have to go against his wishes one more time. I hid my black suit in the back of a closet at the house, so I wouldn't have to carry it all over Europe the next year.

CHAPTER 53

THE VUELTA HAD just started, so I checked the news to see how my friends were doing. The opening stage was a team time trial, a notoriously high-speed and dangerous event to begin with, but the course included sections of dirt, sand, rubber mats, bridges, ramps, fire-breathing dragons, and a Wendy's drive-through (I'm only joking about the last two). Teams protested and finally there was a compromise: everyone would ride it, but the stage wouldn't count toward the overall standings. Vincenzo Nibali took over the headlines on the next day for holding on to a car after he missed the front group—a race favorite, blatantly cheating on live TV.

Jonas must have missed that Nibali was kicked out of the Vuelta, because he still wanted me to take a sticky bottle when I crashed that weekend at the Reading 120 just outside of Philadelphia. I'd slid my overinflated tires into the winning breakaway before I finally lost it on a set of wet train tracks, but I got back up and finished twelfth—one last effort for the team. I crossed the line shivering and bruised, but happier than I'd been in weeks, because four hours of suffering in the bike race was a vacation from the real world. It was sad to think that the season was over, that it would be months before I could race again.

Toms Skujiņš finished second in Reading. I heard that he signed to Cannondale and was more worried than ever that my offer would disappear, but the contract showed up that week. I was glad that JV gave me, Woodsy, and Skujiņš a chance—that I didn't have to be mad at him anymore—until I saw that the salary was $65,000 instead of the $70,000 he'd offered over the phone. It's true that my results in Utah and Colorado were less than we'd expected, but he knew why, and either way, we had an agreement. Was this the "your dad is dying" tax? Did Vaughters really need that $5,000, or did he see a chance to kick me when I was down?

When he started the "clean team," many said that JV didn't really care about the health of the sport, and the antidoping angle was just a marketing ploy for sponsors. They said that he was like Whole Foods: they don't sell organic fruit because they care about the environment—they do it because some sucker might pay $4 for an apple. Vaughters was a flawed vessel who'd done so much good, cleaning up pro cycling and making my dreams come true, I'd always wanted to give him the benefit of the doubt, but now it was like I'd pulled back the curtain to meet the Wizard of Oz, and one thing was certain: the salad bar at Whole Foods is delicious. What was I talking about?

Woods's contract came through higher than what he'd agreed to, perhaps thanks in part to my pay cut. I told Mike that he owed me a coffee, and then Mavic offered me a three-year shoe contract for $5,000 a year, which brought me back to Princeton's recommended salary. Athletes can form relationships with companies like you would with people, and I feel the same about those yellow shoes as I would about an old friend who bailed me out of jail.*

I'd never forgive Vaughters, but I didn't care about the money,

---

* Hypothetically.

because I was back in the Show. Returning to the *Wizard of Oz* analogy: remember when Dorothy opens the door and suddenly everything is in color? That's how it felt to rejoin the WorldTour.* I was reborn. My dream was alive.

JV wasted no time, sending me on another Tour de Phil, but I DNFed this one after ten "stages" and jumped on another Southwest flight to Atlanta, because my dad had died. They said he had a year, but he only made it two months. Joanna came to help me through the funeral, and when we got back to Toluca Lake, my bike had two flat tires in the garage. They say these things come in threes.

"Drinking camp" with my new/old team was at the end of October, and boy, did I need it. We stayed at the Little Nell, a five-star resort in Aspen where you get a tour of your room when you check in, as if you couldn't find the bed by yourself. The first day, we played touch football, and the Europeans kept kicking it and didn't know where to stand. I was sprinting full speed toward the end zone for what should have been a touchdown, except I had to dive into the grass because I was about to run over Pierre Rolland—one of the team's marquee signings. He was supposed to podium the Tour de France or something, but he sure looked fragile on the ten-yard-line. I think I came close to ending his season before it started.

The other big signing for the team looked anything but delicate next to Pierre: Colombian Rigoberto Urán. After a hard youth in Medellín, I couldn't judge Rigo if he did take that bribe from Vinokourov at the 2012 Olympic road race, but it pissed me off that Vaughters would sign him. Overall, the team seemed to be a bunch of good dudes, and I'm pretty sure there were no dopers whatsoever.

Our truly clean roster would have been touching if it didn't make me feel so old. JV had signed a batch of talented youngsters, like Lawson Craddock, who transferred from Giant-Shimano.

---

* Dorothy doesn't have to go back to metric, though.

Living in Austin and coming up on the LiveStrong development team, Lawson was friends with Lance, arriving in Aspen with road rash on his thigh from sliding during a kickball game at his house. Maybe Lawson was too young to realize how much Lance's actions had cost him, or perhaps if you eat enough nachos and watch football at someone's mansion, you don't mind that he's the reason you have to pee in a cup for authorities all the time, or that you live in a much smaller house—that you're renting. Then again, if I could be friends with Danielson, who am I to judge?* I'll even admit to this: we live in a world of nuance, and there's a chance that Lance isn't as evil as I want him to be.†

With all the new faces, there were some old ones missing, like Nathan Haas and Dan Martin, who'd both moved to other teams but promised to train with me when I got to Girona. The team's title had changed from Garmin-Sharp to Cannondale-Garmin to just Cannondale, but mostly it felt the same—like I went out to lunch and it took a year.

We hiked, we rode mountain bikes, we ate fancy dinners in Aspen, and then we hit the bars with the staff and directors, because this was drinking camp, and someone made a rule that if you went to bed before two, we'd break into your room and flip your mattress. The schedule included core exercises at seven a.m., which were optional, but you didn't want to show weakness by sleeping through it. I hadn't had a drink since July, so I remember being in the back of the exercise room with Howes one morning, trying to figure out why we were stumbling through yoga poses.

"Wait a minute. We're still drunk!" he whispered. Then we giggled and fell over.

---

* Jesse Anthony rides with Dave Zabriskie. We always joke that "my doper is better than your doper."
† Lance engaged me in a weird Twitter fight around that time. It made me wonder what it would take for cycling to forgive him. Do I just keep hating him until he kills himself? The guy did some damage, but he's not a serial killer, and you also hear stories about him paying for someone else's cancer treatment.

Like real professional athletes, we even trashed the hotel. We threw tomatoes off the roof at soigneurs, overturned a flowerpot in Pierre's bed, and streaked the Little Nell's hallways—really living the dream. One night, we had to flip Talansky's mattress for leaving the bar at midnight, but he'd dead-bolted his door, so Toms Skujiņš climbed across the balcony, dangling three stories high from the neighboring room to get in through the porch. I told you he was Batman.

We did have some sponsor work in Aspen, and each rider had the meeting with directors to discuss his race schedule. I was sharing a hotel room with Woodsy, who casually mentioned that they told him to peak for his first race—the Tour Down Under in January—a WorldTour stage race where he'd be team leader. It's a good thing that Mike was too much of a rookie to know how crazy that was, but I liked that JV had enough faith to give him the opportunity.*

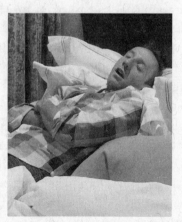

Mike Woods at drinking camp.

---

* He raced head-to-head with some of the best in the world and finished fourth overall, so never underestimate a guy who doesn't know what he can't do. But whatever. I *won* my first race in the WorldTour.

The team had less faith in me, so my spring schedule was almost identical to my program from 2014. That's how much I'd progressed in two years, and in case I didn't know where I stood, they sent a bunch of guys to the track in Los Angeles for bike fits and aerodynamic testing, and I wasn't invited. When I asked if I could drive over to join in, the coach said no.

They spelled my name right on the laundry bag this time, but my height and weight were reversed in the "stats" section of the trading cards, and the race results were all wrong. Some of my biggest wins were left off and they had me listed as second place in the KOM competition at a race I'd never even attended. So somebody made up a result for me, *and it wasn't even a win*. It gave me a bad feeling about my career prospects, but that was nothing new, and I was too excited and motivated to let anything get me down. I could pay for a bike fit myself and I knew from experience that the race schedule wasn't set in stone. I didn't have crazy dreams of winning a Grand Tour anymore, but I was good enough to start one, and Team USA had asked for my clothing sizes, because I was on the long list for the *Olympics*.

Whatever happened, I knew what I was getting into this time and how to do it right. I'd train hard and do the best I could with the legs I had, but I'd keep my perspective and balance. I'd enjoy the adventure with Joanna, and if I found myself chasing a team car down a mountain in the rain, I'd give it plenty of room, because it's not worth dying over—or taking a sticky bottle. I'd rent out the house in Toluca Lake, so I'd have two pirate ships, which would be more than enough for a nice apartment in Old Town Girona and a meal for two at Can Roca. Everything is so simple in October.

I was exhausted when I flew back to Los Angeles, with a hangover and a head full of possibilities, but when Joanna picked me up at the airport she wanted to talk. With more of her friends getting engaged, she had to reiterate that I shouldn't get my hopes up about setting a wedding date anytime soon, and she still wasn't sure about the whole "marriage thing."*

That was the last night I'd lose sleep over Joanna. Being with me meant a lot of sacrifice and compromise, and while she said she wanted to stay together, it seemed like she'd been sabotaging our relationship, because deep down, she couldn't do it anymore. My emotional energy was stretched thin, and I had to spend what was left on my mom, so I gave Joanna a month to move out.

A breakup is never easy, but nothing bothers you after your dad dies, and looking at the next year, order and control would be more important than romance. I wouldn't get a third shot at the WorldTour, and if I failed, I needed it to be my fault. Stefano and Katie and Jesse instituted mandatory "chosen family dinners" once a week to cheer me up, Koschara called regularly to check in, and coach Frank sent me on "Soul Rides" for training, where I'd go out all day and cruise in the canyons or do group rides with Matt Wikstrom and my friends in Toluca Lake. I was surrounded by great people, and it wasn't hard to see that what tied them all together was my biggest relationship of all: bikes. Sure, we had our ups and downs, but cycling was my home, my classroom, my sanctuary, and my social circle, and I didn't need anything else. Besides, being single meant that I could sleep around again, like a real pro athlete (it's not as good as being in a relationship, but it's close).

When you put yourself out there with a book, you start getting e-mails from readers. Most of them were great, but if I believed the compliments I'd also have to believe the occasional hater, so I'd tried to tune it all out, giving quick responses and moving them all to a folder in my Gmail.

That winter, I finally went through that folder and discovered

---

* Cruel at it seems, I have to give Joanna credit for this. I wanted to marry her pretty bad and she never caved, which was merciful if you think about it.

SoCal family: Jesse, me, Katie, and Stefano.

another relationship: this is going to sound sappy, but I'm talking about you. Hundreds of strangers had thanked me for making them laugh or inspiring them to get off the sofa and exercise, and a few said that my book helped them through a hard time with a sick family member or a breakup, which hit close to home. The money wasn't much, considering all the hours I'd spent at the computer, but reading those notes was more satisfying than winning a race had ever been, so writing seemed like something I should keep doing. I started carrying a voice recorder, taking notes, and working on book proposals in my spare time. I didn't have the talent to win the big races, but I could tell you what it's like to try.

PART 4

The Long List

CHAPTER 54

BEFORE THE SEASON started, the team doctor sent me to a medical center for a UCI-mandated health test. My resting pulse was 28, and I was diagnosed with "athlete's heart," which basically means that one of the muscles in my old ticker is overdeveloped, so if I ever stop exercising, I'll die (no biggie). Next, they attached a bunch of wires to my chest and put me on a treadmill for a "stress EKG." It was still easy for me when the nurse started to increase the speed and incline, and I noticed that the hallway was crowded with more doctors and staff, peeking into my room, pointing and whispering, excited to see what a pro athlete would do in a test they normally administered to the elderly. Most patients run until failure, but the UCI only needed my heart rate up to 160, so I told myself I'd stop there. *No need to give these jerks a show. I'm not a damn zoo animal, here for your entertainment.*

A few minutes later, sweat poured down my face, I'd tuned out the beeping of the machines, and all there was in the world was the echo of my breath and my "athlete's heart," pounding through my skull at 190 beats a minute. I guess I couldn't help it.

Twenty-nine years old and I still had to test my limits. When my body gave out, I was back in a lab in Denver, doubled over, surrounded by wide-eyed doctors who were trying to decide if I was okay.

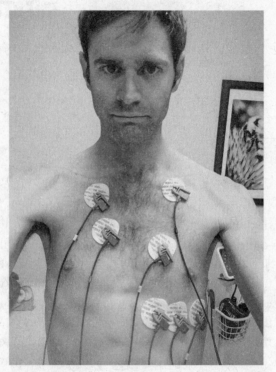

Lab rat.

I was in good shape for the Tour de San Luis and one of the strongest in the team time trial the first day, but instead of winning a stage like I had two years before, I flipped over a median at sixty kilometers an hour and lost most of the skin from the right side of my body. I probably should have dropped out, but I helped my teammates for six more days and finished the race dressed

like a mummy, spending my evenings in the doctor's room. He
said he brought "a Grand Tour's worth" of gauze and used it all up
that week, just on me. He also said I have one of the highest pain
thresholds he'd ever seen, which I took as a compliment. *I'm a
man! I'm tough!*

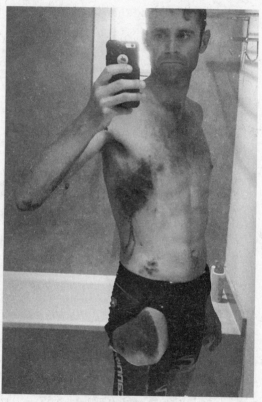

Road rash in San Luis.

When I got back to L.A., still bruised and swollen on my thirtieth birthday, my gift to myself was breakfast at a café, where
I enjoyed an expensive cookie and an espresso. That night, I
rented out the "Gold Room" at a pool hall in Burbank, invited

all my friends, and ate a cannabis cookie. Marijuana is only banned in-competition, so to test positive you basically have to be high *during* the race. It was only my second time trying it, but lots of pros partake in the off-season, between races, or even on training rides. I once saw a very well-known rider on a climb outside of Girona, wearing his team bib shorts, a T-shirt, no helmet, and Beats by Dre. I'm guessing that weed had something to do with that.

Birthday cookie.
Don't change. Just get better.

I set ten alarms before my birthday party, and I don't remember anything from my flight to Barcelona in the morning. I landed and went to baggage claim, wondering if I'd checked my luggage. *Good one, Phil,* I thought with a smile when they came out.

Danielson gave up his place in Girona, but the team's chef said he had the stuff I'd left in the closet back in 2014, so I packed light, but it turns out that things get lost when you abandon them for two years. Here's what was left when I finally got my bags:

- Vitamins (left with a guy who said he tested positive for tainted vitamins, so they went in the trash)
- The old seventeen-inch Hewlett-Packard laptop
- A framed photo of my mom and dad
- A framed photo of Joanna
- A box of condoms, expiring in exactly two weeks*

So I had to buy sheets, towels, new clothes, and condoms (just in case), hiking across town four times with a full backpack from the mall, but I settled in to a nice apartment in a building right next to the cathedral in Old Town Girona, with a creaky wood door and a stone wall built in AD 800. The property manager had advertised that Wi-Fi was included, and then told me to knock on my neighbor's door and offer them 50 euros for their password. I should have been angry, but I just smiled. It was nice to get Spained again.

Kiel Reijnen made his way to the WorldTour with Trek, so I trained and socialized with him, Woods, Skujiņš, Haas, Talansky, Howes, and lots of other great folks in town. We'd hurt each other on the climbs, relax with a coffee and a sandwich, and then go out and do it again.

I chose a two-bedroom apartment, purely because Mom said she wanted to visit, and when she booked her flight, I sent an e-mail to Can Roca, still ranked the number one restaurant in the world. Either I got lucky or that year-long waiting list doesn't

---

* Again—not believable. But it happened.

Ride with Kiel and Woods in Girona.

apply to WorldTour riders, because we got in right away.* The fourteen-course meal for two was $600 with the wine pairing, but every bite was an incredible experience—more like visiting an art museum than a restaurant.

That weekend, Mavic needed me in France to test some wheels on short notice. When I told them that Mom was still in town, they invited her, rented me a BMW, and put us up at a swanky

---

* Other perks of being a pro athlete: when you complain on Twitter about an airline, if you have enough followers, they send you a phone number where they take care of you immediately. I almost made a new post complementing their service, but then I realized something: everyone should have that phone number.

hotel. I did some nice rides with the famous yellow support car behind me, and shared a crepe with my mother on the Mediterranean.

The second dessert course at Can Roca.

Mavic was just one of many sponsor obligations I had that spring—filming an ad for stationary trainers, attending the launch of Cannondale's new disc brake bike, etc. The trips added up, and a month went by without a big week of riding. When I finally went to a race (Haut Var—the hardest bike race you've never heard of) I felt unprepared, but when the team told me to bring back the early breakaway, I closed down a one-minute gap on a ten-minute climb, and the pack was shattered behind us.

I raced well and I was climbing pretty close to Woods and Talansky on training rides, but I kept getting flicked from the roster for WorldTour events. Those weeks, I'd train alone and have gelato in the evenings with Elly Woods, Laura Fletcher, other wives and girlfriends, or loser riders like myself who were sick, injured, or deemed unworthy of racing.

With my mom and gray hairs in my beard.

JV had warned me that I'd have a light race schedule, but he also said he'd keep his eyes open, so every time I had a good race, I'd send him power files to make my case, only to be ignored, sent wherever they needed a body. I actually enjoyed the first stage at Three Days of West Flanders this time, and that night, a Norwegian teammate asked for translation help when he was composing a tweet.

"What do I say if I really want to suffer for the team tomorrow?" he asked.

"Say you're excited to fist yourself," advised a soigneur.*

He took it well when the whole team reposted it.

We laughed through dinner, but something didn't get along with my stomach, and the cold rain and wind didn't agree with my skinny climber's build the next day. I was dropped early and got lost when the cars were out of sight, so I found a highway and followed signs to the city where the race finished. Cannondale

---

* Another soigneur got our Italian bus driver to offer a woman a "handjob" when she was carrying a heavy suitcase.

didn't have a bus for the smaller races, so I went to the local YMCA, where I sat in my wet tights next to a space heater for four hours, waiting for my team to arrive. Age-group races took place before the pros, so a steady parade of junior riders stared through the window as I shivered in my WorldTour jersey. *That's right, kids, if everything goes well, in ten years you can be like me, right here where you already are, except without dry clothes to change into or your parents to give you a hug and a ride home.*

CHAPTER 55

W HEN THE TEAM finally sent me to Critèrium International, a hilly stage race that suited me, I covered breakaways all day and still finished eleventh on the final stage and the overall GC, but it wasn't enough to earn a start at the Tour of the Basque Country the next week, so I headed back to Girona to train for the Ardennes classics. On the list for Amstel and reserve for Flèche and Liège, I sprinted up short climbs, visualizing myself delivering Woods and Howes to the front of the pack with 1k to go, and then I got a phone call: the team needed me at Paris–Roubaix. In forty-eight hours.

Here's the thing about Paris–Roubaix: it would be an honor to line up at such a historic race and I was excited for it, but sending a climber to Roubaix is sort of an insult: the equivalent of benching a baseball player (if the bench is painful and 260 kilometers long) or putting a draft animal out to pasture. Half of our sprinters were sick and JV would be hit with a 5,000-euro fine from the UCI if he didn't start a full team, so when I finally got the call for a race I'd dreamed of as a teenager, it wasn't because I was ready and they needed me. It was more of a booty call—when a douchebag strikes out at the bar and just wants someone to come over ("Yo! You awake?").

Well, I was awake, leaving Girona with just a backpack containing my passport, one set of race clothes, spare underwear, a T-shirt, and a bar of dark chocolate. My teammates felt bad for me when I arrived, but they patted me on the back for having the guts, and the media loved the story of my last-minute call-up, starting a #prayforphil campaign on Twitter (someone compared it to losing my virginity to Ron Jeremy). There was no time to try out the Roubaix-specific bike or preview the cobblestone sectors, but let's not pretend that one ride would have made me any more prepared. In fact, you could argue that it would spoil the surprise. Confession: that night, I still imagined myself winning.

View from the stage at Paris-Roubaix.

I teased the guys as they taped their knuckles before the race, like boxers getting ready for a fight, some puffing prescription asthma inhalers or taking Advil like it would make a difference. Wouter Wippert and Ryan Mullen had been targeting this race, and they were glad I was there to help everyone relax, but even I got nervous when Wegelius told me to make the early break.

The breakaway is a tall order when a hundred guys are fighting to get there, but guess what? This climber fucking did it. I fought for the front and read the attacks, and I even got on TV if anyone in the States happened to be awake at three a.m. Then the break got caught, and the rest of my day was a perfect metaphor for my racing career: if you're not in the top twenty going into a cobble section, you're just part of a mile-long line of shrapnel. Someone crashes, you slam your brakes, work your way around them, and catch up to the front guys just as the next cobbles start, so you can get stuck behind crashes again. You repeat this process until you can't see the front anymore, and soon you're just riding as hard as you can, dodging drunk fans in the streets while team cars work their way around you.

If you're me, your seat slipped when you hit a pothole five minutes into the race, so your balance is off and your muscles are cramping from a tweaked position. You're also cross-eyed from an hour in the breakaway, you've never ripped a turn on that bike (or the Roubaix-specific wheels and tires), and you weren't even supposed to be there that day, so of course you slide into a hay bale in a dusty turn.*

I kept riding, just hoping to finish, until I realized I'd missed one of the 325,987,239,842 turns and I'd gone off course somehow.

---

* Cancellara crashed twice, so I didn't feel bad. If you don't bleed a little at Roubaix, you're not getting the full experience. I never figured out what it was, between tire pressure, rim width, and just being in my own head, that made me crash so much in 2015, but my skin was mostly intact with Cannondale, and I felt great on descents.

I was about to ask a stranger for directions when the team car happened to pass me on the way to the feed zone.

I'd never felt more defeated than when I climbed into that backseat, but the soigneurs cheered me up. They said they were pounding the roof, yelling "Legend!" when they heard my name in the break—a reminder that friends were surely cheering and toasting me at McKiernan's Irish Pub in Girona, and what more can you really ask for? They posted a photo of me safely in the backseat with a Coke, captioned "He's alive! #prayforphil." My flight home wasn't first class, but the team did spring for a seat with extra legroom, and I ate the whole bar of dark chocolate.

I was still beat up from Roubaix a few days later when I pinned my number for Brabantse Pijl, the warm-up race for the Ardennes monuments. It was pouring rain, so to stay safe for Amstel at the end of the week, I didn't go crazy fighting for wheels. I rode support for my teammates and came out of the pack with 20k to go, cruising in to the finish. Nate Brown lost the front group 10k after I did, and when the team car passed him, they said he had my spot for Amstel.

I couldn't believe they'd make the decision to take me out of my first monument *during a race*, without even talking to me first, and I begged Johnny Weltz to go to bat for me, but he said the decision had already been made, and he was sorry.

"Dreams don't come true, eh?" he said.*

Adding insult to . . . well, ten other insults, I was still on the reserve list for the Ardennes, so rather than letting me go back "home" to Girona, the team had me stay at the hotel for a week in Genk, Belgium, in case someone got sick.

It's a good thing Joanna and I weren't together anymore, because bouncing around Europe with no say in your schedule and

---

* I swear he looked me in the eye and said those words. A kindergarten teacher would gasp.

no plan makes it hard to be an adult, and it certainly would have strained a relationship. But as a single dude, my week in Belgium was a great opportunity to explore and catch up on training. I knocked out six hours every day, enjoying the steep hills and bike paths, crossing the border into the Netherlands, and stopping for coffee in Maastricht.

One afternoon, the bike path led to a restaurant by a river. It looked familiar, with a waterwheel at the entrance, so I stopped and called my mom.

"Remember when we rode bikes in the Netherlands? That windy day when I was a kid? Where was that exactly?"

"I don't know," she said. "Somewhere near Maastricht."

I'm sure there are lots of restaurants with waterwheels around there and there's no way of knowing if this was the same place, but it's not important. What matters is that the yellow pancake was delicious, and this time, I didn't need a push to make it back through the headwind.

They dropped me off at the airport as some teams were arriving for Amstel, so I sat with my bags as a parade of pro cyclists came in, said hi, and then asked why I was headed the other way. It was a pro cyclist's walk of shame and a dark day for my career, but Matt Wikstrom cheered me up, offering his guest room in L.A. for a few weeks since my house was rented out. I spent time with him, recharged, and harnessed my anger for three brutal weeks in Big Bear in May, training specifically for the Tour of California's time trial, and the big mountaintop finish on Gibraltar, where I'd first been humbled by "Rusty Woods."

CHAPTER 56

STAGE ONE OF the Tour of Cali passed JC's old apartment in San Diego, where I'd bummed in 2008 as an amateur, with my stuff on his porch because there wasn't enough floor space. Looking up at the window, I wished I could have gone back in time to tell that poor, desperate loser that everything would be okay. Then I'd tell him to have his dad get cancer screenings every month, talk to his girlfriend about marriage *before* he proposes, and which lottery numbers to play.

Stage two started in Pasadena, where I had a full cheering section and a ridiculous quantity of cookies, and I didn't miss the "local boy" introduction. Ben King took the GC lead when he won the stage out of a breakaway, so we had to control the race on the way to Gibraltar on stage three. I was disappointed when Wegelius told me to pull on the front, ready to waste me before the climb he knew I'd been preparing for. Once again, I'd miss an opportunity, but I worked my way up, ready to do my job, until Talansky grabbed my jersey and held me back. Andrew didn't care what our director said. We'd been training together, and he knew I was better than the team gave me credit for. "Stay here, Phil," he said. "We're saving you for the climb."

So I didn't get to race for my own result, but at the bottom of Gibraltar, with .000000001 percent of the world watching, I took the front and tore that pack apart.

"Yeah, Phil!" said Talansky at 450 watts. "Show 'em you belong here!"

The time trial was the same course I'd done on my road bike in 2014 after the airline broke my Cervélo, so I was excited for another crack at it, but the team said I should ride easy, to save my legs to help our leaders the next day. So all the wind tunnel experts and bike fits, the $9,000 bicycle, the speed suit, the aerodynamic helmet, the shaved legs—not to mention my many hours of training in that uncomfortable position—culminated in a twenty-four-kilometer ride at 80 percent effort, smiling and waving to spectators who cheered for the "cookie monster."

WorldTour riders train hard, but no workout compares to the demands of competition, so ultimately your race program determines your fitness. By May, I was the only one on the team with no WorldTour races under my belt (half of Roubaix doesn't count), but I still broke all my power records at the Tour of Cali, so I sent Vaughters the files. He knew that my schedule had been a handicap, but here was proof that I'd put in the work—that I was still in the game, a good team player, and I deserved a shot at some tough, mountainous events like the Tour de Suisse or the Dauphiné.

I flew all the way to Europe for a photo shoot instead, at a Cannondale event in Austria, followed by the Ster ZLM Tour—another windy, flat, five-day race in Belgium, where eight guys squeezed into a rented camper. It never stopped raining and I lost any momentum I had in my fitness, but I rode well.

To make me feel better—or to tease me—when I headed back to the States for the Tour of Utah, they put me on the long list for the Vuelta. I got excited and did another three weeks in Big Bear, including heat-specific training to prepare for the broiling August in northern Spain.*

I got stronger and leaner, sat through a few days of PowerPoint lectures at yet another sponsor event, rode well in Utah, flew to Spain for my Grand Tour debut, and was taken off of the roster. Pierre Rolland had a disappointing Tour de France and wanted to salvage his season at the Vuelta, so my next race—and final race of the year—would be the Tour of Alberta.

What would be my final departure from Girona.

---

* One day, USADA was waiting when I got home, and I was so dehydrated, I knew it would take an hour to pee. The chaperon wasn't allowed to let me out of his sight, so I showered with the curtain open.

Vaughters confirmed another merger that summer—with Drapac, the Australian team I'd been considering a year before. Cannondale Pro Cycling would take most of their money and just a few riders, but JV was ignoring me again. I took that to mean that my days on the team were numbered, and realized that in a way, I wasn't a pro cyclist at all in 2016. I'd been fooling myself—a glorified salesman in tights. My dream was already dead, but it took half the season to realize it.

I had played a role as rider/ambassador, though, and pathetic as it sounds, I loved being in the WorldTour so much, I begged to JV to let me pretend for another year, to live the life in Girona. I'd raced well enough, sponsors and teammates liked me, and I'm still sure it was in their best interest to keep me for 2017. "Sure, I'm not winning, but you won't find anyone else who can film an ad for trainers, chase down the breakaway on a climb at Haut Var, and make the early break at Paris–Roubaix in the same month," I promised, in one of the many e-mails he ignored.

I reached out to other teams, but after eight months of low-level, flat races, 2016 was my first year without a win, and to be honest, if you look at the WorldTour for 2017, there weren't a lot of teams I'd want to ride for anyway. Oleg Tinkov threw in the towel on his sponsorship, but the prince of Bahrain started a new team, and he's much worse. Most of the other WorldTour programs still had dirty histories or questionable riders, so even if I wanted to ride for them, they wouldn't be into the guy with the CLEAN tattoo. I had some good talks with Dimension Data again, but if that didn't work out, in the big picture, there didn't seem to be much of a place for me in pro cycling anymore.

CHAPTER 57

THE UNITED STATES only qualified two spots for the Olympics, so I never had a chance there, either, and watching the games on Eurosport from my apartment in Girona, I saw things differently than I had as a kid. I was still in awe of the leaders, grimacing to gain every inch, but in 2016, I kept an eye on the ones at the back, and I couldn't help but notice they were smiling. For most Olympians, the victory is just getting selected. They knew they couldn't win, so now instead of suffering to place eleventh, they were enjoying the moment they'd earned.

For the rest of the summer, that was me. I'd worked hard to get to the WorldTour, and now there was nothing to do but savor my time. No one would notice if I wasn't 100 percent on the flat roads in Alberta (where even winning a stage wouldn't help me find a job), which meant there was no reason to train anymore, and I was on an extended, paid vacation.

So what did I do with that time, now that the sport was spitting me out? Did I go to museums? Did I sit on the beach or stay out late at the bars? No. I rode my bike for five hours a day, but I rode slightly slower than usual—with a higher ratio of coffee stops per kilometer—and instead of hooking a U-turn to do another effort up the hill and staring at my power meter, I took a moment at the top to enjoy the view. I wasn't an athlete anymore. I was an explorer, a tourist, seeing the world for the first time.

I'd been an addict for the chemicals you get when you win, but with Vaughters's help, I'd beaten that cold turkey, and despite everything, I never cracked that year, and I didn't set foot in Mc-Donald's. I had dinner with my friends most nights, singing out loud as I walked the streets, and smiling like I'd found $20 in my jeans. It wasn't what I'd expected, but I was living the dream.

I finally had some luck with contracts, as my previous publisher agreed to put out a collection of my monthly magazine column, and the success of my first book caught the eye of Penguin (which is pretty much WorldTour for an English major). Thanks to them, I type this from my 1,200-year-old porch in Girona, sipping sparkling water as the sun sets over the Pyrenees, with the strum of Spanish guitar in the background from a guy in dreadlocks who sits on the cathedral stairs.* You can chase something and you can fail, but maybe a job you love is right next to the one you wanted. Or at the very least, whatever you hoped for and wherever you end up, I bet you can carve out little moments of living your dream, once in a while.

---

* I can also hear a homeless guy who just snorted something, and now he's retching. Shit, he just keeled over. What do I do, call the police? Okay, he's up. He's fine. Let's focus on the guitar, okay?

CHAPTER 58

AFTER MONTHS OF silence, I finally got an e-mail from Vaughters's assistant with a letter attached, informing me that I wouldn't be coming back in 2017. JV's signature was on it, but he never said a word. I'll always wonder why he bothered to hire me in the first place—or again—just to use me where I didn't belong, and then let me go when I performed better than anyone could have expected. If you look at my 2016 schedule, it's like he sat down and planned it to ruin my morale, dangling my dreams in front of me like a carrot on a string. Maybe it's better that I don't understand, because Vaughters is an evil hypocrite, and seeing his side would mean I'm crazy, too. I don't think JV has any real friends, and he only goes out of his way when something's in it for him. I'm proud that I can't understand that, just like I'll never get why Charles Manson wanted to kill people,* but I'm still glad I got to ride for him, because I know I'm better off than if I'd kept floundering in the minor leagues.

I probably shouldn't take it so personally. Instead of blaming my misfortune on someone else and feeling like a victim, it would

---

* Manson probably wants to know why you haven't killed anybody.

feel better to take responsibility, to claim control over my fate. Hanlon's razor says "Never attribute to malice that which is adequately explained by stupidity," and I could take that a step further. Gaimon's razor: "Never attribute to stupidity that which is adequately explained by indifference." Vaughters must feel like a dad with thirty kids, who all need his attention and approval and support. If he'd given me the opportunity to see my full potential, I would've done well, but my very best probably wouldn't have cracked a podium, so it made more sense for him to focus elsewhere and neglect me—to throw me to the cobbles.

At the end of the season, Dimension Data still looked promising, and friends on the team begged their bosses to pick me up, but then one day, they announced their roster for 2017. I'd been talking to their manager for three years and he didn't even bother to tell me no. I just read it in the news and found out it was over. I'd been discarded.

Sticking to the resolution I made after my concussion in 2015, I didn't scramble for jobs from smaller teams, but I still got a couple offers. One would have been the most money I'd ever made as a pro cyclist, but looking at their race schedule, I wasn't inspired. I caught myself thinking about the rider who'd died at a UCI race that year, the four who landed in comas, and the close friend who was hit by a car and had to have a new face put on. Stefano and Katie would be having a baby in the spring, and I wanted to be at the hospital with them, not because I hit my head at some crappy tour in Asia or the Middle East, trying to keep the dream alive another year. I thought about how hungry I was at twenty-three, how I would have killed for those offers, and all the twenty-three-year-olds now who wanted nothing more than a contract that wouldn't mean as much to me. I didn't want to take their spots like Ted King took mine two years before, so it was time to get out of the way. Let someone else try to live the dream, and hope he has it easier than I did.

The media kept referring to my "retirement" when I told them my decision, but that word didn't feel right. Retirement implies career—that it ever even existed, that it wasn't on the verge of sinking at any minute. I have a big box of medals and jerseys and trophies, I own two houses, and I'll have three books on the shelf at Barnes and Noble pretty soon, but I still feel like a failure. Is that my fault, or is that what chasing a dream does to you?

I try to convince myself to be proud. I got further than I ever should have if you know how bad things were when I started. Remember all those guys who were doping when I was an amateur, kicking my ass the first time I raced Redlands and Gila? They never made it to the WorldTour. In the long run, I passed those dickheads and I did it clean. I didn't get as lucky as some guys, but a lot of guys weren't as lucky as me. I didn't do everything I wanted, but I did all I could.

Whenever I saw Howes that year, he'd take a close look at the spots I'd nervously rubbed off of my beard before Utah in 2015.

"It's coming back in, buddy!"* he always said. And it did, eventually. I still have scars on my forehead, my chin, and all over my hips, knees, and shoulders, but I'm the only pro I know who didn't break a collarbone, and despite a couple concussions, my brain still works real good. More importantly, from meeting my heroes, I learned what it means to be a hero, and from missing out on my dreams, I found balance, the value of friendship, and how to carve happiness out of disappointment. I never learned Catalan, but I can say "please," "thank you," "sorry," and "fuck off" in eight languages, and, win or lose, at almost every race for those last few years, some kind stranger brought cookies for me. If that's not living the dream, I don't know what is.

---

* Woodsy got everyone on Cannondale using "buddy," too.

CHAPTER 59

'D THOUGHT ABOUT deleting Danielson's number from my phone, but I stayed in touch with him, hoping for resolution. At first, he was going to sue the team, having his supplements tested, sure that he could trace it back to their doctors. Then he had his sunscreen and water bottles analyzed. Next, he concluded it must have been sabotage, going back to his ex-wife or an angry fan (at one point he said that the FBI was involved). It sounded crazy, but it was exactly the kind of confused, desperate reaction I'd have at a positive drug test—or you would if the cops showed up and arrested you for murder.

In Tom's emotional state, he'd even misunderstood the substance he tested positive for. USADA finally announced that in fact it was DHEA in his system, which was much more plausible for a tainted-supplement excuse. When we're talking about parts per million, if he'd had another bottle of water before the test, that might have diluted him into legal range. Besides, if Tom wanted to cheat, he could have applied for TUEs for substances that were legal and ten times more effective—or he'd have just found some EPO. He wouldn't have gone for DHEA—a cheap, weak steroid, known to barely help muscle recovery and to linger in your system.

They didn't admit it publicly, but I think even USADA knew there was a mistake, because they only banned him for four years instead of the lifetime that's standard for repeat offenders, and they gave him months to try to resolve it. If Tom had kept it all a secret instead of freaking out on Twitter, he could have been racing that whole time. He could have raced the 2015 Tour of Utah, and if he'd proved a tainted supplement, I bet the whole thing would have been swept under the rug.*

For my "image," it would be in my best interest to renounce my friendship and attack Tom in the media like everyone else, but it would make me a liar if I didn't tell the truth as I see it, so here goes: I believe Tom Danielson, I hate myself for not being there for him when he needed me most, I apologized for it, and we don't talk much but we're still friendly.

I've always been pretty good at explaining my feelings and making myself understood, but with this one thing, people either don't get it or they won't listen, so I'm sure someone will call me a hypocrite or a sucker, and if you think you know him better than I do somehow, fuck off in advance. I'm not saying he's a saint, that his reduced suspensions were fair, or that you have to like him. I think the sport was so broken, there is no fair anymore. I do believe that it was time for the EPO generation to go, so the DHEA mix-up was a form of sideways justice—like when Al Capone went to jail for tax evasion. Maybe nobody should get a second chance when so many are waiting for their first.

Tom is running training camps now, coaching other cyclists so they can achieve their goals. He said that crossing the line with me in the San Luis, he realized for the first time how good that felt.

I want to think I left the sport better than I found it, but guys were still testing positive left and right, and hackers exposed TUEs from some of the top riders, showing that many were abusing gray

---

* It makes you wonder: what *is* under that rug?

area medications—similar to what I think Horner was doing to win the Vuelta (marginal gains, my ass, Brad Wiggins). The union kept us from racing in bad weather,* but they couldn't do anything about the camera motorcycles all over the courses—even after one of them killed the guy that year. It was a shame that teams made their riders line up the next day instead of demanding stricter safety measures, and an insult when they got together to protest a few months later—over UCI reforms about the race calendar. Basically, WorldTour teams didn't bother to take action when their employees' safety was in question, but they were able to unite when money was on the line.

There is some hope, though: Brad Huff got his life together and won a bunch of races, Talansky finished fifth at the Vuelta, and Lachlan took the overall at the Tour of Utah,† where the fan with the moose helmet had traded his "Voigt" and "Horner" jerseys for one that said "Reijnen." At the end of the year, both Schlecks were retired (they finally went home, Alex!), as was Fabian Cancellara.‡

When I went for a ride in Tucker that fall, an SUV slowed down next to me and the driver leaned out to yell. I braced myself for a "Get off the road, faggot!" But what I got was a "Good luck with whatever you do next, Phil!"

On Main Street, a new bike shop had opened, and remember those dumb little twigs they'd planted? They're trees now.

---

* Funded in part by a nice donation from George Hincapie.

† I saw Lachlan in a photo with Armstrong that fall, at what looked like a small dinner party in Aspen. He wasn't wearing the "So Dope" shirt.

‡ But only after he won a gold medal in the Olympic time trial. Lance Armstrong tweeted, "Congratulations, Luigi!" referring to the code name on Fabian's Operación Puerto blood bags. Imagine being Lance—a national embarrassment—watching another guy on the Olympic podium, knowing that he did the same stuff (or worse if I'm right about the motor), supported by Trek—a brand that Lance built, which then threw him away. Then I talked to Thomas Dekker about it, and he said that *he* was "Luigi" in the Puerto scandal, and Lance was mistaken. So I give up. No one's ever figuring this out.

AFTERWORD

THIS IS THE part that's supposed to sound like a commencement speech, where I say something inspiring, like you should follow your dreams, too, and everything will work out if you do what you love, even if it's a fringe sport with corrupt leadership and hay bales in the turns. But if you came here for encouragement or life advice, you might be in trouble, and if you try to be a pro athlete or an astronaut or a rock star, it probably won't work out.*

You know who doesn't want you to chase your dreams? Your landlord, because he wants his check on time—or your kids, who need new shoes again. If you roll the dice, you could spend a decent portion of your life and get nothing, and if you ask those lucky few who did achieve everything they wanted, they'll probably tell you it's lonely up there,† and if it doesn't go on forever, I bet it feels like they die twice.

---

* Note to Bob Dylan or Michael Jordan or Oprah Winfrey, in case you're reading this: I'm sorry. You are at the top of the ladder.

† Bob, MJ, and Oprah: You know what I'm talking about, right? No one can ever *really* understand you, can they? I bet you can see why Elvis lost his mind. But hold strong, you guys. It's going to be okay. —

So what's my point? Dream small? Dream reasonable? Don't dream at all? I'm glad that my parents didn't encourage me to make cycling my profession, because if they had, boy, would I be pissed now. I want to resent the old guys who told me to keep going, but I don't, because if they said I should play it safe and take a desk job, I wouldn't have listened. I didn't *decide* to follow a dream—I was kidnapped by it—and if you feel like it's a choice at all, you should choose not to, because the ones who make it either were born with it or felt they'd rather let it kill them than die inside from doing anything else.

Friends asked how I stayed motivated to train all those years, but it would have been much harder to stop, and if that sounds like bragging, please understand that I consider this more of a disease than a gift, and I hope you don't catch it, because I'm jealous if you could be happy with a life of security and attainable goals. I bet that the guy who laced my shoes at Stride Rite would be jealous, too, but we're both better off failing than walking around our whole lives feeling like we had an itch we couldn't reach.

I wish I could say that dreams are dumb, but as I clawed my way to the middle, I got to know a few lucky souls who took theirs all the way.

I didn't make it to the Olympics, but you know who did? Mike Woods. He'd already signed a healthy contract with Cannondale for 2017, but there was a glow to him after the games. He was a new man, full of smiles and energy and stories. Woodsy got what he'd always wanted, and it felt just liked he'd hoped.

You know who else had their Olympic dreams come true? Gwen Jorgensen and Pat Lemieux. I visited them for a week that summer when Gwen was starting her final month of training, and I was amazed at their dedication. You'd think it's just doing the workouts and hurting yourself like Danielson taught me, but she set daily goals in a journal—not results goals like Powers recommended,* but process goals—little things she could control and assess and improve, because at the end, you don't regret the score as much as you'd regret the effort. Gwen's coach lived nearby and she had all sorts of staff and help, with Pat keeping everything organized, buying fresh food every day, planning his life around her needs. There's success that takes Real Talent, and there's another level I'd never imagined, that takes a team of two of the most hardworking, impressive people I'd ever met, with complementary Talents, all-in on a single mission.

In Rio, she swam with the leaders, she rode smart on the bike, and I got goose bumps when she pushed the pace on the run and found herself alone in the lead. I was sure she'd trip and twist an ankle or someone would come from behind, because nothing works out so perfect in the real world, but then suddenly she's crossing the line and there's a gold medal around her neck. She's crying, and I know that Pat's on the sidelines crying, along with all of their families and friends and coaches, and I'm alone in my apartment in Girona, and I'm bawling. It got you, too, just now, didn't it? And you don't even know them.

I'm glad I played it safe, but I won't tell you to do the same. Sacrifice everything if you want. Drop out of school and chase the impossible. If I knew what my life would be like as a pro athlete and where I would end up, I'm not sure if I ever would have started, and odds are, it'll shatter you, too. But on the rare occasions when it does work out like it should, and it happens for the right people, it's so big and it feels so great, it makes up for the pain of everyone they beat—of all the suckers like us who went for it and fell short.

I kept hoping there'd be a moment that year where I could pause and feel like I had a good ending for this book. First I thought I could win a race somewhere, but the breakaways didn't

---

* Sorry, buddy. You had it just a bit off.

stick when I needed them to. Then I thought I'd do it vicariously, delivering Howes or Woods or Talansky to a big result, but it never worked out. I was always sure that the next race would be better, and then all of a sudden it was over, and the season had gotten away from me. Most people who chase a dream don't get a happy ending. The best I can do is ride off into the sunset.